# Palgrave Studies in Digital Inequalities

Series Editors
Massimo Ragnedda
Apartment 7
NEWCASTLE UPON TYNE, UK

Laura Robinson
Berkeley, CA, USA

Power, exclusion, and the widening gaps between those with agency and those without is the foremost question of our time among scholars across humanities and the social sciences. This series speaks to the main drivers of power and exclusion in contemporary society: digital technological advances that are rapidly transforming society. Titles in this series will investigate and propose different ways to think, analyse and understand inequalities in the digital age. Themes covered include, but are not limited to, how digital inequalities persist vis-à-vis economic class, gender, sexuality, race and ethnicity, aging, disability, healthcare, education, rural residency, networks, and global geographies, as well as the study of emergent forms of inequality related to AI, digital labor, the platform economy and networked individualism, cybersafety, cybercrime, gaming, and emotional well-being.

Our goal is to create a series at the centre of these debates, pushing the field forward. Thematically, the series will examine both problems and solutions. On the one hand, we welcome monographs that map out how diverse digital technologies are exacerbating inequalities or creating new ones. On the other hand, we also welcome monographs that chart out how these technologies can be used to tackle social exclusions and marginalization.

Maria Laura Ruiu • Massimo Ragnedda

# Digital-Environmental Poverty

## Digital and environmental inequalities in the post-covid era

palgrave
macmillan

Maria Laura Ruiu
Department of Media and Communication
American University of Sharjah
Sharjah, UAE

Massimo Ragnedda
Department of Mass Communication
University of Sharjah
Sharjah, UAE

ISSN 2731-3336 ISSN 2731-3344 (electronic)
Palgrave Studies in Digital Inequalities
ISBN 978-3-031-56183-2 ISBN 978-3-031-56184-9 (eBook)
https://doi.org/10.1007/978-3-031-56184-9



Cover illustration: LuckyStep48 / Alamy Stock Vector

This Palgrave Macmillan imprint is published by the registered company Springer Nature Switzerland AG.
The registered company address is: Gewerbestrasse 11, 6330 Cham, Switzerland

Paper in this product is recyclable.

# Acknowledgments

The review of UK Policies on the Digital Divide has been conducted with the support of Max Posner.

# Contents

# Abbreviations

| | |
|---|---|
| AI | Artificial Intelligence |
| BECTA | British Educational Communications and Technology Agency |
| CCC | Climate Change Committee |
| EKC | Environmental Kuznets Curve |
| EMT | Ecological Modernization Theory |
| DEP | Digital-Environmental Poverty |
| DEPF | Digital-Environmental Poverty Framework |
| DFID | Department for International Development |
| DPA | Digital Poverty Alliance |
| DPF | Digital Poverty Framework |
| EIP | Environmental Improvement Plan |
| GDSA | Government Digital Sustainability Alliance |
| HDI | Human Development Index |
| ICROA | the International Carbon Reduction and Offset Alliance |
| IoT | Internet of Things |
| ICT | Information and Communications Technology |
| ISPs | Internet Service Providers |
| ITU | International Communication Union |
| LDCs | Least Developed Countries |
| MDGs | Millennium Development Goals |
| ML | Machine Learning |
| MPI | Multidimensional Poverty Index |
| OEP | the Office for Environmental Protection |
| OPHI | Oxford Poverty and Human Development Initiative |
| PHDI | Planetary Pressure Adjusted Human Development Index |
| SDG | Sustainable Development Goal |
| ToC | Treadmill of Consumption |

| | |
|---|---|
| ToI | Treadmill of Information |
| ToP | Treadmill of Production |
| WSIS | World Summit of the Information Society |
| UN | United Nations |
| UNDESA | United Nations Department of Economic and Social Affairs |
| UNDP | United Nations Development Programme |
| USO | Universal Service Obligation |
| WEF | World Economic Forum |
| WSIS | World Summit on the Information Society |

# List of Figures

# List of Tables

CHAPTER 1

# Introduction. Between Digital, Socioeconomic, and Environmental Poverty

Beginning with the deconstruction of the concept of poverty, this book explores themes at the intersection of resilience, environmental threats, prosperity, and innovation to demonstrate how digital poverty is connected not only to socioeconomic inequalities but also to environmental poverty. The rapid digital acceleration that has characterized contemporary society in recent decades, notably accelerated by the COVID-19 pandemic, has profoundly reshaped societal structures and dynamics (Amankwah-Amoah et al., 2021; Anandan et al., 2022). It is particularly urgent for both scholars and policymakers to explore the repercussions of digital evolution on social inequalities and the evolving, nuanced nature of poverty in this digital age. To analyze and understand the complexity of digital poverty, there is a need to rethink the concept holistically by considering the intersecting nature of digital, socioeconomic, and environmental poverty.

First, we argue that poverty must be viewed through digital technological access and usage. In today's digital age, technology plays a crucial role in shaping access to information, resources, services, and opportunities. Various socioeconomic factors, such as income, education, and geographic location, play a pivotal role in influencing individuals' access to digital technologies and their capacity to develop digital competencies (Ragnedda et al., 2022), consequently shaping their participation in the digital realm


M. L. Ruiu, M. Ragnedda, *Digital-Environmental Poverty*, Palgrave Studies in Digital Inequalities,
https://doi.org/10.1007/978-3-031-56184-9_1

(van Dijk, 2020a). While economic factors are undoubtedly crucial for ensuring access to technology, they are insufficient when individuals lack the skills and knowledge required to benefit from their use. Inability to participate in the digital world can exacerbate social and economic inequalities, hindering individuals from accessing education, job opportunities, healthcare, and other essential services. Therefore, it is vital to refrain from assessing individuals facing poverty solely in terms of their financial and economic limitations because adopting this perspective offers only a partial solution. We advocate considering the capability to use technology effectively and when needed the most as another critical aspect of poverty. Digital competencies are vital in empowering individuals to navigate the digital landscape, allowing them to improve their livelihoods and engage in a broader socioeconomic fabric (Marr, 2022). As argued elsewhere (Ragnedda & Ruiu, 2020), these two factors—access to digital technologies and the ability to master digital competencies—and their holistic union give rise to digital capital. A scarcity of digital capital can contribute to a certain degree of poverty, given its significant impact on people's socioeconomic prospects and overall well-being (Ragnedda et al., 2022). The concept of digital capital is intrinsically linked to the evolution of the digital divide and its role in perpetuating and exacerbating socioeconomic inequalities (Ragnedda et al., 2020). A person's ability to maximize the advantages offered by digital technology will affect their position within the social structure as well as their interactions and mobility within it.

In addition to accessing and using digital technology, the quality of the natural environment in which individuals reside plays a significant role in determining their poverty levels. People living in impoverished areas often face environmental degradation, inadequate sanitation, and limited access to clean water and green spaces. These environmental factors can have severe implications for physical and mental health, perpetuating a cycle of poverty that affects both the current and future generations. Moreover, a degraded environment can impact the quality of the available digital infrastructure, limiting opportunities for a beneficial digital experience. In contrast, increased digital adoption/penetration can contribute to a better environment and reduction in energy poverty through improved electricity efficiency and reduced reliance on fossil fuels. Many studies have shown how the digital dimension is intertwined with socio-environmental factors (Ha et al., 2022; Hosan et al., 2022; Shift Project, 2019; Irtyshcheva, 2021) by, for example, producing cascading impacts on healthcare, social, and environmental dynamics (Abdul et al., 2021). Digital transformation also has the potential to educate citizens (Loock et al., 2013; Malhotra et al., 2013) about more sustainable behaviors (Hedin et al., 2019) and create new management settings that can either benefit or harm the natural environment (Henkel & Kranz, 2018). The effects of such a digital transformation can be either valuable or harmful to the natural environment, such as increasing electricity demand (Andrae, 2019; Salahuddin & Alam, 2016) and emissions (Strubell et al., 2019). This suggests a need to update our theoretical and policy kits to tackle poverty and promote digital sustainability, intended as the use of digital technologies to promote environmental, social, and economic sustainability that supports a sustainable future for all (Sparviero & Ragnedda, 2021). The emerging scientific debate on digital poverty has considered its interaction with environmental poverty only marginally. This book uses the concept of *Digital-Environmental Poverty*, as it encapsulates the multidimensionality of poverty and includes three pillars at its base: social, digital, and environmental poverty. Importantly, we argue that digital-environmental poverty is not only influenced by the structural conditions of the environment but also by the lack of environmental awareness, understanding, and engagement with policies and governance aimed at reducing the digital footprint and enhancing digital sustainability. Understanding Digital-Environmental Poverty might support policymaking to improve individuals' digital life/health and reduce the pressure on both the health and environmental systems while boosting the economy and business and better protecting the environment, which in turn can lower the costs of healthcare (Van Den Eeden et al., 2022).

Effective governance and policymaking require education, active participation, and understanding from all segments of society, including those experiencing poverty. We argue that marginalized communities often lack the means or opportunities to meaningfully engage in shaping policies that affect their lives. This exclusion can perpetuate a vulnerable status and hinder sustainable development initiatives. In this vein, one of the key aspects of our discussion is that a nuanced approach to framing digital poverty also needs to consider the exposure to environmental degradation/weather extremes, environmental regulation, opportunities to participate in environment-related decision-making and the overall social context, and the capacity, support, and motivations to use digital technologies sustainably. This creates conditions for citizens to understand and engage with the environment, which will, in turn, be reflected in their digital behavior and, consequently, the digital-environmental footprint. To shed light on the intricate nature of poverty in the digital age, with particular emphasis on its multidimensional aspects and the interplay between its three fundamental pillars, this book aims to provide a deeper understanding of the complexities surrounding the evolution of digital inequalities, exploring their connection with digital acceleration and the environmental crisis. In this vein, there is a need to understand what pre-existing social, economic, and cultural determinants are worsening individual digital engagement, which in turn might affect the country's productivity and contribute to failing the Sustainable Development Agenda aimed at ending extreme poverty by 2030 (UN, 2022) by balancing the economic, social, and environmental impacts (Hallegatte et al., 2016).

Building upon the Digital Poverty Framework established by the Digital Poverty Alliance (2022), we elaborate on several key factors that contribute to the manifestation of digital poverty, including the environmental dimension. In summary, *Digital-Environmental Poverty* is divided into three sections. The first section begins by briefly analyzing the concept of poverty, its multidimensionality, and the need to comprehend it in terms other than economic, to situate poverty in the context of contemporary digital-environmental evolution. We theorize the evolution of poverty by framing the concept of poverty and discussing its evolution in the digital age. The second section specifically focuses on the environmental dimension of poverty. After framing and redefining the concept of poverty, keeping in mind the environmental and digital aspects, Section III presents case studies to illustrate how this concept might be useful in making sense of the interrelated relationship between social, digital, and environmental poverty. Finally, the conclusions provide recommendations for anticipating and reducing the risk of experiencing digital-environmental poverty.

More specifically, Chap. 2 starts by analyzing digital poverty beyond the mere dichotomic conceptualization—access versus no access or digital poor versus digital rich—and by focusing on the multilayered skills needed for e-inclusion. This first section argues that when determining whether people can fully participate in an increasingly digital society, the gaps to be considered extend beyond the initial facet of the digital divide (Ragnedda & Muschert, 2013), which is characterized by limited access to ICTs and digital infrastructure (the first level of the digital divide). They also involve deficiencies in digital skills and competencies (the second level of the digital divide) and an uneven distribution of benefits derived from accessing and using ICTs (the third level of the digital divide). In other words, this section considers the so-called digital divide as a complex issue involving the intricate interplay of various factors, including different levels of skills and benefits gained through the use of ICTs, consistent access, quality of connectivity, types of devices being used, digital skills, motivation, confidence in using ICTs, the ability to protect personal privacy and safety, and the capacity to enhance the quality of life and well-being through the use of ICTs. In the context of the COVID-19 pandemic, transformation has taken place wherein digitalization has emerged as a crucial requisite for survival (De' et al., 2020; Xie et al., 2020). Rapid digital acceleration has disproportionately affected marginalized groups, such as low-income communities, rural populations, and disadvantaged minorities. Accessing and using digital technologies has become a civil right (Ragnedda, 2020), as it provides access to resources, opportunities, and knowledge that are often not accessible otherwise, including access to digital public services, health, job possibilities, and the ability to work remotely and socialize (Van Dijk, 2020b). Specifically, digital skills are associated with benefits for individuals and the economy in terms of improved employment prospects, financial capability, better health outcomes, and civic participation (Borda et al., 2022). In addition to being a barrier to entering the workforce, a lack of digital skills poses a threat to the nation's system as a whole, raising issues of concern for its ability to compete internationally (International Labour Organization, 2021). We also address the exacerbation of social inequalities due to global digital inequalities. At this level, certain countries have advanced significantly in terms of digital infrastructure, access to technology, and digital literacy, while others remained on the "wrong side" of the global digital divide (Norris, 2001). Countries with strong digital infrastructure and capabilities have a competitive advantage in the global economy, access a wealth of information and knowledge, and the ability to participate actively in the digital age. Conversely, countries with limited access to digital technologies find themselves marginalized, facing barriers to development, education, and opportunities (Ragnedda & Gladkova, 2020).

Chapter 3 goes in depth to conceptualize digital poverty and approaches to addressing digital inequalities. Moreover, this chapter also introduces algorithmic gaps and the Artificial Intelligence divide due to automatic judgments, which can be deceptively biased and operate invisibly. Escaping digital poverty also involves recognizing how algorithms influence daily life activities and avoiding being trapped in the digital cage created by predictive technologies. Considering these interconnected aspects, Chap. 3 introduces the Digital Poverty Framework developed by the Digital Poverty Alliance (2022) to identify the constitutive determinants of digital poverty at multiple levels (structural/macro, circumstantial/meso, and individual/micro).

Finally, the first section introduces environmental poverty and its interplay with socioeconomic poverty. It refers to theoretical approaches from different disciplines that more or less optimistically interpret the relationship between economic development and environmental respect. We shall look into some existing approaches used to investigate the connections between poverty and the natural environment by simultaneously exploring two perspectives: one more oriented to how production processes and structural properties interact with individual behavior and one on how consumer practice can produce change. The chapter also explores the ecological values and consumption practices that shape individuals' environmentally conscious choices.

Section II adopts a comprehensive approach to examining Environmental Digital Poverty, recognizing the interconnectedness of social, digital, and environmental poverty. This section explores their interdependence as unified and encompassing concepts and phenomena. Specifically, Chap. 5 connects environmental transformation to digital transformation and draws on the Digital Poverty Alliance Framework by adding the environmental component to all levels included in the model. This chapter adds the status of the natural environment and its regulation as a structural determinant at the macro level. These structural determinants contribute to several factors, such as the available digital infrastructure (e.g. environmental conditions) and the existence of specific policies aimed at increasing digital efficiency in environmental terms. The natural environment also contributes to shaping the circumstances in which social actors operate (meso level) due to, for example, experiencing adverse environmental conditions/events (which in turn can affect the digital infrastructure) and opportunities available to citizens to participate in environmental decision-making. The possibility of engaging in the decision-making process related to digital sustainability and the experience of environmental degradation is added at the circumstantial level. Moreover, the revised version of the Digital Poverty Alliance Framework model adds environmental awareness/engagement, social networks, and motivation to use digital technologies sustainably as individual determinants. While intrinsic aspects might play a pivotal role in motivating users to engage with digital tools in an eco-friendly way, external social forces should also be considered. These encompass the influence that social networks and shared values can have in shaping individual digital behaviors by determining acceptability. Therefore, individual motivation, environmental awareness, and engagement are essential for developing eco-friendly digital practices and savvy use of technologies to safeguard themselves and the surrounding environment. Our approach emphasizes the importance of fostering digital literacy and cultivating effective skills and competencies in leveraging digital tools to enhance quality of life, both at the individual and societal levels, while safeguarding the environment.

Chapter 6 adopts a Bourdesian perspective to focus on the circumstantial level of the new model, which is interpreted here as the point of interaction between structural and individual properties. It also defines the digital-environmental habitus as the result of such interaction but is also characterized by a transformative potential. This section concludes with some reflections on the long-term sustainability of digital consumption-based capitalism contextualized in a marked ecological degradation, also reflecting on the support needed at both the macro and micro levels while considering the intersection between the two types of intervention. In the last chapter of this second section, we provide some examples for each level considered by the revised Digital-Environmental Poverty Framework (micro/individual-meso/circumstantial-macro/structural). These examples aim to facilitate readers' comprehension of how efforts to address digital poverty can be integrated into initiatives against environmental poverty, highlighting the need for a holistic approach to address digital-environmental poverty.

Section III delves into case studies and best practices to reflect on effective approaches that combine digital post-pandemic recovery with environmental benefits. The section begins with a chapter that evaluates policies geared toward addressing digital poverty and environmental poverty in the UK. We briefly discuss the evolution of the UK policies aimed at tackling the inequalities arising from the diffusion and adoption of digital technologies. Chapter 9 offers a case study based on research conducted by the authors, investigating the digital-environmental habitus of individuals who may be at risk of digital poverty in England. This study sheds light on the complex relationship between digital access, environmental consciousness, and socioeconomic vulnerability, providing valuable insights into potential interventions. The third section concludes by presenting the lessons learned from the case studies and existing legislation. This final chapter aims to formulate guidelines that can orient future policymaking and initiatives, by analyzing successful examples of policies aimed at reducing the digital divide while promoting environmental sustainability. It uses the Action Plan developed by the Coalition for Digital Environmental Sustainability—CODES (2022), "Sustainable Planet in the Digital Age", to contextualize the policies and examples discussed in this book, both from Western and non-Western countries. This plan provides a framework for advancing digital sustainability through collaborative efforts between private and public sectors. Through these case studies and policy insights, Section III seeks to contribute to the development of well-informed strategies that promote inclusive digital recovery, while safeguarding the environment and individuals. The aim is to identify pathways that maximize the potential for digital advancements to serve as a force for positive change while simultaneously addressing social inequalities and environmental challenges. Finally, Chap. 11 offers key takeaways and their corresponding policy recommendations, derived from the content presented in the book. This chapter seeks to present actionable insights that can inform and guide future policy considerations.

Overall, the book reflects upon the main drivers of poverty in the digital age by analyzing the interaction between recovery and environmental threats and exploring the potential educational power of the post-COVID era toward sustainable and efficient use of technologies in individuals' everyday lives. Automation and robotization may result in societal and environmental regression, high unemployment rates, and significant inequities. However, there are scenarios of social independence, efficiency, and emancipation. The direction we go will be greatly influenced by how digital technologies are integrated into the social structure, how we use them to protect the environment, and, overall, our capacity to use digital technologies rather than being used by them.

## References

Abdul, K., Hangjung, Z., & Ananth, C. (2021). Digital transformation and environmental sustainability. *Sustainability, 13*. https://www.mdpi.com/2071-1050/13/3/1530

Amankwah-Amoah, J., Khan, Z., Wood, G., & Knight, G. (2021). COVID-19 and digitalization: The great acceleration. *Journal of Business Research, 136*, 602–611. https://doi.org/10.1016/j.jbusres.2021.08.011

Anandan, R., Suseendran, G., Chatterjee, P., Jhanjhi, N. Z., & Ghosh, U. (2022). *How COVID-19 is accelerating the digital revolution*. Springer.

Andrae, A. S. G. (2019). Comparison of several simplistic high-level approaches for estimating the global energy and electricity use of ICT networks and data centers. *International Journal of Green Technology, 5*, 50–63.

Borda, M., Grishchenko, N., & Kowalczyk-Rólczyńska, P. (2022). Impact of digital inequality on the COVID-19 pandemic: Evidence from European Union countries. *Sustainability, 14*(5). https://doi.org/10.3390/su14052850

CODES. (2022, November 14). *Action plan for a sustainable planet in the digital age*. https://www.sparkblue.org/CODES

De', R., Pandey, N., & Pal, A. (2020). Impact of digital surge during Covid-19 pandemic: A viewpoint on research and practice. *International Journal of Information Management, 55*, 102171.

Digital Poverty Alliance. (2022). *How we define digital poverty & inequality*. https://digitalpovertyalliance.org/ukdigital-poverty-evidence-review-2022/introduction-myths-and-shifts/

Ha, L. T., Huong, T. T. L., & Thanh, T. T. (2022). Is digitalization a driver to enhance environmental performance? An empirical investigation of European countries. *Sustainable Production and Consumption, 32*, 230–247.

Hallegatte, S., Bangalore, M., Bonzanigo, L., Fay, M., Kane, T., Narloch, U., Rozenberg, J., Treguer, D., & Vogt-Schilb, A. (2016). *Shock waves: Managing the impacts of climate change on poverty. Climate change and development*. World Bank. http://hdl.handle.net/10986/22787

Hedin, B., Katzeff, C., Eriksson, E., & Pargman, D. (2019). A systematic review of digital behavior change interventions for more sustainable food consumption. *Sustainability, 11*(9). https://doi.org/10.3390/su11092638

Henkel, C., & J. Kranz (2018, December 13 16). Pro-environmental behaviour and green information systems research—Review, synthesis and directions for future research [Paper Presentation]. *39th international conference on information systems (ICIS)*.

Hosan, S., Karmaker, S. C., Rahman, M. M., Chapman, A. J., & Saha, B. B. (2022). Dynamic links among the demographic dividend, digitalization, energy intensity and sustainable economic growth: Empirical evidence from emerging economies. *Journal of Cleaner Production, 330*. https://doi.org/10.1016/j.jclepro.2021.129858

International Labour Organization. (2021). *Changing demand for skills in digital economies and societies literature review and case studies from low- and middle-income countries*. Prodoc. https://www.ilo.org/wcmsp5/groups/public/%2D%2D-ed_emp/%2D%2D-ifp_skills/documents/publication/wcms_831372.pdf

Irtyshcheva, I. (2021). The effect of digital technology development on economic growth. *International Journal of Data and Network Science, 5*, 25–36.

Loock, C.-M., Staake, T., & Thiesse, F. (2013). Motivating energy-efficient behaviour with green IS: An investigation of goal setting and the role of defaults. *MIS Quarterly, 37*(4), 1313–1332.

Malhotra, A., Melville, N., & Watson, R. (2013). Spurring impactful research on information systems for environmental sustainability. *MIS Quarterly, 37*(4), 1265–1274.

Marr, B. (2022). *Future skills: The 20 skills and competencies everyone needs to succeed in a digital world.* John Wiley & Sons.

Norris, P. (2001). *Digital divide: Civic engagement, information poverty, and the internet worldwide.* Cambridge University Press.

Ragnedda, M. (2020). *Enhancing digital equity: Connecting the digital underclass.* Palgrave.

Ragnedda, M., & Gladkova, A. (Eds.). (2020). *Digital inequalities in the global south.* Palgrave Macmillan.

Ragnedda, M., & Muschert, G. (Eds.). (2013). *The digital divide: The internet and social inequality in international perspective.* Routledge.

Ragnedda, M., & Ruiu, M. L. (2020). *Digital capital. A bourdieusian approach to digital divide.* Emeralds Publishing.

Ragnedda, M., Ruiu, M. L., & Addeo, F. (2020). Measuring digital capital: An empirical investigation. *New Media and Society, 22*(5). https://doi.org/10.1177/146144481986960

Ragnedda, M., Ruiu, M. L., & Addeo, F. (2022). The self-reinforcing effect of digital and social exclusion: The inequality loop. *Telematics and Informatics, 72*, 101852. https://doi.org/10.1016/j.tele.2022.101852

Salahuddin, M., & Alam, K. (2016). Information and communication technology, electricity consumption and economic growth in OECD countries: A panel data analysis. *International Journal of Electrical Power and Energy Systems, 76*, 185–193.

Shift Project. (2019). *LEAN ICT. Towards digital sobreity.* https://theshiftproject.org/wpcontent/uploads/2019/03/Lean-ICT-Report_The-Shift-Project_2019.pdf

Sparviero, S., & Ragnedda, M. (2021). Towards digital sustainability: The long journey to the sustainable development goals 2030. *Digital Policy, Regulation and Governance, 23*(3), 216–228.

Strubell, E., Ganesh, A., & McCallum, A. (2019). Energy and policy considerations for deep learning in NLP. In *Proceedings of the 57th annual meeting of the association for computational linguistics.* 10.18653/v1/P19-1355.

UN. (2022). *The sustainable development goals report 2022.* https://unstats.un.org/sdgs/report/2022/The-Sustainable-Development-Goals-Report-2022.pdf

Van Den Eeden, S. K., Browning, M. H. E. M., Becker, D. A., Shan, J., Alexeeff, S. E., Ray, G. T., Quesenberry, C. P., & Kuo, M. (2022). Association between residential green cover and direct healthcare costs in northern California: An individual-level analysis of 5 million persons. *Environment International, 163*, 107174. https://doi.org/10.1016/j.envint.2022.107174

van Dijk, J. A. G. M. (2020a). *The digital divide*. Polity Press.
van Dijk, J. A. G. M. (2020b, August 4–7). *Closing the digital divide—The role of digital technologies on social development, well-being of all and the approach of the covid-19 pandemic* [Virtual Expert Group UN Meeting]. Socially just transition towards sustainable development: The role of digital technologies on social development and well-being of all. www.un.org/development/desa/dspd/wp-content/uploads/sites/22/2020/07/Closing-the-Digital-Divide-by-Jan--A.G.M-van-Dijk-.pdf
Xie, B., Charness, N., Fingerman, K., et al. (2020). When going digital becomes a necessity: Ensuring older adults' needs for information, services, and social inclusion during COVID-19. *Journal of Aging & Social Policy, 32*(4–5), 460–470.

PART I

# Theorizing Digital Poverty

CHAPTER 2

# From Poverty to Digital Poverty

## 2.1 Introduction

This chapter reviews the main debate and findings on the intersection between traditional forms of poverty and the rise of digital technologies. It starts by introducing the concept of poverty, albeit briefly (for a more comprehensive debate around poverty see Blocker et al., 2023; Lister, 2021; Spicker, 2007), acknowledging its multidimensional nature and emphasizing the need to analyze and understand it beyond the mere lack of financial resources or household income. This chapter aims to identify potential new dimensions that should be included in this concept, fostering a more comprehensive approach to addressing poverty in the digital age. It delves into the transformative influence of digital technologies as they intertwine with the daily experiences of individuals, influencing the definition and manifestations of poverty. Our focus is directed toward key definitions discussed in the literature related to digital disadvantages, including digital inequalities, digital exclusion, digital capital, and the digital divide. We posit that the conventional understanding of poverty necessitates a revision to account for the pervasive influence of digital technologies. In so doing, we reflect on the emergence of a new social group: the digital underclass. This marginalized segment of the population faces the risk of being left behind, primarily due to the rapid technology advancements imposed by the pandemic and the subsequent economic



M. L. Ruiu, M. Ragnedda, *Digital-Environmental Poverty*, Palgrave Studies in Digital Inequalities,
https://doi.org/10.1007/978-3-031-56184-9_2

crisis. We also discuss how different digital experiences may underpin diverse levels of poverty in the digital age. Finally, we briefly focus on the evolution of digital inequalities at a global level.

## 2.2 Defining Poverty

Poverty is a multidimensional concept that encompasses a range of dimensions. It is characterized by scarcity (Blocker et al., 2023) or insufficiency of resources to secure fundamental human needs such as food, clothing, and shelter (Spicker, 2007). However, its scale extends beyond mere material scarcity and encompasses the deprivation of opportunities and essential services (Narayan, 2000). The concept of poverty is, therefore, a multifaceted, dynamic, and context-dependent phenomenon, which manifests differently in various socioeconomic settings. It is shaped by factors such as economic systems, governance structures, cultural norms, historical legacies (Alsop, 2005), and resource availability. Its ramifications extend to both industrialized and less industrialized nations, affecting populations worldwide, as its impact is not confined to economically disadvantaged countries alone. It manifests in a variety of forms, including income inequality, limited access to healthcare and education, and social marginalization (de Haan, 1997). It is not merely attributable to an individual's behavior or personal characteristics. Instead, it is deeply entrenched within industrial societies (Jenkins & Siedler, 2007). The consequences of poverty reach well beyond an individual's personal circumstances, affecting entire communities, societies, and even nations. This highlighted the interconnected nature of socioeconomic challenges. Addressing poverty involves breaking a vicious cycle of poverty and social exclusion. For instance, a lack of access to essential services such as healthcare, education, and overall opportunities and resources, among marginalized and underprivileged segments of the population, can lead to a complex web of social issues, including increased crime rates (Larsson, 2006), mental health problems (Wahlbeck et al., 2017), environmental exploitation/degradation (Le Billon, 2015), and weakening of social cohesion (Nolan & Whelan, 2014). Poverty is not a straightforward or uniform condition, and it should not be viewed as an inevitable fate, but rather as a matter of social injustice and political choice. For this reason, we argue that poverty should be framed and tackled as a consequence of political decisions and ideologies, rather than an unavoidable reality. Addressing and mitigating poverty aligns with the implementation of human rights (Somers, 2008).

Over time, diverse policies, regulations, and initiatives have been proposed and implemented to address and tackle various manifestations of poverty. People and households are deemed to be in poverty if their income is below a certain poverty level (Streeten, 1984). A government or other public institutions set standards, represented by, for example, the poverty threshold, often known as the poverty line, as the minimum income required to meet essential needs (Lipton & Ravallion, 1995). The debate around absolute (minimum level of income below which a family can be considered in poverty) and relative poverty (a percentage below the median income of a community) has been discussed by development economists and sociologists (Townsend, 1985). However, social scientists emphasize the structural criticalities of the conventional indicators used for measuring both absolute poverty (for not considering time and geographical distribution that can affect living costs and individual needs) and relative poverty (for shifting the focus from what should be defined as essential needs) (see Mishra & Das, 2022 for a review on the debate).

The definition of poverty is constantly under scrutiny due to its dynamic nature, which is dependent on cultural, technological, and societal evolution. Laderchi et al. (2003) emphasized the importance of refining the definition of poverty through comprehensive review processes to formulate policies that are relevant and effective in contrasting and alleviating poverty in specific times and places. Poverty is frequently linked to social exclusion, as pointed out by Hickey and du Toit (2013, p. 135), who defined it as "the process through which individuals or groups are wholly or partly excluded from the society they reside in." Similarly, Sen (2000, p. 29) characterizes poverty as "unfavorable inclusion," suggesting how economically disadvantaged individuals are integrated into society in a way that undermines their well-being and potential for success. This unfavorable inclusion affects a person's life in several ways, leading to restricted access to quality housing, healthcare, and civic engagement. A variety of factors contribute to poverty, including a lack of access to education and job training, limited economic opportunities, and inadequate infrastructure and government services. Natural disasters, conflicts, and other crises can also contribute to poverty by abruptly disrupting the lives, livelihoods, and circumstances of entire countries, communities, or individuals. A livelihood includes skills, resources, claims, and activities required for subsistence (Chambers & Conway, 1992, p. 6). The Sustainable Livelihoods Framework, developed by the UK Government's Department for International Development (DFID), is the most commonly referenced and employed framework. There are other popular livelihood frameworks created by various non-governmental organizations, as well as Ellis' (2000) version of Scoones and DFID's frameworks (see Asheley & Carney, 1999, for a review). Ellis modified Chambers and Conway's definition to emphasize the issue of "access," with access being shaped by institutional structures and social relationships. "A livelihood comprises the assets (natural, physical, human, financial and social capital), the activities, and the access to these (mediated by institutions and social relations) that together determine the living gained by the individual or household" (Ellis, 2000, p. 10). Furthermore, in the attempt to update and clarify the definition of livelihood, Scoones (1998, p. 5) defined it as "the capabilities, assets (including both material and social resources) and activities required for a means of living. A livelihood is sustainable when it can cope with and recover from stresses and shocks, maintain or enhance its capabilities and assets, while not undermining the natural resource base."

Specifically, the importance of natural resources and the ability to access and utilize them as required have become vital in contemporary societies. The quality of life is increasingly influenced by the availability of these resources and the ability to influence policy decisions that regulate their use. As we delve further into this discussion, we see how these factors have become integral to the revised definition of poverty. The accessibility and utilization of natural resources have a profound impact on various aspects of life, including nutrition, healthcare (Jimenez et al., 2021; Shannon et al., 2022), housing (Ben et al., 2023; Toufu et al., 2022), and overall well-being (Bratman et al., 2019; Capaldi et al., 2015; Schertz & Berman, 2019). Individuals, or communities, with easy access to clean water, fertile land, digital technologies, and sustainable energy sources tend to have improved living conditions and greater social, cultural, and economic opportunities. Conversely, regions, both at the national and international levels, facing scarcity or limited access to such resources often face significant challenges in meeting basic needs and achieving sustainable development (UN, 2020, 2023). Furthermore, the capacity to influence policy decisions concerning the management and allocation of these resources is vital in defining quality of life. Communities and individuals who can contribute, directly or indirectly, to policymaking processes can advocate for sustainable practices, environmental conservation, and equitable distribution of resources. On the other hand, marginalized groups lacking such influence may suffer from resource exploitation, environmental degradation, and socioeconomic disparities.

## 2.3 The Multidimensionality of Poverty in the Digital Age

Building on the previous paragraph, we understand poverty not only in terms of monetary wealth, but also as the deprivation of vital resources, opportunities, and the ability to shape one's living conditions. This definition of poverty acknowledges that the quality of life is contingent on access to natural and digital resources, the capacity and willingness to utilize them cautiously, and the empowerment to participate in decision-making processes. Reviewing the concept of poverty, Delia (2021) describes how until the 1970s, poverty was measured by using households' income as a proxy, and their need in terms of food, fuel, accommodation, and clothing (UNDESA, 2015). However, such an approach was soon replaced by more integrated frameworks that go beyond food and shelter and include human needs related to healthcare and education (Jolly, 1976). Social science debate around poverty criticized the reductive character of such a definition flattened on minimal material survival requirements (Vu, 2010). By contrast, the focus has been progressively shifted toward considering poverty in relation to individual "capabilities" to achieve human development (Sen, 2000). Such an approach overcomes economic indicators to understand poverty, by also including the conditions that enable individuals to preserve their well-being (Nunan, 2015). From that point, approaches to poverty have been increasingly focused on its multidimensionality. Attempts to contain such multidimensionality are represented by the introduction of both the Human Development Index (HDI) (UNDP, 1990) to assess the development of a country and the Multidimensional Poverty Index (MPI) (OPHI, 2020) based on micro-data, beyond mere economic factors. In particular, the HDI is the most well-known of the numerous indicators of poverty (Palmer, 2011). It ranks nations based on measures of adult literacy, gross enrolment, and GDP per capita as well as indications of health, education, and living standards (McGillivray, 2004).

However, even though both the HDI and MPI include dimensions related to health, education, and living standards at different scales, they do not tend to consider factors related to the environment or the digital experience. Only the 2020 UNDP Human Development Report, based on the HDI, for the first time, proposed the Planetary Pressure-Adjusted Human Development Index (PHDI) to evaluate countries' human development. PHDI is "the level of human development adjusted by carbon dioxide emissions per person (production-based) and material footprint per capita to account for the excessive human pressure on the planet" (UNDP, 2022). Moreover, first under the Millennium Development Goals (MDGs) (UN, 2000), which include 8 combined goals including eradicating poverty (Goal 1) and ensuring environmental sustainability (Goal 7), and then under the 17 Sustainable Development Goals (SDGs) (UN, 2015), both the environmental dimension and the digital dimension are somehow considered to improve both the living conditions and opportunities of individuals living in vulnerable conditions. However, the SDGs do not refer to any specific goals connected either to digital poverty or environmental poverty, but they include several goals related to sustainability (goal 11), natural resources (goals 6, 14 and 15), energy and consumption (goals 7 and 12), and climate action (goal 13), and there is an implicit assumption that Information and Communications Technology (ICT) serves all the 17 SDGs. Goal 9.c specifically refers to "significantly increase access to ICT and strive to provide universal and affordable access to the Internet in least developed countries by 2020." Goal 17, which refers to "Revitalize the global partnership for sustainable development," also includes references to technology development (and communication technologies). This section mainly refers to the development of synergies between North and South. More specifically, sub-goal 17.7 refers to the promotion of "development, transfer, dissemination and diffusion of environmentally sound technologies to developing countries." In parallel to the definition of such goals, first in 2003 in Geneva and then in 2005 in Tunis, the World Summit of the Information Society (WSIS) advanced a program of action for the achievement of the Millennium Development Goals. In 2015, the United Nations General Assembly reviewed the WSIS advances over the past ten years in its "WSIS+10 Review" and renewed the mandate of The Internet Governance Forum (a space for developing ICTs-related debates and policies) for ten years. However, this document refers to ICTs as enablers of MDGs, implying their relevant role as contextual determinants in the fight against poverty. It invites "the UN system organizations and all stakeholders within their respective roles and responsibilities to take full advantage of ICTs in addressing the development challenges of the 21st century and to recognize them as cross-cutting enablers for achieving the three pillars of sustainable development" (WSIS, 2014). However, considering ICTs exclusively as cross-cutting enablers might be reductive because such a conceptualization neglects the role of socioeconomic and environmental variables in contributing to poverty.

Therefore, there is still a need to reframe the multidimensionality of poverty taking into account the human essential need (and right) to access environmental and digital resources. They both contribute to redefining the concept of poverty in the digital age. This is because in contemporary societies human development also directly depends on and contributes to both environmental and digital structures and conditions. Hence, as it will become clearer throughout the book, to escape some levels of poverty in the digital age, individuals need to possess the capability to navigate the digital landscape with confidence, actively engage as digital citizens, influence policies through digital technologies, and be aware of their digital footprint.

## 2.4 Emergence of the Digital Underclass: Navigating the Challenges of the New Poor

As the previous paragraph highlighted, there is a pressing need to broaden the conceptualization of poverty to include both digital and environmental challenges across all levels of society. This paragraph focuses specifically on the digital component of inequalities (Gurumurthy et al., 2019), emphasizing how the literature has recognized digital access and skills as fundamental human rights to prevent the marginalization experienced by individuals belonging to a "digital underclass."

At the beginning of the ICT revolution, digitalization was seen as a way to reduce existing inequalities by providing underprivileged and isolated groups with access to information, goods, and services that were previously inaccessible (Rheingold, 1993; Negroponte, 1995). However, the equitable distribution of affordable, high-quality ICTs did not occur, revealing enduring socioeconomic disparities (DiMaggio & Hargittai, 2001), hence affecting the development of poverty in the digital age.

Inequality stands as one of the dominant global challenges, raising substantial apprehensions regarding the role of digital technology in exacerbating disparities (UN, 2020). The disparity in access to and proficiency in utilizing digital tools and resources has become a critical concern. These digital inequalities have been witnessed both within and between nations, contributing to a broader spectrum of inequalities encompassing economic, educational, and societal dimensions. Against this drawback, the last decades have witnessed the rise of a new underprivileged class in the digital society, commonly known as the "digital underclass." In contrast to the concept of the underclass provided by Murray (1996), which depicted the underclass as individuals who choose a lifestyle of minimal work and heavily rely on government welfare benefits, the concept discussed here pertains to how individuals living in disadvantaged circumstances engage with and are affected by digital technologies regardless of their motivations (Ragnedda, 2020). Digital underclass encompasses not only vulnerable populations who rarely or never use the Internet and have limited digital engagement (Helsper, 2012, 2014), but also those lacking the essential digital skills to use the Internet efficiently and effectively. They are excluded (or have limited access to) from a world full of opportunities and resources, thus reinforcing the mechanism of social exclusion and social inequalities (Ragnedda, 2020). Moreover, as we will elaborate in Chap. 3, these individuals face additional challenges due to the emergence of Artificial Intelligence (AI) and algorithms, which tend to adversely impact their living conditions, intensifying their underprivileged status and exacerbating disparities in the digital age. The rise of AI requires more sophisticated skills, including the ability to avoid surveillance, protect privacy, enhance security, and, most importantly, escape the predefined paths within which algorithms confine individuals.

Delving into the realm of digital inequalities, it becomes evident that their origins are far from straightforward or linear; rather, they stem from a complex interplay of dynamic variables (van Dijk, 2020; Asmar et al., 2022). The landscape of digital inequalities is intricate and constantly shifting, presenting a myriad of challenges (Livingstone et al., 2022; Van Deursen et al., 2017). These challenges evolve in response to the ever-changing dynamics of technology's social and economic utilization (Van Deursen & van Dijk, 2014). As our relationship with technology advances, the nature and scope of these digital inequalities transform, underscoring the need for ongoing assessment and adaptation in our strategies to bridge these inequalities effectively and not create a digital underclass (Ragnedda, 2020).

Due to their exclusion from or restricted access to the digital arena, this emerging underprivileged class is also deprived of the opportunities to engage and participate in the civic and political spheres. They are not fully exercising their rights in the digital society, and not because of their choices, but due to the lack of hardware (for example, devices, infrastructures, connections) and software (for example, digital competencies, skills, and literacy). To some extent, the digital underclass can be seen as "incomplete citizens," as their full participation in the economic, political, and cultural domains is hindered by their exclusion (or limited access) from the digital sphere, where a significant number of these activities has migrated. The transformative shift of essential societal activities into the digital realm means that those lacking sufficient levels of digital capital (Ragnedda & Ruiu, 2020) are denied a complete engagement with the core aspects of digital society (Somers, 2008). This includes accessing economic opportunities online (Francis & Weller, 2022; Sanchez-Diaz et al., 2021), engaging in digital democracy and governance (Reedy & Parker, 2018), and participating in the evolving cultural and leisure landscape (Woodrow & Moore, 2021) that has shifted to the digital arena (Shek, 2021; Zhao et al., 2022).

For instance, during the first wave of COVID-19 in the spring of 2020 around 1.6 billion young people were impacted by closures and the prohibition of face-to-face education (UNESCO, UNICEF, The World Bank, and OECD, 2021). Around 463 million children globally (Unicef, 2020) were unable to learn remotely, mainly because of a lack of devices and a reliable Internet connection, but also due to a low level of digital skills and family support. The students, along with their families, find themselves at a distinct disadvantage with a limited level of digital capital. This low level of digital capital hinders their ability to navigate the digital arena with confidence, impeding access to the full spectrum of opportunities and resources available online. The pandemic was an additional obstacle for individuals who were already struggling with economic and social inequality before the outbreak. The shift to distance learning had detrimental effects on students who lacked the necessary resources or access to quality connections. This situation has undermined the equitable role of education. The pandemic, however, did not originate this new reality; instead, it exacerbated and intensified pre-existing disparities, which are the source of digital inequalities in the field of education (Wulff, 2021). According to several studies, social inequalities in society stem from various demographic and socioeconomic factors, and the pandemic has enlarged educational gaps (Mariya et al., 2022; Vurayai, 2022). This intensification has further increased the vulnerability of communities disadvantaged in social, cultural, and economic terms. This heightened vulnerability is especially noticeable in the health sector. The inadequacy of stable digital access and a lack of essential digital skills, meaning a low level of digital capital, have hindered marginalized communities from accessing crucial health information and healthcare (Eruchalu et al., 2021; Eruchalu et al., 2022; Noori et al., 2022). These marginalized segments of the population are now confronted with an additional set of challenges. In other words, those with limited digital capital struggle to keep up with the rapidly evolving digital landscape, further widening the gap in health disparity (Choudhury & Asan, 2022; Matamanda et al., 2022).

At the same time, digital technologies have the potential to serve as a means of fostering social inclusivity, granting citizens the ability to leverage these tools for inclusive objectives and to elevate their societal standing. Achieving social inclusivity through digital technologies is a nuanced and gradual process, not a binary state of being either completely integrated into or excluded from the digital world (Office for National Statistics, 2019). For this reason, digital inclusion must not be conceived as a mere dichotomy—access versus no access—but in terms of the degree to which e-inclusion improves the well-being of individuals, communities, and society (Ragnedda, 2017). Simply having access to digital infrastructure does not guarantee digital inclusion or an upward shift on the social ladder, transcending the disadvantaged positions individuals may find themselves in due to their social, economic, or demographic characteristics. We need to reiterate that social and digital inequalities are strongly intertwined and influence and reinforce each other. Several studies highlighted the different ways in which individuals use the Internet to enhance their "social inclusion" (Manzoor & Vimarlund, 2018; Arroyo, 2020; Asmar et al., 2020; Reisdorf & Rhinesmith, 2020). However, despite their access to the Internet, individuals at risk of social exclusion are more likely to lack the digital experience necessary to fully harness the opportunities that the Internet can offer (Van Deursen & Helsper, 2018; Ragnedda et al., 2022a). Similarly, those who tend to gain greater benefits from Internet usage are typically younger, highly educated, and have higher incomes, further reinforcing their already privileged social status (Ragnedda et al., 2022b; Van Deursen & Helsper, 2015). This suggests that the use of ICT capabilities varies among individuals based on their position in the social hierarchy. Therefore, the digital divide not only reflects inequalities in terms of access and uses of ICT but also exacerbates pre-existing inequalities, perpetuating societal privileges at the expense of the digital underclass (Helsper & Reisdorf, 2017). Furthermore, as the digital field undergoes constant innovation, digital competencies can quickly become obsolete, but in any case, essential for participating in the social, economic, and political life of the community or society of reference. This makes digital illiteracy crucial for economic (Bejaković & Mrnjavac, 2020), educational (Boulton, 2017), civic engagement (Reedy & Parker, 2018), and more broadly for everyday life activities (Reddy et al., 2020). Nonetheless, as will become more evident in Chap. 3 when we will delve into this topic, exclusion from the digital realm implies exclusion from the social sphere due to the increasingly blurred distinction between these two domains and the intertwined relationship between social and digital inequality (Calderón Gómez, 2020; Merisalo & Makkonen, 2022). Hence, it is important to acknowledge digital inequalities as a crucial aspect when conceptualizing and understanding contemporary poverty. These disparities encompass not only access to digital technologies but also competencies and the ability to leverage digital experiences to concretely enhance one's quality of life. Recognizing and addressing digital inequalities is essential for a holistic understanding of poverty in the digital age. The following paragraph will delve into the topic of digital inequalities and the emergence of a digital underclass on a global scale, highlighting the need for a multilevel, globally coordinated approach. It will also delve into the intersection between digital poverty and environmental inequalities, emphasizing the potential for digital technology to contribute to environmental sustainability through cleaner innovations.

## 2.5 Digital Inequalities on a Global Scale

As addressed in previous paragraphs, digital inequalities stem from the critical intersection between technology and societal inequities, shaping the evolution of poverty in the digital age. In this vein, the Commission for Social Development recognized the significance of digital technology in combating poverty, achieving sustainable development, and improving lives worldwide (UN, 2021). Digital technologies play a key role in job creation, entrepreneurship, and economic development. In principle, digital technologies offer a chance to enhance social rights, combat social exclusion, reduce social inequities, and promote fairness. However, such progress cannot occur spontaneously. Achieving these goals requires actively promoting digital equity through initiatives and services specifically designed to address and alleviate disparities, both at the national and international levels (Ragnedda, 2020). Adopting a macro perspective on digital inequalities provides valuable insights into the global distribution of the impacts of accelerated technological advancements stemming from the pandemic. How individuals access education and digital literacy, the influence of government laws and regulations, and the challenges posed by linguistic and cultural barriers are all affected by the global digital divide. This macro perspective helps identify the countries that are most affected by this digital acceleration and those that, on the contrary, are consolidating their hegemonic position in the global arena (Ayanso et al., 2010; Armenta et al., 2012; Heeks, 2018; Ragnedda & Gladkova, 2020). The lack of suitable infrastructure and costs has historically been the main barriers to a quality connection in the Global South (Pype, 2021). This creates a first level of global digital divide depending on the type of access and connection.

Analyzing the macro-level differences and similarities between developed and developing countries in terms of digital inequalities provides insights into how the data infrastructure conditions affect access for impoverished individuals in less affluent nations. Additionally, this perspective sheds light on the nuances of the digital experience's quality within developed nations. In this vein, several scholars have dedicated their efforts to comprehend the impact of technologies on poverty, particularly in the context of developing countries (Fuchs & Horak, 2008; Gebremichael & Jackson, 2006; Manduna, 2016; Mariscal, 2005; Mecinas Montiel, 2016; Yuan & Guo, 2021). ITU's analysis underscores a critical disparity in achieving universal and meaningful connectivity, defined as the ability for all individuals to enjoy a secure, gratifying, enriching, and cost-effective online experience (ITU, 2023). This prospect remains distant for the Least Developed Countries (LDCs). For instance, in the year 2022, merely 36% of the population within LDCs utilized the Internet, signifying a substantial lag compared to the global average of 66%. Furthermore, a notable 17% of the population in these countries lacked access to both fixed and mobile broadband networks, denoting a significant access gap. It is noteworthy to emphasize that accessing the Internet in LDCs proves to be financially burdensome when juxtaposed with other regions globally (ITU, 2023).

These prevailing digital inequalities at the global level show the risk of relegating developing nations to a "global digital underclass" due to inadequate access to digital technologies and a lack of innovative solutions. Limited digital access can impede the flow of communication and the availability of essential information, hindering the ability of individuals in these areas to connect with the broader global community. The consequences of this digital isolation extend beyond mere inconvenience, impacting the ability to participate in the global economy, access educational resources, and benefit from advancements in healthcare. Similar to what we have described when referring to the emergence of a digital underclass within specific societies, studies on the global digital divide (Pisa & Polcari, 2019; Coleman, 2019; Kwet, 2019) highlight discrepancies not only in access but also in proficiency. Digital inequalities remain a persistent societal and global challenge that hinders progress toward social inclusion, despite the rise in digital ownership and access to ICTs on a global scale. For example, a study conducted by Dodel in Brazil (2023) showed that despite the increasing expansion in mobile devices in lower-income countries, the possession of these tools does not enhance their interaction with the government online generating "e-government" divides. However, the importance of acquiring digital skills goes beyond the individuals and it affects the whole country and its competitiveness internationally (International Labour Organization, 2021). In 2021, worldwide deficiency was on the rise, rather than decreasing (Spiegel & Chow, 2021). This widening gap is attributed to several key factors. Firstly, the rapid growth of tech talent is surpassing the already limited supply, further exacerbating the deficit of skilled professionals. Secondly, the high costs and fragmented approaches to traditional education are serving as significant impediments, creating barriers to accessible learning in the digital domain. Lastly, socioeconomic status is a critical factor limiting access to both digital infrastructure and the development of essential digital skills, contributing to the widening digital skills gap on a global scale. Furthermore, the World Economic Forum (WEF, 2020) highlighted the significant increase in data usage during the pandemic, particularly in areas such as healthcare (with a 490% surge in telemedicine urgent care visits), socialization, retail, and online transactions. These findings underscore the importance of both access to and proficiency in navigating the digital landscape to fully benefit from it.

Moreover, according to the 2023 WEF Jobs report, technology adoption is anticipated to continue as a pivotal catalyst for business transformation in the forthcoming five years. The report reveals that a significant majority of organizations have underscored the heightened importance of embracing new and cutting-edge technologies and are focusing on broadening access to these technologies, reflecting the pervasive recognition of their transformative potential (WEF, 2023). However, when entire regions of the world lack access to these opportunities, it widens the income gap and exacerbates inequalities between countries.

The economic and social stability of countries relies heavily on the presence of robust digital skills and the capacity of the individuals, state infrastructures, and business communities to employ them in their everyday activities and services. The acquisition of digital skills plays a crucial role in empowering individuals to leverage the Internet effectively and enhancing their ability to transform the utilization of digital technologies into a favorable advantage. Research conducted by the International Telecommunication Union (ITU, 2019) across 84 countries revealed that in 40 of them, less than half of the population possesses basic ICT skills such as copying files or sending emails with attachments. While additional data is required for comprehensive analysis, preliminary results suggest a pronounced and urgent requirement for governmental emphasis on initiatives aimed at cultivating digital skills, especially within developing nations.

Furthermore, beyond the issues of access, and the competencies to use digital technologies to enhance the quality of life, global digital poverty is intertwined with the environment. Digital poverty also shows variations contingent upon a country's level of both socioeconomic and environmental poverty. Existing studies predominantly focus on the relationship between technologies and the environment within the context of firms' activities and innovation processes, shedding light on how green technological innovations in OECD countries can have positive environmental impacts, particularly through the reduction of carbon emissions (Nesta et al., 2014; Fernández-Martínez et al., 2019; Koçak & Ulucak, 2019). Additionally, digitalization processes have been recognized as valuable tools for governments to monitor the environment, such as measuring ambient pollutant concentrations using satellite-based sensors (The World Bank, 2022). A report by the WEF highlights the potential of digital technologies to contribute to a global reduction in carbon emissions by up to 15% (Ekholm & Rockstrom, 2019). Concrete examples of technology applications aimed at minimizing environmental impact can be observed in various contexts. For instance, in factory settings, the implementation of automated systems for heating, ventilation, air conditioning, light control, and building management, as seen in Ericsson's 5G Smart Factory, has led to reduced energy and water consumption compared to conventional buildings. Similarly, the advent of 5G technology has facilitated the emergence of smart agriculture, utilizing sensors to optimize resource utilization and improve production efficiency. These advancements help minimize the need for environmentally harmful inputs such as nitrogen fertilizers that can pollute underground water (Ekholm, 2021).

Understanding the intersection of digital poverty and the environment necessitates considering the broader scope of technological impacts beyond firms' activities. It requires a multiscale and multidimensional approach that recognizes and addresses these digital-environmental interconnections. It involves recognizing the potential for technology to contribute to environmental sustainability through cleaner innovations, as well as addressing social behaviors and consumption practices that contribute to environmental degradation. More recent approaches (Pestre, 2019) emphasize the need for a holistic perspective that involves not only the development of cleaner technologies but also social behaviors, lifestyles, and consumption patterns. These approaches acknowledge that consumption plays a significant role in environmental degradation, particularly in terms of carbon emissions exacerbating climate change. However, Ericsson (2020) forecasted that by the end of 2026, there will be around 3.5 billion 5G subscriptions globally, but 80% of 5G users will be in North America and only 5% in sub-Saharan Africa. This scenario has frequently led to the Global North reaping the benefits of the digital revolution, while the Global South pays the environmental costs. Therefore, the increasing divide between advanced and disadvantaged digital users makes filling these inequalities difficult.

## 2.6 Conclusion

This chapter highlighted that the concept of poverty extends beyond mere material deprivation. It encompasses life chances and well-being, which are also shaped by access to opportunities and services, both in the online and offline realms. These aspects are, in turn, influenced by economic systems, cultural norms, environmental health, historical legacies, and geographical configuration, generating hierarchies at both international and national levels. One of the key points in this chapter is the emergence and integration of digital technologies into our societies and how they have transformed various aspects of our lives, offering unprecedented opportunities for progress, communication, and connectivity. However, the introduction of these technologies has also brought forth significant challenges, particularly in the form of inequalities and poverty. This multifaceted issue stems from inequalities in access, skills, and usage, and it has the potential to exacerbate existing social inequalities both within countries and across global regions.

The chapter adopted a definition of poverty that goes beyond purely economic factors highlighting the significance of access to technology. It also emphasized the value of digital skills in utilizing the Internet to its full potential and minimizing its negative effects. Moreover, the chapter stressed the impact of varied digital experiences on different levels of poverty. This issue is multidimensional intersecting with economic, social, educational, and cultural inequalities. It not only prevents individuals from accessing opportunities but also deepens their exclusion from society in a world increasingly dependent on digital technologies. Specifically, we have seen how the primary social axes of social inequality, such as age, gender, income, education, and social classes, have a significant impact on this connection and penalize segments of the population. Given that governmental administration and private services are moving online, having access to the Internet and having digital skills is essential for equal opportunities in education, socialization, the workplace, and more broadly in everyone's daily life.

The evolving landscape of digital poverty reveals a complex web of interrelated factors that contribute to its perpetuation. From unequal access to digital infrastructure and the Internet to the varying degrees of digital literacy among individuals, and the insidious impact of biased algorithms in perpetuating discrimination, the consequences of digital poverty are extensive. Those already living at the margins of society find themselves further penalized and excluded, as technology shapes their opportunities, resources, and interactions. Furthermore, the global scale of digital poverty exposes a strong contrast and divide between developed and developing nations, as well as the persistent disparities within these regions. While digital technology has the potential to bridge gaps and enhance lives, its benefits are unevenly distributed, leaving a significant portion of the world's population disconnected and disempowered. Efforts to address this challenge must encompass not only access to devices and the Internet but also digital literacy and skills that enable individuals to meaningfully engage with the digital realm. To confront the issues posed by digital poverty, a comprehensive approach is necessary, involving collaboration between governments, private sectors, and civil society.

We also highlighted the need to recognize digital poverty's far-reaching consequences and its intricate connection with societal well-being, environmental sustainability, and overall quality of life. It is important to acknowledge the strong connection between a clean environment, resources, access, and the use of digital technologies to enhance the quality of life and tackle digital poverty. Recognizing these complexities is essential for developing effective strategies and policies that can bridge the digital divide, promote equitable access, and address the underlying inequalities that perpetuate poverty in the digital age. In this direction, initiatives aimed at improving digital infrastructure, enhancing digital literacy, and mitigating algorithmic biases can contribute to a more equitable digital future.

In conclusion, we need to reiterate that access to technology and the Internet are crucial steps in the effort to reduce poverty, as it would empower individuals and enhance the possibilities to access resources and opportunities. However, accessing digital technologies alone is not sufficient to address poverty, and it must be combined with other efforts to address underlying issues such as lack of education, job training and opportunities, environmental interconnections, and access to healthcare and other services. In the following chapter, we delve into the factors that contribute to digital poverty, focusing and further elaborating on the framework presented by the Digital Poverty Alliance. This model considers social structure and individual agency as interconnected elements, highlighting how individuals engage with external structures based on their assimilation and response to these influences. A revised definition of poverty should incorporate access to natural and digital resources, the ability to take care of and use these resources to gain benefits, and the capacity to influence decision-making in terms of environmental choice and well-being.

## References


Alsop, R. (2005). *Power, rights and poverty: Concepts and connections.* The World Bank.

Armenta, A., Serrano, A., Cabrera, M., & Conte, R. (2012). The new digital divide: The confluence of broadband penetration, sustainable development, technology adoption and community participation. *Information Technology for Development, 18*(4), 345–353.

Arroyo, L. (2020). Implications of digital inclusion: Digitalization in terms of time use from a gender perspective. *Social Inclusion, 8*(2), 180–189.

Asheley, C., & Carney, D. (1999). *Sustainable livelihoods: Lessons from early experience.* Department for International Development.

Asmar, A., Mariën, I., & Van Audenhove, L. (2022). No one-size-fits-all! Eight profiles of digital inequalities for customized inclusion strategies. *New Media & Society, 24*(2), 279–310.

Asmar, A., van Aduenhove, L., & Mariën, I. (2020). Social support for digital inclusion: Towards a typology of social support patterns. *Social Inclusion, 8*(2), 138–150.

Ayanso, A., Cho, D. I., & Lertwachara, K. (2010). The digital divide: Global and regional ICT leaders and followers. *Information Technology for Development, 16*(4), 304–319.

Bejaković, P., & Mrnjavac, Ž. (2020). The importance of digital literacy on the labour market. *Employee Relations, 42*(4), 921–932.

Ben, S., Zhu, H., Lu, J., & Wang, R. (2023). Valuing the accessibility of green spaces in the housing market: A spatial hedonic analysis in Shanghai, China. *Land, 12*(9), 1660. https://doi.org/10.3390/land12091660

Blocker, C., Zhang, J. Z., Hill, R. P., Roux, C., Corus, C., Hutton, M., Dorsey, J., & Minton, E. (2023). Rethinking scarcity and poverty: Building bridges for shared insight and impact. *Society for Consumer Psychology, 23*(3), 489–509.

Boulton, H. (2017). Exploring the effectiveness of new technologies: Improving literacy and engaging learners at risk of social exclusion in the UK. *Teaching and Teacher Education, 63*, 73–81.

Bratman, G. N., et al. (2019). Nature and mental health: An ecosystem service perspective. *Science Advances, 5*(7). https://doi.org/10.1126/sciadv.aax0903

Calderón Gómez, D. (2020). Technological socialization and digital inclusion: Understanding digital literacy biographies among young people in Madrid. *Social Inclusion, 8*(2), 222–232.

Capaldi, A. C., Passmore, H., Nisbet, E. K., Zelenski, J. M., & Dopko, R. L. (2015). Flourishing in nature: A review of the benefits of connecting with nature and its application as a wellbeing intervention. *International Journal of Wellbeing, 5*(4). https://doi.org/10.5502/ijw.v5i4.449

Chambers, R., & Conway, G. (1992). *Sustainable rural livelihoods: Practical concepts for the 21st century.* IDS Discussion Paper 296, Institute of Development Studies, Brighton.

Choudhury, A., & Asan, O. (2022). Use of technology for health-related tasks among older adults: Trend analysis of pre-&-during COVID. *Proceedings of the International Symposium on Human Factors and Ergonomics in Health Care, 11*(1), 113–118.

Coleman, D. (2019). Digital colonialism: The 21st century scramble for Africa through the extraction and control of user data and the limitations of data protection laws. *Michigan Journal of Race and Law, 24.* https://repository.law.umich.edu/mjrl/vol24/iss2/6

de Haan, A. (1997). *Poverty and social exclusion: A comparison of debates on deprivation.* Working Paper no. 2, University of Sussex.

Delia, P. (2021). *Merging the poverty and environment agendas.* International Institute for Sustainable Development. Brief 11. https://www.iisd.org/articles/deep-dive/merging-poverty-and-environment-agendas

DiMaggio, P., & Hargittai, E. (2001). *From the 'digital divide' to 'digital inequality': Studying Internet use as penetration increases.* Center for Arts and Cultural Policy Studies.

Dodel, M. (2023). Why device-related digital inequalities matter for e-government engagement? *Social Science Computer Review*. https://doi.org/10.1177/08944393231176595

Ekholm, B. (2021). *COVID-19 showed the importance of 5G for the economy and theenvironment*.https://www.weforum.org/agenda/2021/01/davos-agenda-covid-19-5g-economy-environment/

Ekholm, B., & Rockstrom, J. (2019). *Digital technology can cut global emissions by 15%.Here'show*.https://www.weforum.org/agenda/2019/01/why-digitalization-is-the-key-to-exponential-climate-action/

Ellis, F. (2000). *Rural livelihoods and diversity in developing countries.* Oxford University Press.

Ericsson. (2020). *More than 1 billion people will have access to 5G coverage by the end of 2020 globally.* https://www.ericsson.com/en/press-releases/2/2020/11/more-than-1-billion-people-will-have-access-to-5g-coverage-by-the-end-of-2020

Eruchalu, C. N., Bergmark, R. W., Smink, D. S., et al. (2022). Demographic disparity in use of telemedicine for ambulatory general surgical consultation during the COVID-19 pandemic: Analysis of the initial public health emergency and second phase periods. *American College of Surgeons 107th Annual Clinical Congress.* https://doi.org/10.1097/XCS.0000000000000030

Eruchalu, C. N., Pichardo, M. S., Bharadwaj, M., et al. (2021). The expanding digital divide: Digital health access inequities during the COVID-19 pandemic in New York city. *Urban Health, 98*(2), 183–186.

Fernández-Martínez, M., Sardans, J., Chevallier, F., Ciais, P., Obersteiner, M., Vicca, S., et al. (2019). Global trends in carbon sinks and their relationships with CO2 and temperature. *Nature Climate Change, 9*(1), 73–79.

Francis, D. V., & Weller, C. E. (2022). Economic inequality, the digital divide, and remote learning during COVID-19. *Review of Black Political Economy, 49*(1), 41–60.

Fuchs, C., & Horak, E. (2008). Africa and the digital divide. *Telematics and Informatics, 25*(2), 99–116.

Gebremichael, M. D., & Jackson, J. W. (2006). Bridging the gap in Sub-Saharan Africa: A holistic look at information poverty and the region's digital divide. *Government Information Quarterly, 23*(2), 267–280.

Gurumurthy, A., Chami, N., Bharthur, D., & Singh, P. J. (2019). *Tackling online inequality: Making digital platforms work for inclusive development.* IT for Change.

Heeks, R. (2018). *Information and communication technology for development (ICT4D)*. Routledge.

Helsper, E. J. (2012). A corresponding fields model for the links between social and digital exclusion. *Communication Theory, 22*(4), 403–426.

Helsper, E. J. (2014). *Synthesis report: Harnessing ICT for social action. Peer review in social protection and social inclusion*. EU Commission, DG Employment Report. http://ec.europa.eu/social/BlobServlet?docId=12437&;langId=en
Helsper, E. J., & Reisdorf, B. C. (2017). The emergence of a "digital underclass" in Great Britain and Sweden: Changing reasons for digital exclusion. *New Media & Society, 19*(8), 1253–1270.
Hickey, S., & du Toit, A. (2013). Adverse incorporation, social exclusion, and chronic poverty. In A. Shepherd & J. Brunt (Eds.), *Chronic poverty* (pp. 134–159). Palgrave Macmillan.
International Labour Organization. (2021). *Changing demand for skills in digital economies and societies literature review and case studies from low- and middle-income countries*. Prodoc. https://www.ilo.org/wcmsp5/groups/public/%2D%2D-ed_emp/%2D%2D-ifp_skills/documents/publication/wcms_831372.pdf
ITU. (2019). New ITU data reveal growing Internet uptake but a widening digital gender divide. https://www.itu.int/en/mediacentre/Pages/2019-PR19.aspx
ITU. (2023). ITU's measuring digital development – Facts and figures: Focus on least developed countries. https://www.itu.int/itu-d/reports/statistics/facts-figures-for-ldc/
Jenkins, S. P., & Siedler, T. (2007). The intergenerational transmission of poverty in industrialized countries. *Chronic Poverty Research Centre Working Paper, 75*. https://doi.org/10.1094/PDIS-91-4-0467B
Jimenez, M. P., DeVille, N. V., Elliott, E. G., Schiff, J. E., Wilt, G. E., Hart, J. E., & James, P. (2021). Associations between nature exposure and health: A review of the evidence. *International Journal of Environmental Research and Public Health, 18*(9), 4790. https://doi.org/10.3390/ijerph18094790
Jolly, R. (1976). The World Employment Conference: The enthronement of basic needs. *Development and Policy Review, A9*(2), 31–44.
Koçak, E., & Ulucak, Z. Ş. (2019). The effect of energy R&D expenditures on CO2 emission reduction: Estimation of the STIRPAT model for OECD countries. *Environmental Science and Pollution Research, 26*, 14328–14338.
Kwet, M. (2019, October 13). Digital colonialism is threatening the Global South. *Science and Technology News, al Jazeera*. https://www.aljazeera.com/opinions/2019/3/13/digital-colonialism-is-threatening-the-global-south.
Laderchi, C. R., Saith, R., & Stewart, F. (2003). Does it matter that we do not agree on the definition of poverty? A comparison of four approaches. *Oxford Development Studies, 31*(3), 243–274.
Larsson, D. (2006). Exposure to property crime as a consequence of poverty. *Journal of Scandinavian Studies in Criminology and Crime Prevention, 7*(1), 45–60.
Le Billon, P. (2015). Environmental conflict. In T. Perreault, G. Bridge, & J. McCarthy (Eds.), *The Routledge handbook of political ecology* (pp. 598–608). Routledge.

Lipton, M., & Ravallion, M. (1995). Poverty and policy. In J. Behrman & T. N. Srinivasan (Eds.), *Handbook of development economics* (pp. 2551–2657). Elsevier.

Lister, R. (2021). *Poverty.* Polity Press.

Livingstone, S., Helsper, E. J., & Rahali, M. (2022). The digital lives of children and youth. In *Global connectivity report 2022* (pp. 138–151). ITU Publications.

Manduna, W. (2016). Empirical study of digital poverty: A case study of a University of Technology in South Africa. *Journal of Communication, 7*(2), 317–323.

Manzoor, M., & Vimarlund, V. (2018). Digital technologies for social inclusion of individuals with disabilities. *Health and Technology, 8*, 377–390.

Mariscal, J. (2005). Digital divide in a developing country. *Telecommunications Policy, 29*(5–6), 409–428.

Mariya, S., Ananda, A., Erianjoni, E., & Montesori, M. (2022). Mobile learning-based pocketbook development in educational field practice in increasing the competency of professional teachers. *International Journal of Educational Dynamics, 5*(1), 131–137.

Matamanda, A. R., Nel, V., Leboto-Khetsi, L., et al. (2022). Risk communication in an informal settlement during COVID-19: Case of Dinaweng, Bloemfontein South Africa. *Urban Governance, 2*(2), 296–304.

McGillivray, M. (2004). *Towards a measure of non-economic national well-being achievement: And other constructs. Researching well-being in developing countries.* Hanse Institute for Advanced Study Delmenhorst.

Mecinas Montiel, J. M. (2016). The digital divide in Mexico: A mirror of poverty. *Mexican Law Review, 9*(1), 93–102.

Merisalo, M., & Makkonen, T. (2022). Bourdieusian e-capital perspective enhancing digital capital discussion in the realm of third level digital divide. *Information Technology & People, 35*(8). https://www.emerald.com/insight/0959-3845.htm

Mishra, D. K., & Das, R. J. (2022). *Global poverty. Rethinking causality.* Brill.

Murray, C. (1996). *Charles Murray and the underclass: The developing debate.* Institute for the Study of Civil Society.

Narayan, D. (2000). *Voices of the poor: Can anyone hear us?* World Bank.

Negroponte, N. (1995). *Being digital.* Alfred A. Knopf.

Nesta, L., Vona, F., & Nicolli, F. (2014). Environmental policies, competition and innovation in renewable energy. *Journal of Environmental Economics and Management, 67*(3), 396–411.

Nolan, B., & Whelan, C. T. (2014). The social impact of income inequality: Poverty, deprivation, and social cohesion. Changing inequalities in rich countries. *Analytical and Comparative Perspectives*, 146–168.

Noori, S., Jordan, A., Bromage, W., Fineberg, S., Cahill, J., & Mathis, W. S. (2022). Navigating the digital divide: Providing services to people with serious mental

illness in a community setting during COVID-19. *SN. Social Sciences, 2*(160). https://doi.org/10.1007/s43545-022-00470-0
Nunan, F. (2015). *Understanding poverty and the environment. Analytical frameworks and approaches.* Routledge.
Office For National Statistics. (2019). Exploring the UK's digital divide. https://www.ons.gov.uk/peoplepopulationandcommunity/householdcharacteristics/homeinternetandsocialmediausage/articles/exploringtheuksdigitaldivide/2019-03-04/pdf
OPHI. (2020). *Global Multidimensional Poverty Index.* https://ophi.org.uk/multidimensional-poverty-index/
Palmer, M. (2011). Disability and poverty: A conceptual review. *Journal of Disability Policy Studies, 21*, 210. https://doi.org/10.1177/1044207310389333
Pestre, D. (2019). "Environment and Social Innovation: Why Technology Never Was the Solution," Creative Economy. In S. Lechevalier (Ed.), *Innovation beyond technology* (chapter 0, pp. 175–194). Springer.
Pisa, M., & Polcari, J. (2019). *Governing big tech's pursuit of the "next billion users"*. CGD Policy Paper 138, Center for Global Development.
Pype, K. (2021). (Not) in sync – Digital time and forms of (dis-)connecting: Ethnographic notes from Kinshasa (DR Congo). *Media, Culture and Society, 43*(7). https://doi.org/10.1177/0163443719867854
Ragnedda, M. (2017). *The third digital divide. A Weberian analysis of digital inequalities.* Routledge.
Ragnedda, M. (2020). *Enhancing digital equity: Connecting the digital underclass.* Palgrave.
Ragnedda, M., & Gladkova, A. (2020). *Digital inequalities in the global south.* Palgrave.
Ragnedda, M., & Ruiu, M. L. (2020). *Digital capital. A bourdieusian approach to digital divide.* Emeralds Publishing.
Ragnedda, M., Ruiu, M. L., & Addeo, F. (2022a). How offline backgrounds interact with digital capital. *New Media & Society.* https://doi.org/10.1177/14614448221082649
Ragnedda, M., Ruiu, M. L., & Addeo, F. (2022b). The self-reinforcing effect of digital and social exclusion: The inequality loop. *Telematics and Informatics, 72*, 101852.
Reddy, P., Sharma, B., & Chaudhary, K. (2020). Digital literacy: A review of literature. *International Journal of Technoethics, 11*(2), 65–94.
Reedy, K., & Parker, J. (2018). *Digital literacy unpacked.* Facet.
Reisdorf, B., & Rhinesmith, C. (2020). Digital inclusion as a core component of social inclusion. *Social Inclusion, 8*(2), 132–137.
Rheingold, H. (1993). *The virtual community: Homesteading on the electronic frontier.* Addison-Wesley.

Sanchez-Diaz, I., Altuntas Vural, C., & Halldórsson, Á. (2021). Assessing the inequalities in access to online delivery services and the way COVID-19 pandemic affects marginalization. *Transport Policy, 109*, 24–36.

Schertz, K. E., & Berman, M. G. (2019). Understanding nature and its cognitive benefits. *Current Directions in Psychological Science, 28*(5). https://doi.org/10.1177/0963721419854100

Scoones, I. (1998). *Sustainable rural livelihoods: A framework for analysis*. https://opendocs.ids.ac.uk/opendocs/bitstream/handle/20.500.12413/3390/Wp72.pdf?sequence=1

Sen, A. (2000). Social exclusion: Concept, application, and scrutiny. *Social Development Papers, 1*(1), 1–60.

Shannon, N. Z., Tabak, L. A., & Pérez-Stable, E. J. (2022). *Food accessibility, insecurity and health outcomes*. National Institute on Minority Health and Health Disparities. https://www.nimhd.nih.gov/resources/understanding-health-disparities/food-accessibility-insecurity-and-health-outcomes.html#resources

Shek, D. T. L. (2021). COVID-19 and quality of life: Twelve reflections. *Applied Research in Quality of Life, 16*(1), 1–11.

Somers, M. (2008). *Genealogies of citizenship: Markets, statelessness, and the right to have rights*. Cambridge University Press.

Spicker, P. (2007). *The idea of poverty*. Policy Press.

Spiegel, S., & Chow, C. (2021). *54% believe technology will advance faster than the skills of the workforce*. https://www.salesforce.com/news/stories/tech-skills-research/

Streeten, P. (1984). Basic needs: Some unsettled questions. *World Development, 12*, 973–978.

Toufu, H., Quingyun, H., & Xiao, O. (2022). The capitalization effect of natural amenities on housing price in Urban China: New evidence from Changsha. *Frontiers in Environmental Science, 10*. https://doi.org/10.3389/fenvs.2022.833831

Townsend, P. (1985). A sociological approach to the measurement of poverty: A rejoinder to Professor Amartya Sen. *Oxford Economic Papers, 37*, 659–668.

UN. (2000). *Millenium development goals*. https://www.un.org/millenniumgoals/

UN. (2015). *Sustainable development goals*. https://www.un.org/sustainabledevelopment/blog/2015/12/sustainable-development-goals-kick-off-with-start-of-new-year/

UN. (2020). *Recover better. Economic and social challenges and opportunities*. United Nations, Department of Economic and Social Affairs.

UN. (2021). *More must be done to close digital divide, end poverty, speakers say, as social development commission continues debate*. https://press.un.org/en/2021/soc4895.doc.htm

UN. (2023). *Water*. https://www.un.org/en/global-issues/water
UNDESA. (2015). Multidimensional poverty. *Development Issues, 3*. https://www.un.org/en/development/desa/policy/wess/wess_dev_issues/dsp_policy_03.pdf
UNDP. (1990). *Human Development Index (HDI)*. https://hdr.undp.org/data-center/human-development-index#/indicies/HDI
UNDP. (2022). *Planetary pressures–Adjusted Human Development Index (PHDI)*. https://hdr.undp.org/planetary-pressures-adjusted-human-development-index#/indicies/PHDI
UNESCO, UNICEF, The World Bank, & OECD. (2021). *What's next? Lessons on education recovery: Findings from a survey of Ministries of Education amid the COVID-19 pandemic*. http://covid19.uis.unesco.org/wp-content/uploads/sites/11/2021/07/National-Education-Responses-to-COVID-19-Report2_v3.pdf
UNICEF. (2020). *Covid-19: Are children able to continue learning during school closures?* https://data.unicef.org/wp-content/uploads/2020/08/COVID-19-Remote-Learning-Factsheet_English_2020.pdf
Van Deursen, A. J., & Helsper, E. J. (2018). Collateral benefits of Internet use: Explaining the diverse outcomes of engaging with the Internet. *New Media & Society, 20*(7), 2333–2351.
Van Deursen, A. J. A. M., & Helsper, E. J. (2015). The third-level digital divide: Who benefits most from being online? In L. Robinson, S. R. Cotton, J. Schulz, et al. (Eds.), *Communication and information technologies annual* (pp. 29–52). Emerald Group Publishing Limited.
Van Deursen, A. J. A. M., & van Dijk, J. A. G. M. (2014). The digital divide shifts to differences in usage. *New Media & Society, 16*(3), 507–526.
Van Deursen, A. J. A. M., Helsper, E., Eynon, R., & Van Dijk, J. A. G. M. (2017). The compoundness and sequentiality of digital inequality. *International Journal of Communication*, 452–473.
van Dijk, J. A. G. M. (2020). *The digital divide*. Polity Press.
Vu, C. M. (2010). The influence of social science Theories on the conceptualization of poverty in social welfare. *Journal of Human Behavior in the Social Environment, 20*(8), 989–1010.
Vurayai, S. (2022). COVID-19 pandemic and the narrative of the digital divide gap in universities in Sub-Saharan Africa. *African Studies*. https://doi.org/10.1080/14725843.2022.2122398
Wahlbeck, K., Cresswell-Smith, J., Haaramo, P., & Parkkonen, J. (2017). Interventions to mitigate the effects of poverty and inequality on mental health. *Social Psychiatry and Psychiatric Epidemiology, 52*, 505–514.
WEF. (2023). *Future of jobs report*. https://www3.weforum.org/docs/WEF_Future_of_Jobs_2023.pdf

Woodrow, N., & Moore, K. (2021). The liminal leisure of disadvantaged young people in the UK before and during the COVID-19 pandemic. *Journal of Applied Youth Studies, 4*, 475–491.

World Bank. (2022). *Getting down to earth are satellites reliable for measuring air pollutants that cause mortality in low- and middle-income countries?* World Bank Group.

World Economic Forum. (2021, September 22). *Why Carbon Offsetting doesn't cut it.* https://www.weforum.org/agenda/2021/09/greenpeace-international-carbon-offsetting-net-zero-pledges-climate-change-action/

WSIS. (2014). *WSIS+10 statement on the implementation of the WSIS outcomes. Final agreed draft.* https://www.itu.int/net/wsis/review/inc/docs/final/wsis10.statement.pdf

Wulff, A. (2021). Global education governance in the context of COVID-19: Tensions and threats to education as a public good. *Development, 64*, 74–81.

Yuan, J., & Guo, L. (2021). Investigation and analysis of digital poverty among adolescents in China. *Journal of Documentation, 77*(6), 1265–1285.

Zhao, L., Cao, C., Li, Y., & Li, Y. (2022). Determinants of the digital outcome divide in E-learning between rural and urban students: Empirical evidence from the COVID-19 pandemic based on capital theory. *Computers in Human Behavior, 130*, 107177.

CHAPTER 3

# Determinants of Digital Poverty

## 3.1 Introduction

In the previous chapter, we started analyzing the evolution of poverty, introducing the implications of digital inequalities and their contribution to the nature of poverty in the digital age. In this book, the concept of digital poverty is intricately linked to the three levels of the digital divide (Ragnedda, 2017). Digital poverty extends beyond basic access to digital technologies, the lack of which is commonly defined as the first level of the digital divide, as we will delve into more extensively. Access to digital technologies alone is insufficient to guarantee a meaningful digital experience. Digital poverty also encompasses the second level of the digital divide, involving the lack of necessary digital skills to fully engage with the Internet. Moreover, digital poverty acknowledges the third level of the digital divide, which pertains to the ability to navigate the Internet effectively and mitigate potential negative consequences associated with its use. This layered nature of digital poverty suggests that social inequalities are both the outcomes of and triggers for different forms of digital and social exclusion.

Furthermore, to better understand how poverty is evolving according to the digital transformation, we will discuss how the introduction of cutting-edge technologies, such as AI and the pervasive influence of


M. L. Ruiu, M. Ragnedda, *Digital-Environmental Poverty*, Palgrave Studies in Digital Inequalities,
https://doi.org/10.1007/978-3-031-56184-9_3

predictive algorithms, is significantly impacting digital inequalities and further redefining the concept of poverty in the digital age. Particularly, this chapter sheds light on the implications of an increasingly predictive and data-driven digital landscape on marginalized groups, emphasizing the pressing need for equitable technological access and ethical deployment of AI in society. In this vein, we shall see how being digitally disadvantaged also entangles disparities in terms of knowledge, access, and skills in utilizing digital technologies, leaving these users more vulnerable and exposed to biased algorithms, privacy infringements, limited access to information and exposure to misinformation, and the risks associated with cybercrime or cyberbullying. All these aspects are discussed in light of additional attributes of digital inequalities such as in the specific case of "data poverty" (lack of sufficient sources to afford private and secure mobile or broadband data for essential needs) (Lucas et al., 2020) or "information poverty" (a gap between digitally disadvantaged groups and mainstream society across various levels) (Chatman, 1996; Yu, 2006).

This chapter delves into the digital poverty concept and its determinants, and it focuses on the theoretical paradigm established by the Digital Poverty Alliance (2022) and further developed by Ruiu et al. (2023). This model suggests that individuals' behavior is shaped by the way external structures are assimilated, emphasizing the inseparable relationship between social structure and human agency. Our attention is then directed toward recognizing the significant challenges posed by agency, motivation, social support, and societal organization, which can hinder the effective utilization of digital technology. Specifically, in our attempt to uncover and explain the underlying factors contributing to digital poverty, we employ a model that, as articulated by Greenhalgh and Stones (2010) and Stones (2005), transcends the conventional dichotomy between social structure and human agency. Instead, following this model we suggest that these elements are inextricably intertwined, with individuals acting within the framework of their assimilated external structures. This conceptualization draws inspiration from Dahlgren and Whitehead's renowned "determinants of health" framework, often referred to as the "rainbow model" (1991). Originally designed to explain the intricate socioeconomic and environmental factors influencing health outcomes, this healthcare model has been adapted to the examination of digital poverty. It operates on a theoretical foundation structured around three distinct layers: (Individual) Determinants, Circumstantial Determinants, and Structural Determinants. Within this framework, ***Individual Determinants*** encompass elements such as Device and connectivity, Access, Capabilities, Motivation, and Support. *Circumstantial Determinants* delve into the complexities of living conditions, economic stability, family dynamics, health, sociodemographic context, psychosocial factors, lifestyle, and behaviors. *Structural Determinants* scrutinize the broader socioeconomic and political underpinnings that shape our digital landscape. In this model, Individual Determinants correspond to individual lifestyle factors, Circumstantial Determinants reflect the influence of social networks, and Structural Determinants encapsulate the general socioeconomic, cultural, and environmental conditions that underlie the phenomenon of digital poverty. Consequently, the interaction between personal, social, and technological contexts transcends the simplistic dichotomy of users and non-users, as posited by Neves et al. (2018). As we delve deeper into this chapter, the intricacies and interplay of these determinants become more apparent, shedding light on the multifaceted nature of Digital Poverty. This chapter serves as a foundational precursor to the subsequent chapters. In the upcoming sections, we delve deeper into this model, expanding our perspective by incorporating the environmental dimension. Our objective is to develop a comprehensive understanding of digital-environmental poverty, thereby enriching our overall conceptual framework. This exploration sheds light on the intricate interplay between technology, society, and the environment, offering valuable insights into the evolving landscape of poverty in the digital age.

## 3.2 Conceptualizing Digital Poverty

The origins of digital poverty can be attributed to its capitalist nature (Schiller, 1999, 2001) which has made ICTs indispensable for capitalist development and political-economy structure. The increasing interweaving of digital dimensions in the structure of society has been defined in several terms such as "digital economy," "platform economy," "gig economy," and "sharing economy," which draw upon the digital technology-based organization of economy and society. However, digital capitalism (Fuchs & Mosco, 2015; Fuchs, 2019) has already shown an unequal distribution of risks in relation to multiple aspects such as security (privacy/data breach and theft), increased consumerism (through tailored advertising based on personal preferences), price and access discrimination (for example, to medical insurances), and quality of information (Ding & Chai, 2022). Furthermore, in an era where education, employment, social interactions, and nearly every aspect of daily life have consistently migrated online, individuals might find themselves dealing with new challenges. Socially disadvantaged citizens often lack the digital skills and resources needed to study, work, socialize, access information, and conduct business and are, therefore, negatively affected by the pervasive use of digital technologies, accelerated by the COVID-19 pandemic. Specifically, in the midst of and following the pandemic, a unique scenario has unfolded where certain individuals and households, who may not conventionally fall under the category of "digital underclass," are dealing with the consequences of digital acceleration. This acceleration has pushed them into an era where their ability (or lack thereof) to access and navigate the evolving digital landscape has become a critical factor in their lives. These experiences could materialize in various ways. For instance, during the lockdowns, some families encountered difficulties due to the scarcity of digital devices available to accommodate both their children's educational needs and their work requirements (Ruiu et al., 2023). Moreover, unreliable Internet connections could further exacerbate their difficulty, hampering engagement with the digital landscape (Janer & Ricafort, 2022). Limited proficiency in digital competencies could limit their ability to support their children's educational needs, carry out their professional responsibilities, or simply carry out their daily activities in an online setting. As our world increasingly relies on digital technologies, it becomes evident that addressing the complexities of this scenario demands more than mere access and basic digital competencies. Hence, those citizens belonging to the digital underclass and living in digital poverty are prevented from accessing a world full of opportunities and resources that cannot be reached in any other way (Goedhart et al., 2019).

One of the first definitions of digital poverty has been provided by Barrantes (2007) who argues that the concept is based on a minimum of ICT use and consumption as well as income levels necessary to demand ICT products. In this interpretation, digital poverty is interpreted as the cause of the digital divide. Starting from this conceptualization and further developments, Lucas et al. (2020) define digitally poor individuals, households, or communities as those "who cannot afford sufficient, private and secure mobile or broadband data to meet their essential needs." While accurate, this interpretation offers a limited perspective on digital poverty, focusing mainly on one factor, which is access. Such an approach has also been explored empirically by focusing on access and showing different levels of digital poverty (for example, defined as absolute, moderate, and relative by Manduna, 2016) in connection to pre-existing financial poverty, level of education, geographical location, gender, and income. In other terms, this approach to digital poverty seems to focus only on the first level of the digital divide (the uneven access to the Internet), while not taking into account the multidimensionality of digital inequalities. Digital poverty is also intricately linked to a multitude of cultural, social, and political factors, as highlighted by Robinson et al. (2020). It is an intersectional issue that "exacerbates and is exacerbated by other socio-economic, educational, racial, linguistic, gender, and health inequalities" (Allman, 2022).

In this vein, a comprehensive and holistic approach to framing digital poverty should acknowledge that individuals must possess the ability not only to access the Internet but also to utilize it effectively, how and when needed the most, accessing and using resources and opportunities that can significantly enhance their overall quality of life. A lack of ICT experience and knowledge can impact any segment of the population not necessarily affected by economic poverty. It is also affected and determined by the lack of digital skills which will make it harder for individuals to access online services, find employment, or take advantage of opportunities offered by the digital economy. It can also limit their ability to participate in the digital economy, which is increasingly essential for economic growth and development. Analyzing and understanding digital poverty means acknowledging how much the lack of access or lack of digital skills by individuals, groups, and classes can create new social inequalities or exacerbate those already present (Robinson, Ragnedda, and Shulz 2020), to the point of encroaching on a "digital apartheid" (Brown & Czerniewicz, 2010). This digital apartheid excludes specific groups or individuals from the advantages and opportunities provided by digital technology connected, for instance, to education, employment opportunities, healthcare, and political involvement.

In the current historical juncture, digital literacy plays a key role, also in relation to two further pivotal dimensions. The first pertains to the environmentally responsible use of digital technologies, emphasizing the need to adopt digital tools in an ecologically sustainable manner. The second aspect involves mitigating the adverse repercussions stemming from the excessive and improper utilization of digital technologies that, as we have already noted, are related to the third level of the digital divide. The avoidance or mitigation of harmful impacts resulting from the use of digital technologies on the surrounding ecosystem, coupled with the reduction of their potential negative effects on individual well-being, are crucial in addressing and tackling digital poverty. As the subsequent sections of this book will expound upon, reducing the digital footprint and safeguarding personal well-being constitute fundamental competencies in the digital age. These competencies play a pivotal role in significantly enhancing the overall quality of life and, consequently, reducing DEP.

## 3.3 Digital Poverty and the Three Levels of the Digital Divide

The COVID-19 pandemic has shown the detrimental impacts of digital poverty on multiple fronts, encompassing both individual and societal dimensions. It has underscored the imperative of recognizing the urgency in identifying and rectifying existing inequalities, which have fostered the emergence of new vulnerable groups forced to adapt to the evolving technological landscape in diverse ways.

Fighting digital poverty requires challenging a broader digital fragility that is eroding individuals' independence, personalities, and rights to a good living. This is connected to Nunan's strategy to eradicate poverty, which goes beyond using just economic measures to maintain people's wellness (2015). Digital poverty affects well-being and emphasizes the inability (both in terms of resources and abilities) to make use of digital technologies to either improve one's well-being or avoid being negatively impacted by them. Nonetheless, even though digital poverty has gained considerable attention among scholars and policymakers, the existing literature reveals a lack of consensus regarding its definition. This lack of agreement has posed a challenge to both its conceptualization and implementation of policies targeted at alleviating this issue rooted in social inequalities (Donaghy, 2021). Recently, the Digital Poverty Alliance (DPA) has developed an operational definition that characterizes digital poverty as the incapacity of individuals to fully participate in the online world in the necessary manner and extent. This all-encompassing definition acknowledges digital poverty as a phenomenon that both intensifies and is intensified by various disparities in socioeconomic status, education, race, language, gender, and health (Allman, 2022). Digital poverty is a concept that embraces the multifaceted essence of the digital divide overcoming its simplistic interpretation in dichotomic terms (for example, in terms of have and have not access to the Internet). This encompasses not only inequalities in accessing digital technologies but also different degrees of digital proficiency, alongside the tangible outcomes that stem from the utilization of ICTs. Hence, digital poverty can be understood as the outcome arising from what is known as the three levels of the digital divide. These levels, as mentioned above, encompass inequalities in access (first level), disparities in the utilization of digital technologies (second level), and disparities in the social advantages derived from such engagement (third level) (Ragnedda, 2017). Therefore, it has a structural connection to enhancing well-being through both maximizing the positive effects and minimizing the negative impacts of Internet usage. For each level of the digital divide, the disadvantage is heightened by already existing vulnerabilities such as low income or low level of education, which work to create a vicious circle in which offline inequalities reinforce digital inequalities which in turn reinforce further social inequalities (Ragnedda et al., 2022b). The extent of digital poverty, which should be perceived as a spectrum rather than a binary concept, is shaped and determined by the dynamic interaction of these three levels of the digital divide. The more evident the disparities in access, technology usage and skills, and social advantages, the greater the extent of digital poverty experienced by individuals. More specifically, the categories underlying the concept of digital poverty are based on the determinants related to the first level of the digital divide, which encompasses issues of device and connectivity, limitations in access, and motivational barriers (van Deursen & van Dijk, 2019). Furthermore, inequalities in digital skills and digital competencies contribute to the understanding of digital poverty. However, establishing a more refined theoretical connection to the third level, which focuses on tangible outcomes, necessitates further examination and comprehension of the framework proposed by the DPA. As we will elaborate on in subsequent sections, the inequalities in the distribution of tangible outcomes arising from access to and utilization of ICTs are strongly intertwined with the notion of digital poverty, wherein individuals fail to fully capitalize on their digital experiences in equal measure. The extent of social benefits and outcomes individuals can accrue from their engagement with ICTs is contingent upon the interplay between their socioeconomic and cultural backgrounds and their digital encounters (Ragnedda et al., 2022a). Those endowed with greater economic and socio-cultural capital tend to reinforce their privileged positions within society through their utilization of digital technologies, resulting in a phenomenon known as the "Matthew effect" whereby the rich become even richer, thereby exacerbating societal inequalities (Ragnedda et al., 2022b). Moreover, the third level of the digital divide encompasses also the ability to navigate the adverse consequences of the Internet, including addressing cybercrime, combatting cyberbullying, discerning fake news, and managing digital fatigue (for instance, avoiding digital addiction and overuse). Therefore, we are arguing that digital poverty encompasses these three levels of digital stratification, suggesting that bridging the gap solely in terms of device ownership and reliable connectivity is insufficient. Equally crucial is the acquisition of necessary digital skills and competencies that enable individuals to maximize the transformative potential of the Internet for capital-enhancing endeavors while also safeguarding against negative outcomes.

## 3.4 Digital Inequalities and Artificial Intelligence

To understand and unpack the implications of digital tools on the development of poverty, we also need to focus on the latest technologies that might exacerbate already existing social inequalities, thus deeply affecting poverty. Particularly important is the increasingly pervasive role played by AI and Machine Learning (ML), which are in turn based on algorithms. In the rapidly expanding domain of AI and its impact on various fields in our everyday lives (Müller & Bostrom, 2016), it is essential to reflect upon the social implications surrounding this technology and its relationship with social inequalities. In simple terms, AI enables machines to acquire knowledge from experience and perform tasks traditionally requiring human intelligence. At its core, AI relies on algorithms, which serve as instructions guiding a computer's decision-making process (Bucher, 2017). The literature defines algorithms in many different ways, but the common understanding is that algorithms are sets of instructions, steps, or rules that follow a precise order to produce certain outcomes (Kitchin, 2017). One of the most promising developments of AI is represented by ML, which uses a statistically based inductive approach to develop solutions based on the data under analysis and the knowledge previously acquired by the algorithms (see Prodnik, 2021 for a review).

The applications of AI span diverse industries, including healthcare, transportation, finance, and retail. In the healthcare sector, for instance, AI aids in disease diagnosis, drug discovery, and personalized treatment planning, while transportation benefits from self-driving cars and

AI-powered traffic management systems (Secinaro et al., 2021). Finance, likewise, experiences improvements in fraud detection, risk assessment, and customer service through the seamless integration of AI (Goodell et al., 2021). Similarly, AI optimizes retail operations by streamlining inventory management and enhancing customer experiences with personalized recommendations (Ameen et al., 2021). Such algorithm-based technologies play a key role in the economy (for example, AI and ML are estimated to add USD 15.7 trillion to the global economy by 2030) (PwC, 2017). Moreover, the pervasive use of digital technologies facilitates people's everyday lives while decentralizing economic centers of decisional power (for example, blockchain). Citizens can, indeed, be impacted by digital data even if they do not use technologies such as when accessing benefits and housing, which can be based on an algorithmic risk scoring calculated using data from the digital network (Digital Poverty Alliance, 2022). It is vital to recognize and address the risks associated with AI, also in relation to potential job displacement due to automation and privacy concerns arising from extensive data collection, while posing several ethical challenges to decision-making (Jarrahi, 2018). For instance, AI-powered job automation can replace certain occupations, leading to unemployment among low-skilled workers while benefiting those with advanced technical expertise.

Furthermore, it is vital to understand how the AI system works and how it influences social inequalities. Against this backdrop, it is important to underline that the design, training, and deployment of AI systems can perpetuate and amplify biases and discrimination (Eubanks, 2017; Turner et al., 2019; Kordzadeh & Ghasemaghaei, 2022), thereby influencing and amplifying poverty. Algorithms tend to disproportionately penalize and marginalize individuals already situated at the margin of society (Noble, 2018). This dynamic significantly affects individuals' engagement in public spheres (Feezell et al., 2021), shapes the decisions of media consumers (Zarouali et al., 2022), and perpetuates pre-existing biases and discriminatory tendencies, wherein algorithms reinforce stereotypes and discriminatory practices (Hoffmann, 2019; Susser, 2019). Real-world examples can help us understand how AI can perpetuate inequalities. An example is credit scoring (Gsenger & Strle, 2021), where AI-powered models may unintentionally discriminate against minority groups in relation to, for example, race or ethnicity (Bartlett et al., 2022) and gender (Kelly & Mirpourian, 2021). For instance, a report published by Oliver Wyman (2022) found that 19% of Americans are credit invisible. However, Black and Hispanic groups are the most penalized being the most invisible, unscorable, and subprime (meaning that they are either denied or borrow only at significantly elevated interest rates). Black citizens are 1.8 times more likely to not have a credit score and 1.9 less likely to access favorable rates (Hepinstall et al., 2022). In the same vein, a report published by Women's World Banking found that AI-driven credit scoring in the global financial industry is likely to discriminate against women due to gender-biased data sources and data scientists, coders, and developers' unconscious prejudices. Another example is represented by the application of AI recruitment tools such as that employed by Amazon (Oppenheim, 2018). This tool was trained on a historical dataset that exhibited a notable bias toward male candidates. Consequently, the algorithm exhibited a bias in favor of male applicants, even when comparing them to equally qualified female candidates. This inadvertently contributed to the gender gap, further deepening the existing gender inequalities (Dastin, 2022). Similarly, Google Photos' auto-tagging feature, due to its foundation on datasets primarily comprising white individuals, encountered criticism for its tendency to inaccurately classify individuals from non-white ethnic backgrounds (Hosanagar & Miller, 2020). These examples illustrate how the integration of AI can inadvertently reinforce social inequalities, dictating the access, timing, and manner in which specific resources, services or advantages are made available. This aspect of inclusion/exclusion from privilege and resources, or the system of penalties and rewards, is intrinsically linked to the essence of poverty and affects individuals, their families, groups, communities, organizations, specific population segments, and the broader societal fabric (Marjanovic et al., 2022).

AI treats people differently because they draw their knowledge from data that may be under-representative or over-representative of some social categories. The consequences of this over/under-representation are frequently unknown to the public, who lack the knowledge necessary to recognize AI systems (Gran et al., 2021; Gruber et al., 2021; Dogruel et al., 2020), critically understand them (Shin, 2022; Siles et al., 2020), and then, wherever possible, defend themselves and avoid algorithmic intrusion and "suggestions" (Long & Magerko, 2020; Zarouali et al., 2021). AI algorithms are contributing to the emergence of a novel divide (Zarouali et al., 2021), also referred to as the "AI divide" (Carter et al., 2020). This divide highlights disparities in knowledge (Cotter & Reisdorf, 2020) and algorithmic awareness gap (Gran et al., 2021) among individuals who may not fully understand the subtle use of their data and information. These are exploited to create profiles that subsequently shape their day-to-day activities. Hence, algorithm-based systems can produce multiple inequalities in terms of the benefits gained from digital experiences without becoming a "victim" of potential algorithm discriminations (Ragnedda, 2020) dictated by statistical trends. What we are arguing here is that despite its potential, the introduction of digital technologies is contributing to social inequities (Cetindamar et al., 2021; Cetindamar et al., 2022) because socially disadvantaged groups, on average, tend to lack the means and expertise to use them effectively or because they are negatively affected by biased algorithms (Mohamed et al., 2020). Consequently, this further fortifies the existing structural inequalities among users from diverse sociodemographic backgrounds (Cotter & Reisdorf, 2020; Gran et al., 2021; Lutz, 2019; Zarouali et al., 2021). The tangible consequences of these biases underscore the necessity for vigilant consideration and proactive mitigation efforts to cultivate a more equitable and balanced digital arena, one that fosters fair interactions and sustains the well-being of both individuals and business activities.

Therefore, digital poverty is intricately intertwined with more than just the three conventional levels of the digital divide (access-skills-benefits), but it extends to include the disruptive influence of AI and its potential for discrimination. This complex interplay between social disparities, digital inequalities, and the influence of AI is deeply ingrained in the fabric of our social structure and power dynamics (Beer, 2017). In the next paragraph, we dig deeper into the determinants of digital poverty, as outlined by the DP Alliance.

## 3.5 Understanding Digital Poverty Determinants: Structural, Individual, and Circumstantial Determinants

In the attempt to identify the determinants of digital poverty, we employ and revise the model proposed by the DPA (2022), by interpreting social structure and human agency as not separable and absorbed by individuals who act according to their metabolized absorption of external structures (Greenhalgh & Stones, 2010; Stones, 2005). This model (Fig. 3.1) drew upon Dahlgren and Whitehead's "determinants of health" (1991) framework or "rainbow model," which was used to understand the varying socioeconomic and environmental intricacies related to health outcomes.

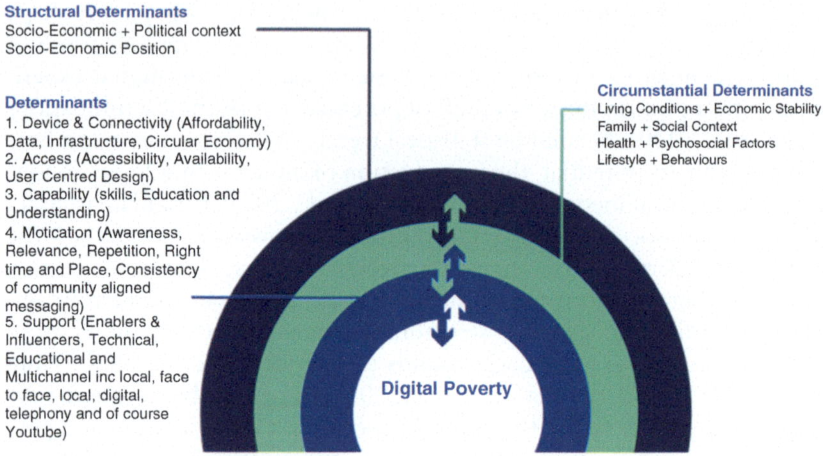


**Fig. 3.1** Determinants of digital poverty (DPA, 2022)

This healthcare model was, in turn, retrofitted to help contextualize the field of study by highlighting the differing social and economic issues that may have direct effects on digital poverty (Allman, 2022).

The DPA has proposed a definition of digital poverty as the "inability [of individuals] to interact with the online world fully, when, where, and how an individual needs to. It exacerbates and is exacerbated by other socio-economic, educational, racial, linguistic, gender, and health inequalities. It is both the product and the cause of other forms of socio-economic disadvantage" (Allman, 2022). This definition is based on a theoretical model that incorporates Five Determinants—Device and connectivity, Access, Capabilities, Motivation, and Support. These determinants are influenced by *Circumstantial Determinants*, including living conditions, economic stability, health, social and family context, psychosocial factors, lifestyle, and behaviors, as well as *Structural Determinants* such as socio-economic and political structures.

In the original model (Fig. 3.1), the Determinants correspond to the outcome of the Circumstantial Determinants and the Structural Determinants. Therefore, they include factors that depend on both structural and individual characteristics. For example, motivation does not only include individual awareness, but also "consistency of community-aligned messaging." In our revised version (see Fig. 3.2), the Five Determinants

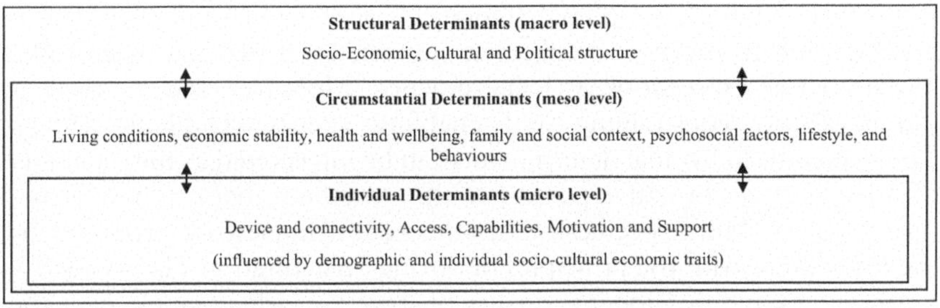


**Fig. 3.2** Revised version of determinants of digital poverty

are characterized as *Individual Determinants* reflecting the individual prerequisites for a digital experience.

In this sense, Device and Connectivity, Access, Capabilities, Motivation, and Support all refer to the specific individual space of manoeuver in the digital realm. These five individual determinants of digital poverty determine what Ragnedda and Ruiu (2020) define as digital capital, which, when combined with the traditional indicators of poverty (individual demographic, socioeconomic, and cultural factors), contributes toward shaping (and is in turn shaped by) circumstances under certain socioeconomic, cultural, and political structures. These individual determinants interact with the structural determinants at the circumstantial level originating different levels of digital poverty. More specifically, we refer to three dimensions of the DPF as *Individual Determinants* (micro level), *Circumstantial Determinants* (meso level), and *Structural Determinants* (macro level).

These reflections suggest that the DPF might be further developed from a sociological perspective as the operationalization of Giddens' conceptualization of the duality of structure. In this sense, the *Structural Determinants* represent the socioeconomic, cultural, and political structural properties of the social system (in terms of resources and rules that shape social practice). The *Circumstantial Determinants* represent the system that produces and reproduces the regular social practice and displays structural properties in time and space through social relations. At the circumstantial level, however, some specifications should be made. Given that the structure is not external to individuals (Giddens, 1984), we interpret the circumstantial level as the point of intersection between the structural and agentic levels. Therefore, all aspects included in this level (such as living conditions, economic stability, health, family and sociodemographic context, psychosocial factors, lifestyle, and behaviors) need to be interpreted as expressions of social practice. Moreover, the structure is simultaneously constraining and enabling agency (Giddens, 1984). Consequently, individual determinants can be interpreted as the capability of subjects (transformative power) to do something that can have structuring power. More specifically, the theoretical framework proposed by the DPA aligns with the principles of Strong Structuration Theory (SST), a concept rooted in Giddens' duality of structure, which emphasizes the interconnectedness of social structure and human agency (Ruiu et al., 2023). Within this framework, these elements are viewed as phenomenologically intertwined and indivisible, absorbed by individuals who, in turn, act according to their assimilated external structures (Greenhalgh & Stones, 2010; Stones, 2005). This perspective also resonates with the Bourdesian notion of habitus (Bourdieu, 1977, 1990), suggesting that individuals develop their internal structures, which in turn are subject to external influences. The intricate interplay between external factors and individuals' inherent predispositions plays a key role in shaping the internal structures of an individual and, in turn, influencing their subsequent actions. This dynamic relationship has the potential to either perpetuate pre-existing disadvantages or open doors to new advantages. This interaction is a complex interplay between the external environment in which individuals find themselves and the personal characteristics and choices that define them. It is this synergy that shapes how individuals navigate the digital landscape, access resources, leverage digital technologies, and protect the surrounding environment. Following the tenets of SST, exploring the outcomes of this interplay between structural factors and agency entails investigating both the intended and unintended consequences, which can encompass change, elaboration, reproduction, or preservation of the structure (internal and external to the agent) (Stones, 2005, p. 84). This implies that structural conditions can either facilitate or hinder the fulfillment of agency purposes. Therefore, our overarching aim in defining and analyzing digital poverty is to untangle the intricate relationships between structural, circumstantial, and individual determinants, shedding light on the multifaceted nature of this pervasive phenomenon. As we shall see in Chap. 5, this model can be reframed by adding the environmental component which plays a key role in determining digital-environmental poverty.

## 3.6 Conclusions

Digital poverty highlights the incapacity and impossibility of engaging with the online realm in a manner that aligns with individual needs, preferences, and circumstances. As emerged throughout the chapter, digital access is pivotal for establishing connections, acquiring knowledge, pursuing employment, and availing oneself of essential services. It has become increasingly evident that lacking access to the digital sphere equates to being denied fundamental aspects of modern life. The consequences of digital exclusion tend to widen pre-existing disparities while also introducing novel forms of inequality that affect poverty. Individuals who are digitally marginalized face substantial obstacles in crucial domains of life, including education, employment prospects, healthcare, and the overarching fabric of social integration. Social inclusion, a cornerstone of well-being, is also compromised by digital exclusion. This chapter reinforced that individuals who experience digital poverty are prevented from fully engaging in the digital world how and when they need to. In an era where social interactions, government services, and community engagement often occur online, those without digital access and lack of digital skills and competencies may find themselves isolated and excluded from vital aspects of society.

Addressing digital poverty is vital for the economic, environmental, and social recovery from the pandemic, as being "digitally included" becomes a key driver not only for the single but for the entire community and society. Understanding such a multifaceted nature of digital poverty is vital to formulating comprehensive and sustainable solutions. Approaches to address it must account for its diverse forms and the dynamic factors that contribute to its persistence. Merely having access to ICTs and possessing basic digital skills is not sufficient within a society that heavily depends on digital resources and technologies. The profound integration of digital technologies into every facet of daily lives has reshaped our culture, economy, and society, ushering in an era of unprecedented convenience and connectivity. However, we should acknowledge that this transformation remains incomplete, as digital inclusion is still an elusive goal. The COVID-19 pandemic exacerbated our increasing reliance on the Internet for everyday tasks, from maintaining social connections to pursuing education and remote work. The pandemic has unmasked the detrimental consequences of digital poverty at both individual and societal levels. This underscores the urgent need to recognize and rectify existing disparities that contribute to the emergence of vulnerable groups struggling to adapt to the evolving technological landscape. Yet, it also laid bare the stark disparities in digital access and utilization, revealing that the advantages of the online world are not equitably distributed throughout society. These disparities extend beyond mere access to encompass the ability of individuals to fully harness the potential of the digital realm, engage meaningfully, and seize new opportunities, while not being penalized or discriminated by AI.

Addressing digital poverty requires a holistic approach that encompasses not only the provision of devices, connectivity, and digital skills but also the creation of an inclusive digital environment where everyone can participate on equal footing. In this chapter, we introduced and revisited the "Digital Poverty Alliance Framework" to identify the determinants of digital poverty. The discussion of such a model and its usefulness will be then connected to the following chapter, which is focused on further developing the concept of digital poverty by including environmental determinants in the framework.

## References


Allman, K. (2022). *UK digital poverty evidence review 2022*. https://digitalpovertyalliance.org/wp-content/uploads/2022/06/UK-Digital-Poverty-Evidence-Review-2022-v1.0-compressed.pdf

Ameen, N., Tarhini, A., Reppel, A., & Anand, A. (2021). Customer experiences in the age of artificial intelligence. *Computers in Human Behavior, 114*, 106548. https://doi.org/10.1016/j.chb.2020.106548

Barrantes, R. (2007). Analysis of ICT demand: What is digital poverty and how to measure it. In *Digital poverty: Latin American and Caribbean perspectives* (pp. 29–53). Practical Action Publishing.

Bartlett, R., Morse, A., Stanton, R., & Wallace, N. (2022). Consumer-lending discrimination in the FinTech era. *Journal of Financial Economics, 143*(1), 30–56.

Beer, D. (2017). The social power of algorithms. *Information, Communication and Society, 20*(1), 1–13.

Bourdieu, P. (1977). *Outline of a theory of practice*. Cambridge University Press.

Bourdieu, P. (1990). *The logic of practice*. Stanford University Press.

Brown, C., & Czerniewicz, L. (2010). Debunking the 'digital native': Beyond digital apartheid, towards digital democracy. *Journal of Computer Assisted Learning, 26*(5), 357–369.

Bucher, T. (2017). The algorithmic imaginary: Exploring the ordinary effects of Facebook algorithms. *Information, Communication & Society, 20*(1), 30–44.

Carter, L., Liu, D., & Cantrell, C. (2020). Exploring the intersection of the digital divide and artificial intelligence: A hermeneutic literature review. *AIS Transactions on Human-Computer Interaction, 12*(4), 253–275.

Cetindamar, D., Abedin, B., & Shirahada, K. (2021). The role of employees in digital transformation: A preliminary study on how employees' digital literacy impacts use of digital technologies. *IEEE Transactions on Engineering Management*. https://doi.org/10.1109/TEM.2021.3087724

Cetindamar, D., Kitto, K., Wu, M., Zhang, Y., Abedin, B., & Knight, S. (2022). Explicating AI literacy of employees at digital workplaces. *IEEE Transactions on Engineering Management*. https://doi.org/10.1109/TEM.2021.3138503

Chatman, E. A. (1996). The impoverished life-world of outsiders. *Journal of the American Society for Information Science, 47*(3), 193–206.

Cotter, K., & Reisdorf, B. C. (2020). Algorithmic knowledge gaps: A new dimension of (digital) inequality. *International Journal of Communication, 14*. https://ijoc.org/index.php/ijoc/article/view/12450

Dahlgren, G., & Whitehead, M. (1991). *Policies and strategies to promote social equity in health: Background document to WHO–Strategy paper for Europe*. Institute for Futures Studies.

Dastin, J. (2022). Amazon scraps secret AI recruiting tool that showed bias against women. In K. Martin (Ed.), *Ethics of data and analytics* (pp. 296–299). Auerbach Publications.

Digital Poverty Alliance. (2022). *How we define digital poverty & inequality*. https://digitalpovertyalliance.org/ukdigital-poverty-evidence-review-2022/introduction-myths-and-shifts/

Ding, X., & Chai, Q. (2022). The rise of digital capitalism and the social changes it caused: How to develop the digital economy in socialist China. *China Political Economy*. https://doi.org/10.1108/CPE-10-2022-0017

Dogruel, L., Facciorusso, D., & Stark, B. (2020). 'I'm still the master of the machine. 'Internet users' awareness of algorithmic decision-making and their perception of its effect on their autonomy. *Information, Communication & Society*.

Donaghy, D. (2021). Defining digital capital and digital poverty. *ITNOW, 63*(1), 54–55.

Eubanks, V. (2017). *Automating inequality: How high-tech tools profile, police, and punish the poor* (1st ed.). St. Martin's Press.

Feezell, J. T., Wagner, J. K., & Conroy, M. (2021). Exploring the effects of algorithm-driven news sources on political behavior and polarization. *Computers in Human Behavior, 116*, 106626. https://doi.org/10.1016/j.chb.2020.106626

Fuchs, C. (2019). Karl Marx in the age of big data capitalism. In D. Chandler & C. Fuchs (Eds.), *Digital objects, digital subjects* (pp. 53–71). University of Westminster Press.

Fuchs, C., & Mosco, V. (2015). *Marx in the age of digital capitalism*. Brill.

Giddens, A. (1984). *The constitution of society. Outline of the theory of structuration*. University of California Press.

Goedhart, N. S., Broerse, J. E., Kattouw, R., & Dedding, C. (2019). 'Just having a computer doesn't make sense': The digital divide from the perspective of mothers with a low socio-economic position. *New Media & Society, 21*(11–12), 2347–2365.

Goodell, J. W., Kumar, S., Lim, W. M., & Pattnaik, D. (2021). Artificial intelligence and machine learning in finance: Identifying foundations, themes, and research clusters from bibliometric analysis. *Journal of Behavioral and Experimental Finance, 32*, 100577.

Gran, A.-B., Booth, P., & Bucher, T. (2021). To be or not to be algorithm aware: A question of a new digital divide? *Information, Communication & Society, 24*(12), 1779–1796.

Greenhalgh, T., & Stones, R. (2010). Theorising big IT programmes in healthcare: Strong structuration theory meets actor-network theory. *Social Science & Medicine, 70*(9), 1285–1294.

Gruber, J., Hargittai, E., Karaoglu, G., & Brombach, L. (2021). Algorithm awareness as an important Internet skill: The case of voice assistants. *International Journal of Communication, 15*, 19.

Gsenger, R., & Strle, T. (2021). Trust, automation bias and aversion: Algorithmic decisionmaking in the context of credit scoring. *Interdisciplinary Description of Complex Systems, 19*(4), 540–558.

Hepinstall, M., Chandrasekhar, C., Carroll, P., Dykstra, N., & Ulucay, Y. (2022). Financial inclusion and access to credit. *Oliver Wyman*. https://images.go.experian.com/Web/ExperianInformationSolutionsInc/%7B63ec9888-37ea-405c-b39d-7492de9143ce%7D_FINALExperian_report_14_01.pdf

Hoffmann, A. L. (2019). Where fairness fails: Data, algorithms, and the limits of antidiscrimination discourse. *Information, Communication & Society, 22*(7), 900–915.

Hosanagar, K., & Miller, A. (2020). Who do we blame for the filter bubble? On the roles of math, data, and people in algorithmic social systems. *After the Digital Tornado: Networks, Algorithms, Humanity*, 103–121.

Janer, S. S., & Ricafort, J. D. (2022). Graduate students' assessment on e-learning during COVID times. *American Research Journal of Humanities and Social Sciences, 5*(9), 25–30.

Jarrahi, M. H. (2018). Artificial intelligence and the future of work: Human-AI symbiosis in organizational decision making. *Business Horizons, 61*(4), 577–586.

Kelly, S., & Mirpourian, M. (2021). *Algorithmic bias, financial inclusion, and gender*. https://www.womensworldbanking.org/wpcontent/uploads/2021/02/2021_Algorithmic_Bias_Report.pdf

Kitchin, R. (2017). Thinking critically about and researching algorithms. *Information, Communication and Society, 20*(1), 1–14.

Kordzadeh, N., & Ghasemaghaei, M. (2022). Algorithmic bias: Review, synthesis, and future research directions. *European Journal of Information Systems, 31*(3), 388–409.

Long, D., & Magerko, B. (2020). What is AI literacy? Competencies and design considerations. *Proceedings of the 2020 CHI Conference on Human Factors in Computing Systems*, 1–16.

Lucas, P. J., Robinson, R., & Treacy, L. (2020). *What is data poverty?* Nesta and Ylab.

Lutz, C. (2019). Digital inequalities in the age of artificial intelligence and big data. *Human Behavior and Emerging Technologies, 1*(2), 141–148.

Manduna, W. (2016). Empirical study of digital poverty: A case study of a University of Technology in South Africa. *Journal of Communication, 7*(2), 317–323.

Marjanovic, O., Cecez-Kecmanovic, D., & Vidgen, R. (2022). Theorising algorithmic justice. *European Journal of Information Systems, 31*(3), 269–287.

Mohamed, S., Png, M. T., & Isaac, W. (2020). Decolonial AI: Decolonial theory as sociotechnical foresight in artificial intelligence. *Philosophy and Technology, 33*(4), 659–684.

Müller, V. C., & Bostrom, N. (2016). Future progress in artificial intelligence: A survey of expert opinion. *Fundamental Issues of Artificial Intelligence*, 555–572.

Neves, B. B., Waycott, J., & Malta, S. (2018). *Journal of Sociology, 54*(2), 236–248.

Noble, S. U. (2018). *Algorithms of oppression: How search engines reinforce racism.* New York University Press.

Nunan, F. (2015). *Understanding poverty and the environment. Analytical frameworks and approaches.* Routledge.

Oppenheim, M. (2018, October 11). Amazon scraps 'sexist AI' recruitment tool. *Independent.* https://www.independent.co.uk/tech/amazon-ai-sexist-recruitment-tool-algorithm-a8579161.html

Prodnik, J. (2021). *Algorithmic logic in digital capitalism.* In P. Verdegem (Ed.), *AI for everyone?* (pp. 203–222). University of Westminster Press.

PwC. (2017). *PwC's global artificial intelligence study: Exploiting the AI revolution.* https://www.pwc.com/gx/en/issues/data-and-analytics/publications/artificial-intelligence-study.html

Ragnedda, M. (2017). *The third digital divide. A Weberian analysis of digital inequalities.* Routledge.

Ragnedda, M. (2020). *Enhancing digital equity. Connecting the digital underclass.* Palgrave.

Ragnedda, M., & Ruiu, M. L. (2020). *Digital capital. A bourdieusian approach to digital divide.* Emeralds Publishing.

Ragnedda, M., Ruiu, M. L., & Addeo, F. (2022a). How offline backgrounds interact with digital capital. *New Media & Society.*

Ragnedda, M., Ruiu, M. L., & Addeo, F. (2022b). The self-reinforcing effect of digital and social exclusion: The inequality loop. *Telematics and Informatics, 72*, 101852.

Robinson, L., Ragnedda, M., & Schulz, J. (2020). Digital inequalities: Contextualizing problems and solutions. *Journal of Information, Communication and Ethics in Society, 18*(3), 323–327.

Ruiu, M. L., Ragnedda, M., Addeo, F., & Ruiu, G. (2023). Investigating how the interaction between individual and circumstantial determinants influence the emergence of digital poverty: A post-pandemic survey among families with children in England. *Information, Communication & Society, 26*(5), 1023–1044.

Schiller, D. (1999). *Digital capitalism*. MIT Press.

Schiller, D. (2001). *Digital capitalism. Networking the global market system*. MIT Press.

Secinaro, S., Calandra, D., Secinaro, A., Muthurangu, V., & Biancone, P. (2021). The role of artificial intelligence in healthcare: A structured literature review. *BMC Medical Informatics and Decision Making, 21*, 1–23.

Shin, D. (2022). How do people judge the credibility of algorithmic sources? *AI & Society, 37*(1), 81–96.

Siles, I., Segura-Castillo, A., Solís, R., & Sancho, M. (2020). Folk theories of algorithmic recommendations on Spotify: Enacting data assemblages in the global South. *Big Data & Society, 7*(1).

Stones, R. (2005). *Old and afraid of new communication technologies? Reconceptualizing and contesting the 'age-based digital divide' Structuration Theory*. Palgrave.

Susser, D. (2019). Invisible influence: Artificial intelligence and the ethics of adaptive choice architectures. *Proceedings of the 2019 AAAI/ACM Conference on AI, Ethics, and Society*, 403–408.

Turner, L. N., Resnick, P., & Barton, G. (2019). *Algorithmic bias detection and mitigation: Best practices and policies to reduce consumer harms*. https://www.brookings.edu/research/algorithmic-bias-detection-and-mitigation-best-practices-and-policies-to-reduce-consumer-harms/

van Deursen, A. J. A. M., & van Dijk, J. A. G. M. (2019). The first-level digital divide shifts from inequalities in physical access to inequalities in material access. *New Media & Society, 21*(2), 354–375.

Wyman, O. (2022). *Driving growth with greater credit access*. https://us-go.experian.com/driving-growth-with-greater-credit-access-white-paper

Yu, L. (2006). Understanding information inequality: Making sense of the literature of the information and digital divides. *Journal of Librarianship and Information Science, 38*(4), 229–252.

Zarouali, B., Boerman, S. C., & de Vreese, C. H. (2021). Is this recommended by an algorithm? The development and validation of the algorithmic media content awareness scale (AMCA-scale). *Telematics and Informatics, 62*, 101607. https://doi.org/10.1016/j.tele.2021.101607

Zarouali, B., Boerman, S. C., Voorveld, H. A. M., & van Noort, G. (2022). The algorithmic persuasion framework in online communication: Conceptualization and a future research agenda. *Internet Research, 32*(4), 1076–1096.

CHAPTER 4

# The Environmental Dimension of Poverty

## 4.1 Introduction

The previous chapter introduced the framework adopted by the DPA in which social structure and human agency are conceptualized as intertwined and metabolized by individuals (Greenhalgh & Stones, 2010; Stones, 2005). In this chapter, we start by introducing the core aspects of environmental poverty and its intrinsic connection with monetary poverty. This helps us understand why the environmental component, intended as inseparable from poverty, should also be considered integral to digital poverty and its related inequalities. The chapter introduces the concept of environmental poverty and the existing approaches to tackle it. It also refers to the literature on ecological values and green consumption, which supports connections with both digital behaviors and digital consumption.

One of the central goals of the whole book is to dig deeper into the DPF and review and expand it by including the environmental dimension. However, before delving deeper into this, it is essential to thoroughly examine the definition of environmental poverty as a state characterized by a degraded environment that poses a threat to human well-being and survival. We emphasize the interconnectedness between socioeconomic poverty and the degradation of the environment, by scrutinizing key



M. L. Ruiu, M. Ragnedda, *Digital-Environmental Poverty*, Palgrave Studies in Digital Inequalities,
https://doi.org/10.1007/978-3-031-56184-9_4

theoretical frameworks, such as the Poverty-Environment Hypothesis, the Ecological Modernization Theory, and the Environmental Kuznets Curve. This helps us to shed light on the dynamic interplay between environmental and economic conditions. We also further critically analyze this interconnectedness by using insights from social sciences and sociological perspectives. This allows us to reflect on how environmental poverty extends beyond mere physical conditions and incorporates the knowledge and perceptions of the environment held by various social actors. We do it by delving into the social construction of the environmental component of poverty.

Overall, this chapter aims to create a more comprehensive and nuanced understanding of the intricate web of relationships between social, economic, and environmental factors.

## 4.2 Definition of Environmental Poverty

Chapter 2 already introduced some aspects of the evolution of poverty over time and its multidimensionality and intersectionality with a variety of social, digital, and environmental aspects. We have also emphasized the need to conceptualize environmental and digital poverty as both independent and interdependent with socioeconomic and cultural aspects of poverty. Wang et al. (2022) showed that digital, social, and environment are strictly intersected, by finding a connection between digital adoption/penetration, a better environment, and a reduction of energy poverty thanks to improved efficiencies in the use of electricity and a reduction of the need for energy from fossil fuels. They also argue that all levels of society, from the government to business and the individual use of digital technologies, play a role in reducing energy demand. Consequently, investigating environmental poverty as a distinct term at the conceptual level may aid in comprehending how it interacts with other forms of poverty, such as digital poverty.

Before going in-depth in expanding the DPF to include the environmental trait in each of its constitutional dimensions/determinants, it might be useful to explore the definition of environmental poverty as a degraded environment that is unfit for human survival (Liu, 2012). Many studies (see Burki et al., 2022 for a review) have connected environmental degradation to high (socioeconomic) poverty levels and inequalities (Boockhin, 2005; Boyce, 2007). Moreover, environmental degradation can contribute toward increasing poverty when the use of resources, which should theoretically alleviate poverty, is redirected to address environmental threats (Asongu & Odhiambo, 2019; Dasgupta et al., 2005). This has direct effects on the welfare of a country by impacting health, living conditions, and household income, which in turn can have a role in inflaming internal conflicts and impacting the most vulnerable segments of the population (Dasgupta et al., 2005). On the other hand, it has been shown that detrimental environmental conditions impact the attractiveness of a country for investors, diminishing the opportunity to improve local economies and citizens' well-being (Akinlo & Dada, 2021). However, traditionally, poverty has been explored in its monetary valence, and this is because poverty reduction approaches have been historically driven by economic growth, which conceptualizes environmental damage as a future cost (Clémençon, 2012) and interprets poorer individuals' preferences in terms of surviving in the present at the cost of the environment conditions (Hagerty, 1999). However, it has been increasingly recognized that poverty intersects with the complexity of society and must be interpreted as multidimensional (Nunan, 2015). Moreover, the interrelationships between environment and poverty have been at the center of discussions since the nineteenth century when Malthus problematized the environmental consequences of population growth at the global level. Since the first UN Environment conference in Stockholm in 1972 and the Institution of the United Nations Environment Programme (UNEP, 1972), environmental and technological inequalities between developed and developing countries have been also at the center of transnational discussions. This was the first time that poverty and the environment were connected in terms of preserving and improving the human environment, for both the benefit and prosperity of all people. Similarly, the major concerted action plans at the global level (Kyoto Protocol and the Paris Agreement) constantly refer to the degradation of the environment as directly connected to the deterioration of human habitats. In fact, despite its multidimensionality, environmental degradation is generally identified in deforestation, air pollution, land degradation, water scarcity/contamination, and biodiversity loss (World Bank, 1992), which have direct effects on human lifestyles. Moreover, first, the Millennium Goals and then the Sustainable Goals set a range of commitments to eradicate poverty that also include multiple environmental aspects (Delia, 2021).

Liu (2012) suggests that environmental poverty differs from ecological poverty and climate poverty. Both ecological poverty and climate poverty refer to a particular type of poverty that derives from the scarcity of ecologically natural resources and the impacts of climate change. Instead, Liu (2012, p. 87) defines environmental poverty as "the lack of a healthy environment needed for society's survival and development, and this lack is mainly recognized as the consequence of environmental degradation caused by human activities." Such a condition is human-induced and caused by the exploitation of natural resources. This definition also reflects the social construction of nature, which is not fixed, but in continuous redefinition (Pellow, 2013). Environmental justice studies have also recognized the intersectional nature of environmental poverty (Magnani & Ryder, 2018; Pellow, 2013) by emphasizing the links between race, class (Downey, 2006; Bullard, 2005; Taylor, 2014), age (Hornberg & Pauli, 2007; Stephens, 1996; Taylor, 2009), but also ethnicity, migration, sexual orientation, and environmental inequality (Chakraborty et al., 2016; Crowder & Downey, 2010), and the need for addressing ecological degradation as a social injustice that mainly affects already marginalized groups (Frey et al., 2019; Martínez-Alier, 2002; Mennis & Jordan, 2005; Nyseth-Brehm & Pellow, 2014). Therefore, environmental problems can be interpreted from a social constructionist perspective as social problems, which are defined not only by objective conditions but are identified, perceived, and defined by shared meanings attached to the issues (Burningham & Cooper, 1999; Taylor, 2012). This also suggests that different framings of environmental discourses can produce different perceptions of the problem. This is also valid for environmental inequality and poverty.

Following this direction, this chapter uses a definition of environmental poverty as both independent in its conceptualization and interdependent with other forms of poverty. As an independent concept, environmental poverty is often used as an umbrella term that refers to unhealthy and degraded environments, which in turn affect living standards and social well-being. Following Nunan (2015) and the Millenium Ecosystem Assessment (2005), the natural environment provides several services that include provisioning functions (for example, food, water, wood), regulating functions (for example, regulation of the climate), cultural functions (for example, recreation and esthetic), and supporting functions (for example, production natural resources). More specifically, adopting and further developing the definition of the level of poverty provided by the United Nations (UN, 1995), we refer to poverty as a condition of deprivation of basic human needs/well-being (including awareness and understanding of the environment) and healthy ecosystems (including degradation of biotic and abiotic components). "It depends not only on income but also on access to services [and a healthy environment]." Therefore, this definition of poverty also includes environmental conditions as constitutive of poverty and enablers of individual "capabilities" to achieve human development (Sen, 2001). As an interdependent concept, it contributes toward defining poverty by including both socioeconomic (including digital chances) and environmental deprivation.

## 4.3 Approaches to Environmental Poverty

The previous paragraph highlighted some interconnections between socioeconomic poverty and environmental degradation by also identifying streams in the literature that connect environmental concerns and their related behavior to aspects linked, for instance, to social class (for example, education, income, and occupation) (Van Liere & Dunlap, 1981). This understanding is generally based on the assumption that individuals will develop attention to the environment, which they will recognize to be connected to their quality of life, once they have met their basic material needs (Andrews & Withey, 1978). Yu and Liu (2022) synthesize the approaches to the relationship between poverty and the environment into three macro-areas: poverty as the cause of environmental degradation (WCED, 1987; World Bank, 1992); poverty as not necessarily related to the environment (Duraiappah, 1998); poverty as a complex concept intertwined with numerous dimensions, including the environment (Leach & Meams, 1991; Rizk & Slimane, 2018).

The Poverty-Environment Hypothesis, which was one of the core aspects highlighted in numerous reports by the Brundtland Commission (WCED, 1987), the World Bank (1992), and the United Nations Environment Programme (UNEP, 1995), assumes that people living in poor conditions are both victims and responsible for environmental degradation for surviving through the overexploitation of natural resources (Angelsen, 1997; Setyadharma et al., 2020). However, such a hypothesis also emphasizes the need for economic growth to break the poverty circle. Linkages between financial poverty and environmental poverty have been confirmed by several studies (Baloch et al., 2020; Masron & Subramaniam, 2019). Despite this recognition, the conceptualization of the natural environment as constitutive of poverty, rather than just an external "determinant," has been scarcely considered (Schleicher et al., 2017). However, similar to modernization approaches in sociology (Mol, 1995, 2001; Mol & Spaargaren, 2000; Mol et al., 2010; Spaargaren, 1997) and approaches inspired by the Environmental Kuznets Curve (EKC) in economics (Grossman & Krueger, 1991, 1995), this hypothesis is optimistic in connecting the improvement of economic conditions to that of environmental conditions. At the same time, several studies have contradicted the assumption that higher income will translate into a better natural environment (Ficko & Bončina, 2019; Stern, 2004, 2017; Shahbaz & Sinha, 2019), and in some cases, middle- and low-income countries were shown to reduce pollution more rapidly than developed countries (see, for example, Dasgupta et al., 2002). World System Theory and scholars (Wallerstein, 1974) have contextualized the interconnections between environmental degradation and socioeconomic impoverishment in the international arena by stressing the unequal exchange of benefits (for wealthy nations) and disadvantages (for the periphery) (Pellow, 2013). Despite the critiques of its Marxist radicalism, world system analysis highlights how social and environmental conditions must be contextualized in the capitalist world economy, which creates a hierarchy. This unequal relationship results in "ecologically unequal exchange" (see, for example, Hornborg, 1998; Jorgenson, 2006; Jorgenson et al., 2009; Jorgenson & Givens, 2013), characterized by the depletion of "natural capital" (Costanza & Daly, 1992; Schumacher, 1973), the externalization of environmentally harmful consequences (for example, deforestation, pollution, greenhouse gas emissions, loss of biodiversity), and limited distribution of the associated benefits in less developed regions. In turn, such an ecologically unequal exchange is tied to unequal socioeconomic development and asymmetrical power relationships in the world system. The socioeconomic poverty of these realities has also generated a dependence of less developed countries on "foreign direct investment," which, in turn, makes them even more vulnerable. This is because they will be more likely to relax the regulatory system about environmental matters (see Jorgenson & Givens, 2013 for a review).

Among the Political Economy perspectives in environmental sociology, the Ecological Modernization Theory (EMT) predicts a natural alignment of industrial development to global environmental challenges. EMT theorizes the decoupling between economic growth and ecological disruption, which seemed to take place from the mid-1980s onward in most developed nations (Mol, 2010). These assumptions go hand in hand with the hypothesis developed in economics by the EKC (Grossman & Krueger, 1991, 1995), which presumes that once a country achieves economic stability, individuals will start demanding environmental protection (Ridzuan,

2019) through regulation of the market in a green direction. However, the EKC hypothesis has been debated as a controversial model of harmonization between economic growth and the environment (Dinda, 2004). Many studies have contested the validity of such assumptions (Dunlap & York, 2008), also considering that the emissions of several pollutants have declined in countries that are not necessarily developed (Anwar et al., 2022).

Following EMT, these dynamics are also reflected at the individual level thanks to the development of an "ecological rationality" (Mol, 1995), which is driven by self-reflexivity typical of modern societies (Giddens, 1984) and by the development of postmaterialist values (Inglehart, 1977, 1990). These assumptions were supported by the institutionalization of governmental departments with environmental tasks, assessment of the environmental health status, an increasing commitment of Non-Governmental Organizations in the environmental sector, the development of environmental laws, and the emergence of green political parties since the 1970s. Nonetheless, the 1990s saw the most evident changes in environmental management thanks to the introduction of a regulatory apparatus that imposed certain norms of conduct (Mol, 2010). However, environmental-related problems, such as in the case of climate change, have been identified as threats to individuals' ontological security due to the erosion of self-identity caused by constant instability and changes in the environment (Norgaard, 2011). Some studies found different results when considering the relationship between environment and income (Boyce, 1994; Scruggs, 1998; Magnani, 2000). Moreover, in some cases, higher economic development was found to be associated with less environmental concern among citizens (Givens & Jorgenson, 2011). In this direction, Ridzuan (2019) found that higher income inequalities delay the turning point of the curve.

Social science has shown a more complex picture of connections to be considered when exploring individual environmental perception and engagement, by emphasizing links with political decisions (Leffel et al., 2023), economic development and income (Givens, 2018; Prell & Sun, 2015; Sinha & Shahbaz, 2018), and subjective value orientations (Dorsch, 2014). Sociology approaches have considered additional factors that influence the relationship between inequality and environmental engagement/awareness such as the unequal circulation of environmental information and environmental issues not being perceived as priorities (Franzen & Meyer, 2010; Stiglitz, 2014; Wilkinson & Pickett, 2010). This suggests that environmental poverty also encapsulates knowledge and understanding of the environment by social actors at multiple levels, once again reinforcing the social construction of the environment. In response to critiques of EMT national-centeredness, which may not apply well in the context of globalization, Mol et al. (2010) points to further developments in these approaches. These developments align with the environmental sociology of networks and flows, drawing inspiration from the work of Castells, Urry, and Sassen since the mid-1990s, but with a specific focus on the environmental interpretation of the concept of flow. The environmental sociology of networks and flows interprets power and inequality as linked to the capacity to access and control the process of flow and related to the flows of capital, information, and subjects that shape and activate environmental reforms. This is an important point that suggests how environmental poverty is also connected to the lack of participation in the decision-making process and control of the circulation of environmental information.

On the other side of the political economy spectrum, the Treadmill of Production (ToP) theory more pessimistically interprets capitalist economies as a treadmill that requires constant economic growth (Gould et al., 2004, 2008; Gould et al., 1996; Schnaiberg, 1980). In so doing, capitalist approaches favor powerful organizations in the process of appropriation of natural resources and the addition of waste and pollution for profit accumulation (Hooks et al., 2021; Schnaiberg & Gould, 1994). The counterlogic highlighted by Schnaiberg emphasizes how the political-economic paradigm of constant growth contrasts both environmental quality and social well-being, which are two sides of the same coin. In contrast to ecological modernization optimism, ToP theory adopts a Marxist stand in criticizing the capitalist system and interprets technological development as an accelerator of production thanks to increasing efficiency. Private actors who benefit from economic growth will require deregulation and try to maximize profit by reducing costs (for example, related to labor and lower taxes) and will invest in technologies that will require minimum costs and maximum profit at the expense of the environment (Gould et al., 2004). The ToP also triggers cascading processes such as the Treadmill of Consumption (ToC), activated by the advertising process, and the positional nature of consumption, but also by its defensive character to protect the well-being attached to it (Curran, 2017). These mechanisms in turn produce relational exchange that increases the purchasing power of specific groups while undermining the possibility of accessing basic goods of other groups. In this direction, Curran (2017) emphasizes that the continuous upgrading of essential commodities for socialization, especially in the case of ICTs, forces people to contribute to the ToC to defend their well-being. Therefore, inequality in the distribution of benefits is at the basis of the ToP, as well as the impoverishment of the natural environment in which the most vulnerable groups are likely to live.

It is, indeed, generally recognized the activation of multiple vicious circles when environmental poverty and income poverty coexist (Angelsen, 1997; Anwar et al., 2022; Malerba, 2020; Nunan, 2015). On the other hand, a strand of the literature referred to the environment-poverty circle as too simplistic to take into account the specificities of the contexts affected by both environmental and financial poverty. It is based on a causal link between improvement in the environment and poverty and does not sufficiently take into account political economy factors that influence such interaction (Nunan, 2015). Despite contrasting results on the causal relationship between environmental poverty and financial poverty, the degradation of the environment has been often identified as affecting the well-being and quality of life of people in sociocultural and economic terms (Anguelovski & Martinez Alier, 2014; Schleicher et al., 2018, Ulucak & Lin, 2017; World Bank, 2000), as in the case of climate change that hinders poverty eradication efforts (Malerba, 2020) and aggravates poverty conditions (see, for example, Hallegatte et al., 2018; Mendelsohn et al., 2006; Hsiang et al., 2017). While the specificities of the context are relevant from a policymaking point of view, these studies seem to suggest that, beyond both the local and international political economy, when the environment is excessively damaged and polluted, living conditions might find it hard to improve (DFID et al., 2002; World Bank, 2008). Since the 1980s, environmental justice research has repeatedly shown how environmental inequities (for example, exposure to pollution and toxic hazards) are connected to existing disadvantaged conditions (Banzhaf et al., 2019b; Brulle & Pellow, 2006; Bullard, 1990, 1993; Pellow, 2017a) and amplifiers of social inequities, poverty, and divisions (Banzhaf et al., 2019a; Magnani & Ryder, 2018; Pellow, 2017b; Pellow, 2013) at both local and international levels (Temper, 2018).

Even though financial poverty cannot be acknowledged as the unique cause of environmental poverty and vice versa, given the increasing threats imposed by the degradation of natural resources, pollution, and climate change, environmental poverty becomes one of the pivotal dimensions that contribute toward the definition of poverty. This is observable in developing countries and rural contexts in which poorer individuals tend to be extremely dependent on the environment for their livelihoods (Barbier, 2010). This is also supported by the Sustainable Livelihoods Framework (Scoones, 1998) and its further developments (see Natarajan et al., 2022 for a review), which include both natural and non-natural resources, as well as capabilities, as means of gaining a living (for example, human capital, natural capital, financial capital, social capital, and physical capital) (Scoones, 1998; Nunan, 2015 for a review). Several studies and reports showed the impact of environmental degradation on poorer people (World Bank, 2019), for instance, in terms of dealing with the most severe consequences of such a degradation (Satterthwaite, 2003a) such as health consequences (Satterthwaite, 2003b; World Bank, 2019) and availability of resources (Satterthwaite, 2003b).

Considering the profound effects of environmental poverty on specific demographics, the following paragraph will delve into the development of ecological values and specific consumption patterns at the individual level.

## 4.4 Ecological Values and Consumption

So far this chapter has mainly explored the interaction between the values promoted by capitalist organizations and environmental consequences at multiple levels of society; this paragraph takes into account the individual perspective and how the production and consumption dimensions interact in the context of environmental poverty. As aforementioned, following socioeconomic approaches inspired by the EKC, ecological rationality is expected to emerge spontaneously when economic prosperity is achieved. However, the previous paragraph also highlighted several contradictions that emerge at both the theoretical and empirical levels when testing this hypothesis. For example, Ewing (2017) argues that the theoretical foundation of ecological rationality is contradictory because it is simultaneously independent of economic rationality and subordinate to it. Such an approach is still in line with ecological modernization theories that interpret the potential of greening capitalist economies via radical resource productivity driven by partnerships between firms and regulators (Hawken et al., 1999; Mol, 1995; Porter & van der Linde, 1995). At the same time, Spaargaren and Van Vliet (2000) refer to the ecological modernization of domestic consumption, which shows how environmental innovations are also induced by the wishes of the consumers.

The scientific debate has shown multiple criticalities related to "green capitalism-inspired approaches" which draw upon the idea of continuous profit and economic growth (Ewing, 2017). The major ethical concerns of such a conceptualization relate to the tangible risk that economic interests might overshadow socio-environmental inequalities and influence power balances between controllers and market organizations. On the one hand, economic approaches tend to focus on the structural influence of economic configuration in influencing individuals' environmental behavior; on the other hand, social-psychological models emphasize the importance of the values and beliefs that drive agentic power. Research in Green Information Systems has increasingly recognized the importance of addressing the impacts of technology use by individuals, groups, and organizations, and in developing eco-sustainable practices (Watson et al., 2010).

What still needs to be explored is the connection between action (micro level) and structure (macro level) (Spaargaren & Van Vliet, 2000). Despite controversies in identifying the factors that influence the emergence of ecological rationality and post-materialistic values, such rationality is reflected in the way in which individuals have come to conceptualize the environment and how they behave. It is also embedded in a specific context that enables individuals to act in certain ways. In fact, looking at the rules and practice of social systems, following Giddens (1979, p. 65), rules need to be understood in their historical development and "as recursively implicated in practices," whereas practices exist in the context of "overlapping and connected sets of rules." Therefore, this duality of the structure expresses the mutual dependency of rules and practices which "exist in conjunction with one another." Applying Giddens' structuration theory, Spaargaren and Van Vliet (2000) position environmental behavior within social practices, emphasizing that environmentally friendly actions cannot be comprehended in isolation but must be contextualized within a system of shared social norms. At the same time, the "duality of structure," central to structuration theory, functions as both a determinant and an outcome of human action, enabling both reproduction and transformation of social structure. However, scarce attention has been given to how structural properties interact with the agentic transformative individual power in the context of environmental poverty. Nevertheless, even scarcer attention has been given to the potential environmental benefits deriving from an increasing application of Internet technologies in the structure of everyday life and individual consumption practices.

Ecological rationality and values are also reflected in consumption practices and behaviors that can become increasingly environmentally friendly depending on the context in which they are situated, their social values and individual predispositions. The literature offers contrasting results regarding the influence of contextual and individual factors on pro-environmental behavior. Green consumption is defined as practices and lifestyles that combine environmental, ethical, and political values (Barnett et al., 2010). In this direction, many green consumption studies have highlighted how attitudes toward pro-environmental behavior are supported by individual values, intrinsic motivations, and personal satisfaction (see, for example, De Young, 1986, 1996; Ejelöv et al., 2022; Helferich et al., 2023; Steg, 2016). Tang et al. (2023) also found that the effect of the legal system on promoting pro-environmental behavior is mediated by intrinsic motivation. At the same time, everyday practices might also be constrained by structural and circumstantial determinants which can contribute toward the creation of group lifestyles (Barr & Gilg, 2006), for example, under the influence of environmental regulation (Porter & van der Linde, 1995), specific social norms (see, for example, Allcott, 2011; Keiser & Schultz, 2018; Smith et al., 2012), and social capital (Wan & Du, 2022). Since Thorstein Veblen's Theory of the Leisure Class (1899), sociologists have increasingly understood the consumption of goods and services as a social and ostentatious/conspicuous practice that marks a status (Douglas & Isherwood, 1979). However, adopting a Bourdesian approach can help reconcile the criticalities of Veblen's approach, which does not consider new "democratized" luxury (Taylor et al., 2009), and is strictly based on economic factors and a "trickle-down" model (emulation of the upper class by the masses) (Simmel, 2011). For example, a strand of literature highlights how low-income consumers tend to spend more on conspicuous items (including trending technologies) (Currid-Halkett, 2017; Eckhardt et al., 2015). A Bourdesian approach can, instead, help focus on the cultural component of taste, which also allows for a "trickle round" of tastes (which can follow multiple directions and not just top-down) (Trigg, 2001). Indeed, Bourdieu (1984/1979) noted a "trickle-up" mechanism where the upper class adopted certain working-class tastes, differentiating themselves from the middle class, which in turn sought to emulate upper-class tastes and distinguish themselves from the working class. A Bourdesian perspective (1984/1979) can help understand the interaction between social practice and agentic power thanks to the concept of taste, which is both a metabolized expression of individuals' backgrounds and the result of how individuals experience the field of action.

Furthermore, the digital dimension of consumption exacerbates a "privatized" form of consumption (Saunders, 1987) with increasing autonomy of choice for the consumer among a variety of products and services that belong to the global market. Such privatization of the consumption practice is also translated into a "private" experience that happens behind screens in the private dimension, which might be helpful to remove the "waste of goods" connected to conspicuous leisure and consumption described by Veblen. Even though this chapter does not aim to focus on ostentation practices of consumption, it is also worth noting that such environmentally damaging behavior might be reproduced in the digital sphere by, for instance, social media-oriented and digital nomad lifestyles (Bonneau & Aroles, 2021). In this direction, the scientific debate has highlighted that information technologies can support, promulgate, but also inhibit conspicuous behavior (Miller, 2018). This is also helpful in terms of understanding the interconnections between digital and environmental dimensions at the individual level, influenced by one's specific taste (which, in turn, is influenced by their belonging to a social group) and how these preferences are expressed in online consumption behaviors.

As an example of how digital forms of consumption are increasingly becoming observably connected to environmental aspects at multiple levels, let us consider the changes produced by digital acceleration due to the pandemic at multiple levels. At a macro level, during the COVID lockdowns, air quality was significantly higher in several UK cities (UKRI, 2020) due to several constraints, such as travel and movement restrictions (and a shift to digital arenas), the slowdown of the economy, and the reduction of industrial waste and fossil fuel consumption (Rume & Islam, 2020). Some comparative studies also showed a positive impact of e-commerce on the environment. However, they have also shown that the nature of these effects depends on the energy and packaging materials used in logistics networks (Scott Matthews et al., 2001) and the model used, for instance, for home delivery (Gee et al., 2020; Siikavirta et al., 2002) and return system (Sievering, 2020). Moreover, many studies have investigated technology emissions and their impact on the energy sector (for example, Shah et al., 2021; Kahouli, 2018; Koçak & Ulucak, 2019). Therefore, individual choices of digital consumption and behaviors made in the private dimension have an impact and simultaneously interact with both circumstantial and structural determinants.

Given such interdependence, it is useful to reflect on the effects of the increasing digitalization of everyday life, which has been accelerated by the COVID-19 pandemic. The next section will do so by exploring the intersections between environmental poverty and digital poverty using the DPF as a model to guide such an understanding.

## 4.5 Conclusion

This section focused on the definition of digital and environmental poverty as both interdependent concepts (intersected with traditional forms of poverty) and independent constructs that can help isolate some main components of their definition. It reviewed several approaches to digital inequalities that helped define and understand digital poverty as a stratifying concept rather than a dichotomic one (such as in the case of the digital divide). Chapter 3 also explored the model proposed by the DPA that identified multiple determinants of digital poverty. This model will be useful in the next section where we will propose the integration of the environmental component, analyzed in this chapter, at each dimension identified by the framework.

The exploration introduced environmental poverty and its vital association with monetary poverty. It also explored several theories from different disciplines that more or less optimistically interpret the relationship between economic development and the protection of the environment. These ideas provide insight into the intricate relationship between poverty and environmental degradation by emphasizing the uneven benefits that are traded and the worsening of economic situations when environmental degradation is widespread. The chapter also delved into ecological values and consumption, acknowledging the duality of structure in shaping individuals' environmentally conscious choices. The intersection of digitalization and environmental concerns was explored, considering how the digital acceleration induced by the pandemic influences consumption patterns and environmental outcomes.

This chapter presented an exploration of environmental poverty, its interconnection with capitalist-oriented societies, and the role of consumption patterns in shaping environmental outcomes. Overall, this chapter shows the need to adopt a comprehensive approach that integrates environmental factors into the concept of poverty. The next section will focus on identifying the interdependence of digital and environmental poverty in contemporary society and the need for integrating such dimensions to understand and tackle inequalities. We will examine the implications of integrating the environmental dimension at micro, meso, and macro levels. In the next section, we will delve into the integration of the environmental dimension into the concept of digital poverty, examining its implications at multiple levels. We will emphasize the necessity of adopting a multilevel and integrated approach that considers interconnected social issues, including digital and environmental poverty.

## References

Akinlo, T., & Dada, J. T. (2021). The moderating effect of foreign direct investment on environmental degradation-poverty reduction nexus: Evidence from sub-Saharan African countries. *Environment, Development and Sustainability, 23*, 15764–15784.

Allcott, H. (2011). Social norms and energy conservation. *Journal of Public Economics, 95*(9–10), 1082–1095.

Andrews, F. M., & Withey, S. (1978). *Social indicators of well being: American's perception of life quality*. Plenum.

Angelsen, A. (1997). The poverty-environment thesis: Was Brundtland wrong? *Forum for Development Studies, 24*(1), 135–154.

Anguelovski, I., & Martinez Alier, J. (2014). The 'Environmentalism of the Poor' revisited: Territory and place in disconnected glocal struggles. *Ecological Economics, 102*, 167–176.

Anwar, M. A., Zhang, Q., Asmi, F., Hussain, N., Plantinga, A., Zafar, W., & Sinha, A. (2022). Global perspectives on environmental Kuznets curve: A bibliometric review. *Gondwana Research, 103*, 135–145.

Asongu, S. A., & Odhiambo, N. M. (2019). Environmental degradation and inclusive human development in sub-Saharan Africa. *Sustainable Development, 27*(1), 25–34.

Baloch, M. A., Salah Ud-Din Khan, D., & Ulucak, Z. S. (2020). Poverty and vulnerability of environmental degradation in Sub-Saharan African countries: What causes what? *Structural Change and Economic Dynamics, 54*, 143–149.

Banzhaf, H. S., Ma, L., & Christopher, C. (2019a). Environmental justice: Establishing causal relationships. *Annual Review of Resource Economics, 11*, 377–398.

Banzhaf, H. S., Ma, L., & Timmins, C. (2019b). Environmental justice: The economics of race, place, and pollution. *Journal of Economic Perspectives, 33*(1), 185–208.

Barbier, E. B. (2010). Poverty, development, and environment. *Environment and Development Economics, 15*, 635–660.

Barnett, C., Cloke, P., Clarke, N., & Malpass, A. (2010). *Globalizing responsibility: The political rationalities of ethical consumption*. John Wiley & Sons.

Barr, S., & Gilg, A. (2006). Sustainable lifestyles: Framing environmental action in and around the home. *Geoforum, 37*(6), 906–920.
Bonneau, C., & Aroles, J. (2021). Digital nomads: A new form of leisure class? In J. Aroles, F. X. de Vaujany, & K. Dale (Eds.), *Experiencing the new world of work* (pp. 157–177). Cambridge University Press.
Boockhin, M. (2005). *The ecology of freedom: The emergence of dissolution of hierarchy*. AK Press.
Bourdieu, P. (1984/1979). *Distinction: A social critique of the judgement of taste*. Harvard University Press.
Boyce, J. K. (1994). Inequality as a cause of environmental degradation. *Ecological Economics, 11*(3), 169–178.
Boyce, J. K. (2007). *Is inequality bad for the environment?* Political Economy Research Institute Working Paper Series, 135. https://doi.org/10.7275/1282709
Brehm, H. N., & Pellow, D. N. (2014). Environmental justice. Pollution, poverty, and marginalized communities. In P. G. Harris (Ed.), *Routledge handbook of global environmental politics* (pp. 308–320). Routledge.
Brulle, R. J., & Pellow, D. N. (2006). Environmental justice: Human health and environmental inequalities. *Annual Review of Public Health, 27*, 103–124.
Bullard, R. (1990). *Dumping in dixie: Race, class, and environmental quality*. Westview Press.
Bullard, R. (2005). *The quest for environmental justice: Human rights and the politics of pollution*. Sierra Clun Books.
Bullard, R. D. (1993). Anatomy of environmental racism and the environmental justice movement. In R. D. Bullard (Ed.), *Confronting environmental racism: Voices from the grassroots* (pp. 15–40). South End Press.
Burki, M. A. K., Burki, U., & Najam, U. (2022). Environmental degradation and poverty: A bibliometric review. *Regional Sustainability, 2*(4), 324–336.
Burningham, K., & Cooper, G. (1999). Beain constructive: Social constructionism and the environment. *Sociology, 33*(2), 97–316.
Chakraborty, J., Collins, T. W., & Grineski, S. E. (2016). Environmental justice research: Contemporary issues and emerging topics. *International Journal of Environmental Research and Public Health, 13*(11), 1072. https://doi.org/10.3390/ijerph13111072
Clémençon, R. (2012). Welcome to the Anthropocene: Rio+20 and the meaning of sustainable development. *Journal of Environment & Development, 21*(3), 311–338.
Costanza, R., & Daly, H. E. (1992). Natural capital and sustainable development. *Conservation Biology, 6*, 37–46.
Crowder, K., & Downey, L. (2010). Inter-neighbourhood migration, race, and environmental hazards: Modelling micro-level processes of environmental inequality. *American Journal of Sociology, 115*(4), 1110–1149.

Curran, D. (2017). The treadmill of production and the positional economy of consumption. *Canadian Review of Sociology, 54*(1), 28–47.

Currid-Halkett, E. (2017). *The sum of small things: A theory of the aspirational class.* Princeton University Press.

Dasgupta, S., Deichmann, W., Meisner, C., & Wheeler, D. (2005). Where is the poverty-environment nexus? Evidence from Cambodia, Lao PDR, and Vietnam. *World Development, 33*(4), 617–638.

Dasgupta, S., Laplante, B., Wang, H., & Wheeler, D. (2002). Confronting the environmental Kuznets curve. *Journal of Economic Perspectives, 16*, 147–168.

De Young, R. (1986). Some psychological aspects of recycling. *Environment and Behavior, 18*, 435–449.

De Young, R. (1996). Some psychological aspects of reduced consumption behaviour: The role of intrinsic motivation and competence motivation. *Environment and Behavior, 28*, 358–409.

Delia, P. (2021). *Merging the poverty and environment agendas.* International Institute for Sustainable Development. Brief 11. https://www.iisd.org/articles/deep-dive/merging-poverty-and-environment-agendas

DFID, EC, UNDP, & The World Bank. (2002). *Linking poverty reduction and environmental management.* World Bank.

Dinda, S. (2004). Environmental Kuznets curve hypothesis. A survey. *Ecological Economics, 49*(4), 431–455.

Dorsch, M. T. (2014). Economic development and determinants of environmental concern. *Social Science Quarterly, 95*(4), 960–977.

Douglas, M., & Isherwood, B. (1979). *The world of goods: Towards an anthropology of consumption.* W.W. Norton.

Downey, L. (2006). Environmental racial inequality in Detroit. *Sociological Forces, 85*(2), 771–796.

Dunlap, R. E., & York, R. (2008). The globalisation of environmental concern and the limits of post-materialist values explanation: Evidence from four multinational surveys. *The Sociological Quarterly, 49*(3), 529–563.

Duraiappah, A. K. (1998). Poverty and environmental degradation: A review and analysis of the nexus. *World Development, 26*(12), 2169–2179.

Eckhardt, G. M., Belk, R. W., & Wilson, J. A. J. (2015). The rise of inconspicuous consumption. *Journal of Marketing Management, 31*(7–8), 807–826.

Ejelöv, E., Bergquist, M., Hansla, A., & Nilsson, A. (2022). Why are they eco-friendly? Attributing eco-friendly descriptive norms to intrinsic motivation increases pro-environmental purchase intention. *PLoS One, 20*(10). https://doi.org/10.1371/journal.pone.0265839

Ewing, J. A. (2017). Hollow ecology: Ecological modernization theory and the death of nature. *Journal of World-Systems Research, 23*(1), 126–155.

Ficko, A., & Bončina, A. (2019). Public attitudes toward environmental protection in the most developed countries: The Environmental Concern Kuznets Curve theory. *Journal of Environmental Management, 231*(1), 968–981.

Franzen, A., & Meyer, R. (2010). Environmental attitudes in cross-national perspective: A multilevel analysis of the ISSP 1993 and 2000. *European Sociological Review, 26*(2), 219–234.

Frey, R. F., Gellert, P. K., & Dahms, H. F. (2019). *Ecologically unequal exchange. Environmental injustice in comparative and historical perspective*. Palgrave Macmillan.

Gaard, G. (2018). Feminism and environmental justice. In R. Holifield, J. Chakraborty, & G. Walker (Eds.), *The Routledge handbook of environmental justice*. Routledge.

Gee, I. M., Heard, B. R., Webber, M. E., & Miller, S. A. (2020). The future of food: Environmental lessons from e-commerce. *Environmental Science & Technology, 54*(23). https://doi.org/10.1021/acs.est.0c01731

Giddens, A. (1979). *Central problems in social theory*. Palgrave.

Giddens, A. (1984). *The constitution of society. Outline of the theory of structuration*. University of California Press.

Givens, J. E. (2018). Ecologically unequal exchange and the carbon intensity of well-being, 1990–2011. *Environ Sociol 4*(3), 311–324.

Givens, J., & Jorgenson, A. K. (2011). The effects of affluence, economic development, and environmental degradation on environmental concern: A multilevel analysis. *Organization & Environment, 24*, 74–91.

Gould, K., Pellow, D. N., & Schnaiberg, A. (2004). Interrogating the treadmill of production: Everything you wanted to know about the treadmill but were afraid to ask. *Organization & Environment, 17*(3), 296–316.

Gould, K., Pellow, D. N., & Schnaiberg, A. (2008). *The treadmill of production*. Paradigm Publishing.

Gould, K. A., Schnaibergand, A., & Weinberg, A. S. (1996). *Local environmental struggles: Citizen activism in the treadmill of production*. Cambridge University Press.

Greenhalgh, T., & Stones, R. (2010). Theorising big IT programmes in healthcare: Strong structuration theory meets actor-network theory. *Social Science & Medicine, 70*(9), 1285–1294.

Grossman, G. M., & Krueger, A. B. (1991). *Environmental impacts of a North American Free Trade Agreement*. Working Paper 3914, NBER.

Grossman, G. M., & Krueger, A. B. (1995). Economic growth and the environment. *Quarterly Journal of Economics, 110*, 353–377.

Hagerty, M. R. (1999). Testing Maslow's hierarchy of needs: National quality-of-life across time. *Social Indicators Research, 46*(3), 249–271.

Hallegatte, S., Fay, M., & Barbier, E. (2018). Poverty and climate change: Introduction. *Environment and Development Economics, 23*, 217–233.

Hawken, P. A. L., Lovins, A. B., & Lovins, H. (1999). The next industrial revolution. In P. A. L. Hawken, A. B. Lovins, & H. Lovins (Eds.), *Natural capitalism: Creating the next industrial revolution* (pp. 1–21). Little, Brown & Co.

Helferich, M., Thøgersen, J., & Bergquist, M. (2023). Direct and mediated impacts of social norms on pro-environmental behavior. *Global Environmental Change, 80*. https://doi.org/10.1016/j.gloenvcha.2023.102680

Hooks, G., Lengefeld, M., & Smith, C. L. (2021). Recasting the treadmills of production and destruction: New theoretical directions. *Sociology of Development, 7*(1), 52–76.

Hornberg, C., & Pauli, A. (2007). Child poverty and environmental justice. *International Journal of Hygiene and Environmental Health, 210*(5), 571–580.

Hornborg, A. (1998). Towards an ecological theory of unequal exchange: Articulating world system theory and ecological economics. *Ecological Economics, 25*(1), 127–136.

Hsiang, S., Kopp, R., Jina, A., Rising, J., Delgado, M., Mohan, S., Rasmussen, D. J., Muir-Wood, R., Wilson, P., & Oppenheimer, M. (2017). Estimating economic damage from climate change in the United States. *Science, 356*, 1362–1369.

Inglehart, R. (1977). *The silent revolution*. Princeton University Press.

Inglehart, R. (1990). *Culture shift in advanced industrial society*. Princeton University Press.

Jorgenson, A. K. (2006). Unequal ecological exchange and environmental degradation: A theoretical proposition and cross national study of deforestation, 1990–2000. *Rural Sociology, 71*(4), 685–712.

Jorgenson, A. K., Austin, K., & Dick, C. (2009). Ecologically unequal exchange and the resource consumption/environmental degradation paradox: A panel study of less-developed countries, 1970–2000. *International Journal of Comparative Sociology, 50*(3–4), 263–284.

Jorgenson, A. K., & Givens, J. E. (2013). The emergence of new world-systems perspectives on global environmental change. In S. Lockie, D. A. Sonnenfeld, & D. R. Fisher (Eds.), *Routledge international handbook of social and environmental change* (pp. 31–44). Routledge International.

Kahouli, B. (2018). The causality link between energy electricity consumption, CO2 emissions, R&D stocks and economic growth in Mediterranean Countries (MCs). *Energy, 145*, 388–399.

Keiser, K., & Schultz, P. W. (2018). Social norms and pro-environmental behaviour. In L. Steg & J. I. M. de Groot (Eds.), *Environmental psychology: An introduction* (2nd ed., pp. 179–188). Wiley Online Library.

Koçak, E., & Ulucak, Z. Ş. (2019). The effect of energy R&D expenditures on CO2 emission reduction: Estimation of the STIRPAT model for OECD countries. *Environmental Science and Pollution Research, 26*, 14328–14338.

Leach, M., & Meams, R. (1991). *Poverty and environment in developing countries: An overview study*. Final report to the ESRC and ODA, University of Sussex, Institute of Development Studies.

Leffel, B., Derudder, B., Acuto, M., & van der Heijden, J. (2023). Not so polycentric: The stratified structure & national drivers of transnational municipal networks. https://doi.org/10.2139/ssrn.4485113

Liu, L. (2012). Environmental poverty, a decomposed environmental Kuznets curve, and alternatives: Sustainability lessons from China. *Ecological Economics, 73*, 86–92.

Magnani, E. (2000). The Environmental Kuznets Curve, environmental protection policy and income distribution. *Ecological Economics, 32*(3), 431–443.

Magnani, S., & Ryder, S. (2018). Developing deeply intersectional environmental justice scholarship. *Environmental Sociology, 4*(1), 1–7.

Malerba, D. (2020). Poverty alleviation and local environmental degradation: An empirical analysis in Colombia. *World Development, 127.* https://doi.org/10.1016/j.worlddev.2019.104776

Martínez-Alier, J. (2002). *The environmentalism of the poor. A study of ecological conflicts and valuation.* Edward Elgar Publishing.

Masron, T. A., & Subramaniam, Y. (2019). Does poverty cause environmental degradation? Evidence from developing countries. *Journal of Poverty, 23*(1), 44–64.

Mendelsohn, R., Dinar, A., & Williams, L. (2006). The distributional impact of climate change on rich and poor countries. *Environment and Development Economics, 11*, 159–178.

Mennis, J. L., & Jordan, L. (2005). The distribution of environmental equity: Exploring spatial nonstationarity in multivariate models of air toxic releases. *Annals of the Association of American Geographers, 95*(2), 249–268.

Millennium Ecosystem Assessment. (2005). *Ecosystems and human wellbeing: Synthesis report.* Island Press.

Miller, H. (2018). Veblen online: Information and the risk of commandeering the conspicuous self. *Information Research, 23*(2). http://InformationR.net/ir/23-2/paper797.html

Mol, A. P. J. (1995). *The refinement of production: Ecological modernization theory and the chemical industry.* International Books.

Mol, A. P. J. (2001). *Globalization and environmental reform.* MIT Press.

Mol, A. P. J. (2010). Ecological modernization as a social theory of environmental reform. In M. R. Redclift & G. Woodgate (Eds.), *The international handbook of environmental sociology* (pp. 63–76). Edward Elgar Publishing.

Mol, A. P. J., Sonnenfeld, D. A., & Spaargaren, G. (2010). *The ecological modernization reader: Environmental reform in theory and practice.* Routledge.

Mol, A. P. J., & Spaargaren, G. (2000). Ecological modernisation theory in debate: A review. *Environmental Politics, 9*(1), 17–49.

Natarajan, N., Newsham, A., Rigg, J., & Suhardiman, D. (2022). A sustainable livelihoods framework for the 21st century. *World Development, 155.* https://doi.org/10.1016/j.worlddev.2022.105898

Norgaard, K. (2011). *Living in Denial: Climate change, emotions, and everyday life*. MIT Press.
Nunan, F. (2015). *Understanding poverty and the environment. Analytical frameworks and approaches.* Routledge.
Pellow, D. N. (2013). An environmental sociology for the twenty-first century. *Annual Review of Sociology, 39*, 229–250.
Pellow, D. N. (2017a). *What is critical environmental justice?* Polity Press.
Pellow, D. N. (2017b). Environmental justice movements and political opportunity structures. In H. Holifield, J. Chakraborty, & G. Walker (Eds.), *The Routledge handbook of environmental justice* (pp. 63–75). Routledge.
Porter, M. E., & van der Linde, C. (1995). Green and competitive: Ending the stalemate. *Harvard Business Review*.
Prell, C., & Sun, L. (2015). Unequal carbon exchanges: Understanding pollution embodied in global trade. *Environmental Sociology, 1*(4), 256–267.
Ridzuan, S. (2019). Inequality and the environmental Kuznets curve. *Agris, 228*(21), 1472–1481.
Rizk, R., & Slimane, M. B. (2018). Modelling the relationship between poverty, environment, and institutions: A panel data study. *Environmental Science and Pollution Research, 25*(31), 31459–31473.
Rume, T., & Islam, S. M. D. (2020). Environmental effects of COVID-19 pandemic and potential strategies of sustainability. *Heliyon, 6*(9). https://doi.org/10.1016/j.heliyon.2020.e04965
Satterthwaite, D. (2003a). The ten and a half myths that may distort the urban policies of governments and international agencies. *International Institute for Environment and Development*. https://www.iied.org/g03188
Satterthwaite, D. (2003b). The links between poverty and the environment in urban areas of Africa, Asia, and Latin America. *The Annals of the American Academy of Political and Social Science, 590*(1), 73–92.
Saunders, P. (1987). *Social theory and the urban question*. Unwin Hyman.
Schleicher, J., Schaafsma, M., Burgess, N. D., Sandbrook, C., Danks, F., Cowie, C., & Vira, B. (2017). Poorer without It? The neglected role of the natural environment in poverty and wellbeing. *Sustainable Development, 26*(1), 83–98.
Schleicher, J., Schaafsma, M., Burgess, N. D., Sandbrook, C., Danks, F., Cowie, C., & Vira, B. (2018). Poorer without It? The neglected role of the natural environment in poverty and wellbeing. *Sustaintainable Development, 26*, 83–98.
Schnaiberg, A. (1980). *The environment: From surplus to scarcity*. Oxford University Press.
Schnaiberg, A., & Gould, K. (1994). *Environment and society: The enduring conflict*. West Blackburn Press.
Schumacher, E. F. (1973). *Small is beautiful: Economics as if people mattered*. Harper et Row.

Scoones, I. (1998). *Sustainable rural livelihoods: A framework for analysis*. https://opendocs.ids.ac.uk/opendocs/bitstream/handle/20.500.12413/3390/Wp72.pdf?sequence=1

Scott Matthews, H., Hendrickson, C. T., & Soh, D. L. (2001). Environmental and economic effects of e-commerce: A case study of book publishing and retail logistics. *Transportation Research Record, 1763*(1), 6–12.

Scruggs, L. (1998). Political and economic inequality and the environment. *Ecological Economics, 26*(3), 259–275.

Sen, A. (2001). *Development as freedom*. Oxford University Press.

Setyadharma, A., Oktavilia, S., Nihayah, D. M., Bowo, P. A., & Wahyuningrum, I. F. S. (2020). The trade-off between poverty and environmental degradation: Evidence from Indonesia. *IOP Conference Series: Earth and Environmental Science*. https://doi.org/10.1088/1755-1315/448/1/012065

Shah, S. A. A., Longsheng, C., Solangi, Y. A., Ahmad, M., & Ali, S. (2021). Energy trilemma based prioritization of waste-to-energy technologies: Implications for post-COVID-19 green economic recovery in Pakistan. *Journal of Cleaner Production, 284*, 124729. https://doi.org/10.1016/j.jclepro.2020.124729

Shahbaz, M., & Sinha, A. (2019). Environmental Kuznets curve for CO2 emissions: A literature survey. *Journal of Economic Studies, 46*(1), 106–168.

Sievering, O. (2020). The environmental impact of shopping via the Internet. *Central and Eastern European eDem and eGov Days, 338*. https://doi.org/10.24989/ocg.v.338.2

Siikavirta, H., Punakivi, M., Kärkkäinen, M., & Linnanen, L. (2002). Effects of e-commerce on greenhouse gas emissions: A case study of grocery home delivery in Finland. *Journal of Industrial Ecology, 6*(2), 83–97.

Simmel, G. (2011). *The philosophy of money*. Routledge.

Sinha, A., & Shahbaz, M., (2018). Estimation of environmental Kuznets curve for CO2 emission: Role of renewable energy generation in India. *Renewable Energy, Elsevier, 119*(C), 703–711.

Smith, J. R., Louis, W. R., Terry, D. J., Greenaway, K. H., Clarke, M. R., & Cheng, X. (2012). Congruent or conflicted? The impact of injunctive and descriptive norms on environmental intentions. *Journal of Environmental Psychology, 32*(4), 353–361.

Spaargaren, G. (1997). *The ecological modernization of production and consumption: Essays in environmental sociology*. Wageningen Agricultural University.

Spaargaren, G., & Van Vliet, B. (2000). Lifestyles, consumption and the environment: The ecological modernization of domestic consumption. *Environmental Politics, 9*(1), 50–76.

Steg, L. (2016). Values, norms, and intrinsic motivation to act proenvironmentally. *Annual Review of Environment and Resources, 41*, 277–292.

Stephens, S. (1996). Reflections on environmental justice: Children as victims and actors. *Social Justice, 4*(66), 62–86.

Stern, D. I. (2004). The rise and fall of the Environmental Kuznets Curve. *World Development, 32*(8), 1419–1439.
Stern, D. I. (2017). *The Environmental Kuznets Curve*. Oxford University Press.
Stiglitz, J. E. (2014). Reconstructing macroeconomic theory to manage economic policy. *National Bureau of Economic Research*. https://doi.org/10.3386/w20517
Stones, R. (2005). *Old and afraid of new communication technologies? Reconceptualizing and contesting the 'age-based digital divide' Structuration Theory*. Palgrave.
Tang, X., Yuan, J., & Zeng, X. (2023). Influencing factors of community residents' pro-environmental behavior in East Dongting Lake National Nature Reserve under the policy intervention. *Scientific Reports, 13*(6076). https://doi.org/10.1038/s41598-023-32553-0
Taylor, D. E. (2009). *The environment and the people in American cities, 1600s–1900s. Disorder, inequality, and social change*. Duke University Press.
Taylor, D. E. (2012). The raise of the environmental justice paradigm: Injustice framing and the social construction of environmental discourses. *American Behavioral Scientist, 43*(4). https://doi.org/10.1177/0002764200004300400
Taylor, D. E. (2014). *Toxic communities: Environmental racism, industrial pollution, and residential mobility*. NYU Press.
Taylor, J., Harrison, D., & Kraus, S. (2009). *The new elite: Inside the minds of the truly wealthy*. American Management Association.
Temper, L. (2018). Globalizing environmental justice: Radical and transformative movements past and present. In R. Holifield, J. Chakraborty, & G. Walker (Eds.), *The Routledge handbook of environmental justice* (pp. 490–503). Routledge.
Trigg, A. B. (2001). Veblen, Bourdieu, and conspicuous consumption. *Journal of Economic Issues, 35*(1), 99–115.
UKRI. (2020). *Impact on the environment*. https://www.ukri.org/our-work/tackling-the-impact-of-covid-19/researching-the-impact-of-coronavirus/impact-on the-environment/
Ulucak, R., & Lin, D. (2017). Persistence of policy shocks to Ecological Footprint of the USA. *Ecological Indicators, 80*, 337–343.
UN. (1995). United Nations report of the World Summit for Social Development. http://www.un.org/documents/ga/conf166/aconf166-9.htm
UNEP. (1972). Declaration of the United Nations Conference on the Human Environment. http://www.unep.org/documents.multilingual/default.asp?documentid=97&articleid=1503
UNEP. (1995). *Poverty and the environment: Reconciling short-term needs with long-term sustainability goals*. UNEP.
Van Liere, K., & Dunlap, R. (1981). Environmental concern: Does it make a difference how it's measured? *Environment and Behaviour, 13*(6), 651–676.

Veblen, T. (1899). *The theory of the leisure class.* Dover Publications.

Wallerstein, I. (1974). *The modern world system. Capitalist agriculture and the origins of the European world-economy in the sixteenth century.* Academic Press.

Wan, Q., & Du, W. (2022). Social capital, environmental knowledge, and pro-environmental behavior. *International Journal of Environmental Research and Public Health, 19*(3). https://doi.org/10.3390/ijerph19031443

Wang, P., Han, W., Kumail, S., Rizvi, A., & Naqvi, B. (2022). Is Digital Adoption the way forward to Curb Energy Poverty? *Technological Forecasting and Social Change, 180.* https://doi.org/10.1016/j.techfore.2022.121722

Watson, R. T., Boudreau, M.-C., & Chen, A. J. (2010). Information systems and environmentally sustainable development: Energy informatics and new directions for the community. *MIS Quarterly, 34*(1), 23–38.

WCED. (1987). *Our common future.* Oxford University Press.

Wilkinson, R., & Pickett, K. (2010). The spirit level: Why equality is better for everyone. *Journal of Social Policy, 42*(4), 840–842.

World Bank. (1992). *World development report.* Oxford University Press.

World Bank. (2000). *World development report 2000/01: Attacking poverty.* World Bank.

World Bank. (2008). *Poverty and the environment: Understanding linkages at the household level.* World Bank.

World Bank. (2019). *Understanding poverty 2019.* https://www.worldbank.org/en/topic/poverty/overview

Yu, Y., & Liu, Q. (2022). An empirical study on the correlation among poverty, inclusive finance, and CO2 emissions in China. *Environmental Science and Pollution Research, 29,* 71400–71411.

PART II

# Environmental Poverty and Its Interconnections with Digital Poverty

CHAPTER 5

# The Environmental Determinant of Digital Poverty from Macro to Micro Perspectives

## 5.1 Introduction

The previous chapter reviewed the debate concerning the link between economic and environmental poverty, highlighting contrasting findings on their causal relationship, especially due to the complexity of intersecting variables that can influence poverty conditions at multiple levels (from macro to micro levels). The identification of such interdependencies is critical for tackling poverty holistically. However, the previous chapter problematized environmental poverty as a relevant factor influencing living conditions and well-being. The definition of environmental poverty as conceptually distinct from, but also integral to, poverty helps broaden the understanding of poverty beyond economic indicators. As a result, it views poverty as multidimensional, including both economic and environmental components (Nunan, 2015). It also emphasizes the environment's role as one of the enablers of individual "capabilities" for human development (Sen, 2001). This chapter explores the possibility of embedding the environmental component into the concept of digital poverty at the macro, meso, and micro levels, as described in Chap. 3. In this chapter, we further emphasize the interconnections between environmental poverty and digital poverty by problematizing the need for integrating an environmental



M. L. Ruiu, M. Ragnedda, *Digital-Environmental Poverty*, Palgrave Studies in Digital Inequalities,
https://doi.org/10.1007/978-3-031-56184-9_5

variable when exploring digital inequalities. More specifically, we integrate the revised three dimensions of the DPF (Individuals, Circumstantial, and Structural) with the environmental dimension.

Therefore, throughout this chapter, we suggest further conceptualization of the micro area related to individual determinants. This involves expanding motivations (including environmental motivations to use digital technologies) and social support (including environmental models and network values) and adding environmental awareness and engagement. We also propose to expand the circumstantial determinants by including the experience of adverse environmental conditions and opportunities for citizens to participate in the decision-making process. We finally suggest that the structural determinants should include the environmental structural property of society. This is due to the increasing digitalization of everyday life and the shift of social practices online, which might be damaging to the environment. The final paragraph specifically focuses on the meso dimension represented by the circumstantial level by using the concept of digital-environmental habitus to understand how digital-environmental poverty can be tackled.

## 5.2 Connecting Digital Transformation to Environmental Transformation

The current paragraph attempts to explain why the environmental dimension should be included in the definition of digital poverty as one enabler of digital capability. The first step in this direction is considering how the digital and environmental dimensions are interconnected at multiple levels. Berkhout and Hertin (2004) identify three impacts of ICTs on the environment related to the (i) direct effects of production processes and use of ICTs (for example, resource exploitation, pollution deriving from production of both infrastructure and devices, electricity consumption, and waste disposal); (ii) indirect effects of ICTs on production processes, products, and distribution systems (such as de-materialization and new ways of communicating that can substitute travel); and (iii) structural/behavioral effects, especially at the economic level and in terms of lifestyles and value systems. Similarly, Green Information Systems studies have identified three effects that Information Systems can produce on the environment. These are represented by the use of natural sources over the entire lifecycle from production to recycling; support to logistics, mobility, and production processes; and systemic effects of economic structures and behaviors (Kranz et al., 2015; Henkel & Kranz, 2018). All these impacts can be either positive or negative according to how efficient the infrastructure/tools and production and consumption systems are. This suggests that, on the one hand, digitalization processes affect the quality of the environment, but they can also contribute toward developing solutions for both economic development and environmental protection.

The previous chapter referred to different sociology approaches that have optimistically interpreted the relationship between technologies (and digital technologies) and the environment. On the one hand, we argued that ecological modernization approaches tend to emphasize the benefits of Information and Communications Technologies (ICT) development. For instance, ICT can contribute to dematerialization processes, reducing the need for physical movement and transportation through electronic exchanges. Additionally, ICT facilitates the creation of automated control systems that improve efficiency, enhances the capacity for real-time data analysis, and boosts scientific development through global networking and information sharing. Furthermore, ICT provides platforms for activism and advocacy to emerge, thereby supporting various environmental and social causes. All these aspects in turn have positive effects on the environment given their capacity to reduce CO2 emissions (Mol, 2008; Simpson et al., 2019). This is also supported by studies that have shown how the digitalization of certain traditional economic production processes can reduce impacts on the environment (Xu et al., 2022) while making businesses competitive (see, for example, Hosan et al., 2022; Irtyshcheva, 2021). As a result, digital transformation has been interpreted as more comprehensive business models and digital platforms that not only influence consumer behavior and organizations but also have cascading effects on healthcare, social, and environmental dynamics (for a comprehensive review, see Abdul et al., 2021). Ha et al. (2022) empirically investigated the effects of digital transformation on environmental performances in 25 European countries, by showing that digital transformation processes (that involve digital skills, business digitization, and digital public services) positively impact environmental performance. For instance, in the context of digital transformation, the use of AI and the Internet of Things (IoT) promotes business models that can interact with the complexity of environmental problems (Ye et al., 2020) with positive outcomes, such as in the case of smart management of natural resources (Balogun et al., 2022; Goralski & Tan, 2019). At the same time, ML has been also emphasized as effective in tackling climate change (Rolnick et al., 2022). For example, since 2019, Climate Change AI (CCAI), a network of academics and industries, has been working on the intersection between ML and environmental protection. Moreover, Esmaeilian et al. (2020) identify the contribution of blockchain to increasing sustainability, in terms of activating incentive mechanisms and tokenization to enhance consumer pro-environmental behavior; tracking the different phases of the product lifecycle; increasing systems efficiency while decreasing operational costs; and implementing monitoring and reporting corporate performance.

Revising the scientific debate on different levels of digital transformation of society, Ha et al. (2022) reference extensive literature that shows how digital technologies can be applied to alleviate pressure on the natural environment (including pollution control, sustainable production, and urban sustainability) also through, for instance, ICTs that can increase public awareness and the efficiency of policies. Digital technologies can facilitate such transformation by, for example, educating citizens (via tools such as applications and other Information Systems for Environmental Sustainability; see, for example, Loock et al., 2013; Malhotra et al., 2013) to more sustainable behaviors (see Hedin et al., 2019 for a review), but other factors also play a role. They include consumer behaviors and expectations, as well as digital competition, and data availability (Abdul et al., 2021). Moreover, the use of applications for sustainable goals (such as energy saving) mostly characterizes Western European countries (Zawieska et al., 2022), which are less affected by the negative consequences of both digital and environmental poverty. On the other hand, in contrast to what is predicted by techno-optimistic approaches, Simpson et al. (2019) developed the concept of the Treadmill of Information (ToI). ToI directly addresses the impact of ICTs on environmental degradation. Investigating the impact of ICT development on CO2 emissions in 113 countries from the years 1990 to 2010, the authors found that in general ICTs increase $CO_2$ in less-developed countries because of fixed telephone development and in developed countries because of Internet use.

Some studies have shown how the increased use of ICTs, as well as an increasingly digitalized economy, has also increased electricity consumption (Salahuddin & Alam, 2016; Sparviero & Ragnedda, 2021). AI systems, for example, are particularly energy-intensive, and training a single AI system can result in carbon emissions that are five times the lifetime emissions of an average car (Strubell et al., 2019). This is also reflected in AI consumption, with rising energy demand (Andrae, 2019). Some studies have identified ICTs as a cause of concern in terms of environmental impacts (Murugesan, 2008). Also, hardware and their related e-waste represent a main concern, especially with great attention given to smartphones, which are also the most used digital technologies to access the Internet and are most quickly substituted (Bordage, 2019; Malmodin & Lundén, 2018; Oo et al., 2023). In 2021, 15 billion smartphones were sold globally, producing "an impact of 900 million tons of $CO_2$, 1.35 billion tons of materials and 204 billion tons of water to produce them" (Unicef, 2021). Another example of a digital habit that is impactful on the environment is represented by video streaming (Andrae & Edler, 2015; Obringer et al., 2021). Watching one-hour video streaming on Netflix can produce emissions of 36g$CO_2$ (Oo et al., 2023), which is approximately equivalent to boiling a kettle (Oo et al., 2023). However, day-long streaming of videos can be 13 times higher than a return flight from Paris to New York (Balogun et al., 2022). Many studies attempted to estimate the carbon footprint, which is the amount of greenhouse gas emissions released directly and indirectly, associated with data storage and transmission. This is due to the enormous consumption of electricity required by the operations of high-demanding computers and servers (see, for example, Aslan et al., 2018; Hintemann & Hinterholzer, 2019; Malmodin & Lundén, 2018).

Therefore, even though digitalization has produced many advantages, especially thanks to its capacity to increase efficiency, such benefits tend to be counterbalanced by the increasing demand and long uses due to the availability of devices, their continuous upgrading, and opportunities to consume, which in turn increases the energy demand, its related greenhouse gas emissions, resources and mineral extraction, electronic waste, radiations, and dependence on digital tools (Oo et al., 2023).

However, the estimation of the impact of digitalization on the environment has produced contrasting results in the scientific debate due to different measurements used. According to Shift Project (2019), increasing digitalization has had an impact on carbon emissions, which increased by 70% from 2013, accounting for approximately 3.7% of global carbon pollution. Despite the contestation of such estimation as overly pessimistic due to its overestimation of energy consumption for data transfer (Kamiya, 2020), Freitag et al. (2021) emphasize that the carbon footprint of ICTs is generally underestimated by 25%. Scholars have started referring to "digital pollution" as a threat equal to air and other forms of pollution, which mainly derives from Internet network operations and the production of hardware (Oo et al., 2023).

From these contrasting interpretations, it emerges that the scientific community has generally interpreted technology (and digital technology) as both a cause and a potential solution to environmental problems (Watson et al., 2010). In any case, digital transformation can interact with the socio-environmental context at multiple levels and in various ways, through, for instance, digitization (automated tasks, for instance, the conversion of analogical into digital information) and digitalization (addition of digital components to products/services). The outcomes of such interactions between the environment and digital tools, however, will be dependent on both structural and agentic factors in a circular process. Regulations in this direction tend to influence both production and consumption practices, which influence cultures, which in turn influence regulation. This is particularly important with the affirmation of Industry 4.0 (Kamarul Bahrin et al., 2016), which has facilitated relationships between individuals and businesses through the development of digital infrastructures and technologies (such as digital platforms, robots, cloud computing, AI, and IoT) that reinforce the affirmation of the digital economy (Xu et al., 2022).

Individual contributions to the digital economy and environmental impact through the use of digital technologies still need investigation in relation to the concepts of both digital poverty and environmental poverty. The principles underlying the digitalized economy are, indeed, currently similar to those underlying traditional economic growth, with social and environmental sustainability playing secondary roles (Beier et al., 2020). This leads to some considerations on how poverty is connected to the power of activating structuration processes that will ultimately contribute toward shaping our digital-environmental system of values and behaviors. In identifying the value of sociology for energy research, Galvin (2020) defines four different types of power, which are ***material power*** (based on money, possessions, and physical means of coercion); ***discursive power*** (based on the capability of controlling the terms of discussion and producing a narrative); ***institutional power*** (based on the control over rule-making); and *people-power* (through activism and advocacy). Galvin (2020) also mentions the possibility that possession of material resources leads to the accumulation of power not only in material terms but also in discursive terms (by controlling the narrative around environmental-related issues through, for example, the media and think tanks) and institutional terms (by supporting certain political ideology and parties). However, recent studies have also shown increasing inequalities in terms of per capita consumption emissions footprints, with the wealthiest individuals (in the richest 1% of the global population) expected to produce emissions 16 times higher than the global average, and the poorest half of the global population to remain below the 1.5 °C compatible level (Gore, 2021). This suggests that those with material power and wealth also have greater transformative capacity because they can influence structural components (getting most of the benefits while relegating to the poorer the negative consequences of their behavior). By contrast, the fourth mode of power, which is that of *people-power*, represents a form of power from the bottom that is supposed to rebalance the terms of this unequal relationship. However, social engagement for social change necessitates knowledge, but there are knowledge gaps that make connecting the environmental and digital levels difficult (George et al., 2021). These gaps are caused by a failure to disseminate accurate and reliable information about the state of the environment and the costs of unsustainable behavior, making it difficult to consider this variable when making individual, business, and political decisions. As a result, such a lack of knowledge shadows sustainable goods and services and jeopardizes the available natural capital. Therefore, the development of *people-power* also relies on the development of a collective consciousness of how structural (socio-economic, cultural, environmental, and digital configurations in terms of rules and resources), circumstantial (circumstances in which human agency is situated as a social relationship, including environmental knowledge and engagement of a specific social system), and individual factors (individual conditions including environmental awareness, engagement, motivations, and absorbed social influences) can affect how digital technologies are used and their impact on the environment.

The review of the DPA framework developed in the next paragraph can help us understand how digital poverty and environmental poverty are interrelated. On a structural level, a lack of information distribution and accessibility undermines the ontological security (intended here as a sense of security deriving from understanding the environment) that allows individuals to make informed decisions. This also makes it difficult to develop structurally transformative policies that can then be accepted, embraced, and become routinized practices at both the collective and individual levels. Moreover, the *institutional power* at the structural level also creates the conditions for enterprises to invest and develop following certain directions shaped by both the regulatory and participatory systems at play. This in turn shapes the digital development and infrastructure available to citizens to experience and take advantage of the digital realm. On a circumstantial level, if the information is not easily accessible, it will increase suspicion, lack of trust, and involvement in environmental matters. This, in turn, may contribute to the consolidation of counterproductive digital practices based on environmental ignorance. At an individual level, it appears that the uses of Internet networks and data centers are even more impactful than manufacturing them (Oo et al., 2023), making individual uses particularly relevant to be studied. While the lack of knowledge is intertwined with the several determinants proposed by the DPA model, it is particularly relevant to also highlight the motivation, social support, and psychological aspects of the digital experience. Indeed, trust, expectations, and potential benefits are aspects to be considered when deciding whether to use technologies sustainably.

These aspects are further developed in the following paragraphs which revise the DPF by including the environmental dimension in the definition of digital poverty.

## 5.3 The Environmental Determinant of Digital Poverty from Macro to Micro Perspectives

This chapter further discusses the connections between digital and environmental dimensions. It highlights how current development models are anchored to continuous economic growth, while poverty remains predominantly tackled in monetary terms. This paragraph adds to the discussion by considering digital and environmental poverty to be two sides of the same coin. Following the DPA, Chap. 3 defined digital poverty as the "inability [of individuals] to interact with the online world fully, when, where, and how an individual needs to. It exacerbates and is exacerbated by other socio-economic, educational, racial, linguistic, gender, and health inequalities. It is both the product and the cause of other forms of socio-economic disadvantage" (Allman, 2022). We also emphasized that such a definition conceptualizes digital poverty as an intersectional issue that is simultaneously the cause and effect of offline social inequalities. On the other hand, we referred to the definition of environmental poverty provided by the UN (1995), as "a condition of deprivation of basic human needs/well-being and healthy ecosystems that depends not only on income but also on access to services [and a healthy environment]." Such a definition broadens the concept of poverty by incorporating the link between human needs, well-being, and the quality of the environment.

This chapter proposes a combined definition of these two dimensions, by intending Digital-Environmental Poverty as a condition of simultaneous deprivation of basic digital and environmental needs. This includes not only material access to these resources but also awareness and the capability of shaping their uses. This combined deprivation reinforces and, in turn, is reinforced by a multitude of other forms of inequality. These include, but are not limited to, inequalities related to socio-economic status, educational opportunities, generational gaps, racial or ethnic backgrounds, linguistic diversity, gender disparities, and disparities in access to healthcare and overall well-being. Hence, at the core of our discussion is that DEP encompasses a multidimensional and interconnected set of challenges, where individuals or communities experience some forms of inequalities not only in their access to and uses of digital technologies (digital poverty) and environmental resources (environmental poverty) but also in their broader socio-economic, educational, and health-related circumstances (socio-economic poverty).

The revised version of the DPF proposed in Chap. 3 is based on three different levels, represented by structure, circumstances, and what we have elaborated as individual traits. It draws upon (Individual) Determinants (device and connectivity, access, capabilities, motivation, and support), Circumstantial Determinants (living conditions, economic stability, health, family and social context, psychosocial factors, lifestyle, and behaviors), and Structural Determinants (socio-economic, cultural, and political configuration). The three levels can be interpreted as dynamic due to the interaction between structure and agentic levels, which can be understood through the duality of the structure described by Giddens (1984). This approach can also help capture how the different levels interact by reproducing (but also potentially transforming) the structural conditions of poverty. As aforementioned, environmental poverty (as well as digital poverty) does not happen in a "social vacuum" but is embedded in a complexity of social norms and regulatory apparatuses. However, the societal structure reproduces and allows for transformation due to its duality as both a determinant and an outcome of human action. In the following paragraphs, we propose reinserting the environmental determinants at each level of the DPF.

### 5.3.1 *Structural Determinants of Digital-Environmental Poverty*

A revisitation of the original Dahlgren-Whitehead "rainbow model," upon which the DPF is based, can support the need for conceptualizing environmental and digital poverty as intertwined. The structural component of this model is represented by the socio-economic, cultural, and environmental conditions. If we conceptualize this meta level as the combination of rules and resources that create the conditions for the system to display patterns of social practice (Giddens, 1984), the environmental component necessitates being incorporated into such a framing level. To separate digital poverty as a distinct concept, the DPF did not include the environmental component. This constitutive element, by contrast, should be reinstalled at all levels to include the multidimensionality of digital poverty, which is also interconnected with the natural environment. Specifically, it should be incorporated into the definition of a more comprehensive concept of DEP. Figure 5.1 illustrates the adjusted framework, where the environmental determinant is reinstated across all levels.

As a structural determinant, it includes the regulatory apparatus framing environmental matters (rules), the environmental conditions (natural capital), and their related available knowledge/understanding (resources), which can either constrain or enhance opportunities. According to this view, *institutional power* (based on the control over rule-making), as

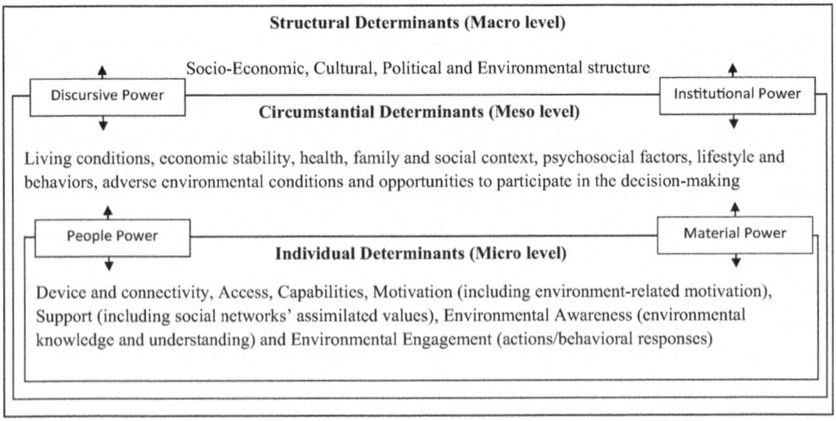


**Fig. 5.1** Digital-environmental poverty framework (DEPF)

introduced in the previous paragraph (Galvin, 2020), can be generated and produce cascading effects on both circumstantial and individual determinants. The structural level, which impacts not only poverty in general but also the sort of digital infrastructure of society, is fundamentally affected by the environment and how it is conventionally interpreted and managed. This is supported by studies that showed how green technology innovation can produce win-win outcomes (in terms of producing, for instance, sustainable development) when it is embedded in a wider vision of ecological advancements (Yi et al., 2022). As we will see later in this section, despite limitations, the Chinese civilization approach offers interesting points of reflection in terms of embedding technology development into an environmental framework, defined by strict regulations and implementation of environmental measures for enterprises. In this direction, some studies found that environmental regulations push enterprises to invest in or buy (Perino & Requate, 2012) green technologies to make the production process more efficient and competitive, which in turn compensates for the initial costs of investment (Guellec & Van Pottelsberghe De La Potterie, 2003; Ma et al., 2022). However, findings in this direction are still controversial and some other studies have shown the negative effects of such environmental regulation on increasing costs for enterprises (see Ma et al., 2022 for a review). In any case, environmental regulations will influence investment decisions (Turken et al., 2020) and have a shaping effect on the context in which the digital experience happens and, therefore, it should be considered as a structuring element of it. Similarly, some studies have shown that the type of approach adopted institutionally can have either encouraging or detrimental effects on societal engagement with environmental matters. Therefore, environmental processes and outcomes are shaped by the structuring power of institutional frameworks. Public authorities' decisions at multiple levels, for example, play a pivotal role in decentralizing administrative responsibilities and initiating dialogue among multiple actors due to their capacity to "allocate and distribute resources, regulate production and consumption [...] and enforce legal frameworks" (Pickering et al., 2022). In doing so, they can institutionalize the power of many actors (not only enterprises) to shape environmental management, a process commonly referred to as governance (Lemos & Agrawal, 2009). Such institutionalization can generate opportunities for collaborative approaches to drive collective efforts to address digital-environmental challenges. Top-down approaches have been shown to have a detrimental effect on stakeholders' commitment to environmental management (for example, tourism enterprises, tourists, local communities, and protected areas authorities in Pakistan) due to a deriving feeling of powerlessness (Imran et al., 2014). By contrast, even though the efficacy of environmental governance is still debated (Bodin, 2017; Kiss et al., 2022; Young et al., 2013), benefits from the participation of a multiplicity of actors such as market actors, state actors, civil-society-based actors, NGOs and local community actors (Lemos & Agrawal, 2009), and citizens (see, for example, Burton & Mustelin, 2013; Nesshöver et al., 2017) have been often highlighted, especially when they empower participants to make decisions (Jager et al., 2019; Schlosberg & Craven, 2019). From this description, it emerges that structural conditions, which also include the set of natural resources, their knowledge, and their regulatory apparatus, can create the conditions for both participatory "circumstances" to emerge at the meso level (as further developed in the next paragraph) and individual predispositions toward the use of (digital) technologies in a pro-environmental direction.

### *5.3.2 Circumstantial Determinants of Digital-Environmental Poverty*

In Chap. 3, we referred to the DPF's Circumstantial Determinants as a point of intersection between the structural and agentic levels, defining them as both constrainers and enablers of both agency and structural evolution (Giddens, 1984). The DPF includes, at this level, living conditions, economic stability, health, family and social context, psychosocial factors, lifestyle, and behaviors. Our revised model, shown in Fig. 5.1, suggests that the environmental determinant should be integrated into this meso-dimension by specifically including societal contact with adverse environmental conditions/events and opportunities for the public to participate in digital-environmental decision-making. If environmental poverty corresponds to unhealthy and degraded environments that affect living standards and deprive basic human needs, a group's direct experience of unhealthy ecosystems represents a circumstance that might mediate and interact with both regulations and societal understanding of environmental problems, including digital challenges. For example, Zhang et al. (2019) demonstrated a positive association between the perception of haze pollution and the intention for green consumption. This suggests that environmental conditions create some circumstances that can play a role in triggering certain pro-environmental behaviors. This holds especially in a scenario where opportunities for both active learning and transformative opportunities about "digital pollution" are present. In fact, given its invisibility, it is generally recognized that awareness about the issue is the first step (Oo et al., 2023). In this direction, the opportunities available for citizens to increase their *citizens' power* (Arnstein, 2007) by taking an active part in the decision-making process are circumstantial elements that need to be considered in addressing environmental poverty. Such opportunities can interact with the individual level, influence the level of knowledge and engagement of citizens, and facilitate both their participation in decision-making and policy responses to environmental degradation. In this regard, Khatibi et al. (2021) review the literature on public engagement in climate-related issues and find an agreement that awareness and knowledge of climate change can contribute to public engagement in decision-making. Increased engagement can, in turn, influence the community's level of awareness and knowledge. At this level, *material power* (based on money, possessions, and physical means of coercion) and *discursive power* (based on the capability of controlling the terms of discussion and producing a narrative) can be produced thanks to access to and use of both material means and knowledge. At the same time, this level also lays the foundation for generating *people-power* (favoring, for example, the rise of activism and advocacy). Digital tools can also provide additional opportunities for environmental participation under certain conditions (involving the acquisition of necessary digital and environmental literacy). They do so by offering citizens e information, creating e-participation opportunities, and empowering citizens with e-decision-making capabilities. However, despite the potentialities, vulnerable groups who might need the most to become "visible" in the decision-making process tend to be extremely penalized because of the lack of knowledge about these opportunities, skills, and digital tools (UN, 2022).

### 5.3.3 Individual Determinants of Digital-Environmental Poverty

Finally, the DPF refers to (Individual) Determinants, which can be interpreted as subjects' ability to do something with transformative power (*people-power*). It includes device and connectivity, access, capabilities, motivation, and support. At this level, Fig. 5.1 adds to the set of existing digital variables both individual awareness of environmental conditions and engagement with environmental problems. Furthermore, when considering motivations to use digital technologies, the motivation to consume/replace/waste technologies in an environmentally friendly manner should be considered (Dahlinger & Wortmann, 2016). This is a pivotal aspect, given that users' devices have been identified by a study conducted by GreenIT.fr (Bordage, 2019) as the main contributors to the global digital-environmental footprint with 34 billion digital devices per 4.1 billion people (more than 8 devices per user, excluding accessories such as USB sticks, earphones, etc.). Chapter 4 referred to some psychology studies that have shown how intrinsic motivations (see, for example, De Youn, 1986, 1996; Ejelöv et al., 2022; Helferich et al., 2023; Steg, 2016; Tang et al., 2023) play a role in promoting pro-environmental behavior also more than formal regulation (Tang et al., 2023). On the other hand, the literature on green consumption emphasizes how also additional social factors (for example, social influence, exchange, inspirational models, and norms; see, for example, Lazaric et al., 2019; Wang et al., 2019) can contribute toward predicting green consumption behavior (Choudhary et al., 2019; Gao et al., 2022). This can be explained by the inspirational model (but also social stigma) that social networks' behaviors can generate (for example, engaging in green consumption or stigmatizing certain antienvironmental behaviors). Therefore, the support component of the DPA model also needs to be reframed by including social networking, intended as valuable to develop not only digital literacy (as suggested by the DPA) but also environmental literacy. Following, the environmental literacy framework developed by Hollweg et al. (2011), an environmentally literate person is someone who makes environmentally informed decisions, acts accordingly, and participates in civic life for the individual and collective well-being and respect of the environment. It considers both awareness and participation in decision-making as essential components for individual enrichment in environmental terms.

Revising the literature on the topic of environmental literacy, Fauville et al. (2020) identify three dimensions of environmental literacy such as knowledge (of ecological systems and its social, political, economic, and cultural intersections), dispositions toward the environment (due to the perception of personal responsibility, self-efficacy, motivation, and intention to act), and competencies (possession of skills related to identifying, analyzing, evaluating, and making choices). The climate change literature agrees on distinguishing between active and passive engagement (Axon, 2016; Nolan, 2010), by separating the cognitive dimension (awareness and understanding) of the problem (about, for example, causes, consequences, and potential solutions), the affective dimension (related to motivation and concern), and the behavioral dimension (actions effectively implemented to mitigate the effects of climate change) (Sutton & Tobin, 2011). As a result, addressing digital-environmental poverty at this level necessitates the metabolization of an understanding of the effects of individual digital practices on the environment. Such absorption of knowledge, values, habits, and social norms in turn affects the engagement in certain behavioral responses that can increase/decrease digital-environmental poverty at the individual level.

## 5.4 Conclusion

The DP framework was used as a starting point in this chapter's exploration of the linkages between environmental and digital factors in contemporary society. It was suggested that digital and environmental poverty should be viewed as two sides of the same coin. A study carried out in India by Jha et al. (2016) offers points of reflection in this regard. This study can be used as an example to better comprehend the links between the various levels that have been discussed thus far. The authors' analysis is based on a social business that uses an ICT platform to address smallholder farmer poverty in Bhubaneswar, which is the capital of Odisha, ranked among the nine poorest states in India by the Global Multidimensional Poverty Index (MPI) 2022. The intense industrialization of the area, based on the extraction of non-renewable resources, has contributed to increasing poverty and vulnerability. At the same time, 70% of the population depends on agriculture and the province is exposed to extreme weather events such as cyclones, floods, and droughts that affect the availability of food (Mahapatra & Birkman, 2021). Digital poverty also exists in this area, where there are 49.09 Internet users per 100 people (as opposed to the national average of 60.73) (Government of Odisha, 2022).

The social business implemented a plan through distinct phases to create a technology-enabled service in the farming community. The case study showed that the creation of both ICT infrastructure (applications, databases, and support for a range of devices) and a space for farmers to develop knowledge and share information contributed toward the coordination of actions gradually generating a robust ecosystem around the platform. The social enterprise's incremental approach also allowed for the incorporation of factors from complementary domains such as agriculture, sanitation, banking, universities, venture capital, and government. Such an integrated approach enhanced addressing complex issues faced by farmers in a coordinated manner by showing the potential benefit of considering environmental and digital poverty as two interconnected dimensions of the complexity of poverty in the digital age.

The case of the social business in Bhubaneswar that uses an ICT platform to address smallholder farmer poverty shows how digital and environmental aspects can positively interact to combat multiple forms of poverty (economic, environmental, and digital). This is accomplished by raising individual and collective awareness and engagement with such digital-environmental interconnection and providing farmers with the tools necessary to capitalize on the opportunities presented by the circumstances (and structural drivers). This also represents a step in a wider process of poverty eradication that has been slowly taking place in the area. Therefore, the relationship between public engagement and the policy instruments is two-way and intersects with individual knowledge and motivation, as well as the social and policy context (Khatibi et al., 2021).

Individual motivation, being part of a social network, environmental awareness, and engagement were shown to be essential for developing eco-friendly digital practices. At the same time, the acquisition of such digital-environmental dispositions is influenced by both structural determinants and the circumstances of the operational field. The environmental structure interacts with individual traits, thanks to the mediation of circumstantial factors such as the direct experience of adverse environmental conditions (Bergquist et al., 2019) and opportunities available for citizens to increase their *citizens' power*. Taken together, these circumstances can be interpreted as the field in which routinized actions take place in a specific time and space. They can produce consequences in more or less "distant" time-space contexts (Giddens, 1984), which can be unintended, by contributing to several factors such as the digital infrastructure available (due, for example, to environmental conditions), assimilation of values among social groups, and the implementation of specific policies aimed at increasing digital efficiency in environmental terms. This can also influence the motivation to use digital tools in a digital sustainable way and reduce individual impacts on the environment. In the next chapter, further attention will be given to the circumstantial level of interaction which is where the agentic power and structural conditions meet and can generate transformative power. Chapter 6 will go more in depth in the exploration of the metabolization of structural and individual determinants by adopting the Bourdesian concept of habitus.

## References

Abdul, K., Hangjung, Z., & Ananth, C. (2021). Digital transformation and environmental sustainability. *Sustainability, 13.* https://www.mdpi.com/2071-1050/13/3/1530

Allman, K. (2022). *UK digital poverty evidence review 2022.* https://digitalpovertyalliance.org/wp-content/uploads/2022/06/UK-Digital-Poverty-Evidence-Review-2022-v1.0-compressed.pdf

Andrae, A., & Edler, T. (2015). On global electricity usage of communication technology: Trends to 2030. *Challenges, 6*(1), 117–157.

Andrae, A. S. G. (2019). Comparison of several simplistic high-level approaches for estimating the global energy and electricity use of ICT networks and data centers. *International Journal of Green Technology, 5*, 50–63.

Arnstein, S. R. (2007). A ladder of citizen participation. *Journal of the American Institute of Planners, 35*(4), 216–224.

Aslan, J., Mayers, K., Koomey, J. G., & France, C. (2018). Electricity intensity of internet data transmission: Untangling the estimates. *Journal of Industrial Ecology, 22*(4), 785–798.

Axon, S. (2016). "The good life": Engaging the public with community-based carbon reduction strategies. *Environmental Science and Policy, 66*, 82–92.

Balogun, A. L., Marks, D., Sharma, R., Shekhar, H., Balmes, C., Maheng, D., Arshad, A., & Batmunkh, A. (2022). Carbon footprint of the most popular social media platforms. *Sustainability, 14*(4). https://doi.org/10.3390/su14042195

Beier, G., Fritzsche, K., Kunkel, S., Matthess, M., Niehoff, S., Reißig, M., & van Zyl-Bulitta, V. (2020). *Green digitized economy? Challenges and opportunities for sustainability.* IASS Fact Sheet 2020/1; Institute for Advanced Sustainability Studies (IASS).

Bergquist, M., Nilsson, A., & Schultz, P. W. (2019). Experiencing a severe weather event increases concern about climate change. *Frontiers in Psychology, 10*, 220. https://doi.org/10.3389/fpsyg.2019.00220

Berkhout, F., & Hertin, J. (2004). De-materialising and re-materialising: Digital technologies and the environment. *Futures, 36*, 906–920.

Bodin, Ö. (2017). Collaborative environmental governance: Achieving collective action in social-ecological systems. *Science, 357*(6352), eaan1114.

Bordage, F. (2019). The environmental footprint of the digital world. *GreenIT.fr.* https://www.greenit.fr/wpcontent/uploads/2019/11/GREENIT_EENM_etude_EN_accessible.pdf

Burton, P., & Mustelin, J. (2013). Planning for climate change: Is greater public participation the key to success? *Urban Policy and Research, 31*(4), 399–415.

Choudhary, S., Nayak, R., Kumari, S., & Choudhury, H. (2019). Analysing acculturation to sustainable food consumption behaviour in the social media through

the lens of information diffusion. *Technological Forecasting and Social Change, 145*, 481–492.
Climate Change AI. (2019). *About climate change AI.* https://dl.acm.org/doi/10.1145/3485128
Dahlinger, A., & Wortmann, F. (2016). *Fostering pro-environmental behaviour with green consumer is: The effects of is-induced construal and general is usage motivations.* Research-in-Progress Papers, 60. http://aisel.aisnet.org/ecis2016_rip/60
De Young, R. (1986). Some psychological aspects of recycling. *Environment and Behavior, 18*, 435–449.
De Young, R. (1996). Some psychological aspects of reduced consumption behaviour: The role of intrinsic motivation and competence motivation. *Environment and Behavior, 28*, 358–409.
Ejelöv, E., Bergquist, M., Hansla, A., & Nilsson, A. (2022). Why are they eco-friendly? Attributing eco-friendly descriptive norms to intrinsic motivation increases pro-environmental purchase intention. *PLoS One, 20*(10). https://doi.org/10.1371/journal.pone.0265839
Esmaeilian, B., Sarkis, J., Lewis, K., & Behdad, S. (2020). Blockchain for the future of sustainable supply chain management in industry 4.0. *Resources, Conservation and Recycling, 163.* https://doi.org/10.1016/j.resconrec.2020.105064
Fauville, G., Queiroz, A. C. M., & Bailenson, J. N. (2020). Virtual reality as a promising tool to promote climate change awareness. In J. Kim & H. Song (Eds.), *Technology and health: Promoting attitude and behavior change* (pp. 91–108). Academic Press.
Freitag, C., Berners-Lee, M., Widdicks, K., Knowles, B., Blair, G. S., & Friday, A. (2021). The climate impact of ICT: A review of estimates, trends and regulations. *Patterns, 2*(9). https://doi.org/10.1016/j.patter.2021.100340
Galvin, R. (2020). Power, evil and resistance in social structure: A sociology for energy research in a climate emergency. *Energy Research & Social Science, 61.* https://doi.org/10.1016/j.erss.2019.101361
Gao, B., Li, Z., & Yan, J. (2022). The influence of social commerce on ecofriendly consumer behavior: Technological and social roles. *Journal of Consumer Behaviour, 21*, 653–672.
George, G., Merrill, R. K., & Schillebeeckx, S. J. (2021). Digital sustainability and entrepreneurship: How digital innovations are helping tackle climate change and sustainable development. *Entrepreneurship Theory and Practice, 45*(5), 999–1027.
Giddens, A. (1984). *The constitution of society. Outline of the theory of structuration.* University of California Press.
Global Multidimensional Poverty Index. (2022). *Unpacking deprivation bundles to reduce multidimensional poverty.* United Nations Development Programme

and Oxford Poverty and Human Development Initiative. https://ophi.org.uk/global-mpi-report-2022/
Goralski, M. A., & Tan, T. K. (2019). Artificial intelligence and sustainable development. *The International Journal of Management Education, 18*. https://doi.org/10.1016/j.ijme.2019.100330
Gore, T. (2021). Carbon inequality in 2030: Per capita consumption emissions and the 1.5°C goal. *Institute for European Environmental Policy and Oxfam.*
Government of Odisha. (2022). *Odisha economic survey 2021–22.* Directorate of Economics and Statistics Planning and Convergence Department Government of Odisha.
Guellec, D., & Van Pottelsberghe De La Potterie, B. (2003). The impact of public R&D expenditure on business R&D*. *Economics of Innovation and New Technology, 12*(3), 225–243.
Ha, L. T., Huong, T. T. L., & Thanh, T. T. (2022). Is digitalization a driver to enhance environmental performance? An empirical investigation of European countries. *Sustainable Production and Consumption., 32*, 230–247.
Hedin, B., Katzeff, C., Eriksson, E., & Pargman, D. (2019). A systematic review of digital behaviour change interventions for more sustainable food consumption. *Sustainability, 11*(9). https://doi.org/10.3390/su11092638
Helferich, M., Thøgersen, J., & Bergquist, M. (2023). Direct and mediated impacts of social norms on pro-environmental behavior. *Global Environmental Change, 80*. https://doi.org/10.1016/j.gloenvcha.2023.102680
Henkel, C., & Kranz, J. (2018, December 13–16). *Pro-environmental behaviour and green information systems research—Review, synthesis and directions for future research.* [Conference Presentation]. 39th International Conference on Information Systems (ICIS).
Hintemann, R., & Hinterholzer, S. (2019, June 10–14). *Energy consumption of data centers worldwide—How will the internet become green?* [Conference Presentation]. ICT4S. https://ceur-ws.org/Vol-2382/ICT4S2019_paper_16.pdf
Hollweg, K. S., Taylor, J. R., Bybee, R. W., Marcinkowski, T. J., McBeth, W. C., & Zoido, P. (2011). *Developing a framework for assessing environmental literacy.* North American Association for Environmental Education.
Hosan, S., Karmaker, S. C., Rahman, M. M., Chapman, A. J., & Saha, B. B. (2022). Dynamic links among the demographic dividend, digitalization, energy intensity and sustainable economic growth: Empirical evidence from emerging economies. *Journal of Cleaner Production, 330*. https://doi.org/10.1016/j.jclepro.2021.129858
Imran, S., Alam, K., & Beaumont, N. (2014). Environmental orientations and environmental behaviour: Perceptions of protected area tourism stakeholders. *Tourism Management, 40*, 290–299.

Irtyshcheva, I. (2021). The effect of digital technology development on economic growth. *International Journal of Data and Network Science, 5*, 25–36.

Jager, N. X., Newig, J., Challies, E., & Kochskämper, E. (2019). Pathways to implementation: Evidence on how participation in environmental governance impacts on environmental outcomes. *Journal of Public Administration Research and Theory, 31*(3), 616. https://doi.org/10.1093/jopart/muab006

Jha, S. K., Pinsonneault, A., & Dubé, L. (2016). The evolution of an ICT platform-enabled ecosystem for poverty alleviation: The case of ekutir. *MIS Quarterly, 40*(2), 431–446.

Kamarul Bahrin, M. A., Othman, M. F., Nor Azli, N. H., & Talib, M. F. (2016). Industry 4.0: A review on industrial automation and robotics. *Journal Teknologi, 78*, 137–143.

Kamiya, G. (2020). The carbon footprint of streaming video: Fact-checking the headlines analysis. https://www.iea.org/commentaries/the-carbon-footprint-of-streamingvideo-fact-checking-the-headlines

Khatibi, F. S., Dedekorkut-Howes, A., Howes, M., et al. (2021). Can public awareness, knowledge and engagement improve climate change adaptation policies? *Discover Sustainability, 2*(18). https://doi.org/10.1007/s43621-021-00024-z

Kiss, B., Sekulova, F., Hörschelmann, K., Salk, C. F., Takahashi, W., & Wamsler, C. (2022). Citizen participation in the governance of nature-based solutions. *Environmental Policy and Governance*. https://doi.org/10.1002/eet.1987

Kranz, J., Kolbe, L. M., Koo, C., & Boudreau, M.-C. (2015). Smart energy: Where do we stand and where should we go? *Electronic Markets, 25*(1), 7–16.

Lazaric, N., Le Guel, F., Belin, J., Oltra, V., Lavaud, S., & Douai, A. (2019). Determinants of sustainable consumption in France: The importance of social influence and environmental values. *Journal of Evolutionary Economics, 30*(5), 1337–1366.

Lemos, M. C., & Agrawal, A. (2009). Environmental governance and political science. In M. S. Delmas & O. R. Young (Eds.), *Governance for the environment. New perspectives* (pp. 69–97). Cambridge University Press.

Loock, C.-M., Staake, T., & Thiesse, F. (2013). Motivating energy-efficient behaviour with green is: An investigation of goal setting and the role of defaults. *MIS Quaterly, 37*(4), 1313–1332.

Ma, R., Li, F., & Du, M. (2022). How does environmental regulation and digital finance affect green technological innovation: Evidence from China. *Frontiers in Environmental Science, 10*. https://doi.org/10.3389/fenvs.2022.928320

Mahapatra, S. and Birkman, L. (2021). *India's climate conundrum: Addressing the climate-food-poverty nexus in Odisha province. The Hague Centre for Strategic Studies*. http://www.jstor.org/stable/resrep38746

Malhotra, A., Melville, N., & Watson, R. (2013). Spurring impactful research on information Systems for Environmental Sustainability. *MIS Quarterly, 37*(4), 1265–1274.

Malmodin, J., & Lundén, D. (2018). The energy and carbon footprint of the global ICT and E&M sectors 2010–2015. *Sustainability, 10*(9), 3027.

Mol, A. P. J. (2008). *Environmental reform in the information age: The contours of informational governance.* Cambridge University Press.

Murugesan, S. (2008). Harnessing green IT: Principles and practices. *IT Professional, 10*(1), 24–33.

Nesshöver, C., Assmuth, T., Irvine, K. N., Rusch, G. M., Waylen, K. A., Delbaere, B., Haase, D., Jones-Walters, L., Keune, H., Kovacs, K., Külvik, M., Rey, F., van Dijk, J., Vistad, O. I., Wilkinson, M. E., & Wittmer, H. (2017). The science, policy and practice of nature-based solutions: An interdisciplinary perspective. *Science Total Environment, 579*, 1215–1227.

Nolan, J. M. (2010). "An inconvenient truth" increases knowledge, concern, and willingness to reduce greenhouse gases. *Environment and Behaviour, 42*(5), 643–658.

Nunan, F. (2015). *Understanding poverty and the environment. Analytical frameworks and approaches.* Routledge.

Obringer, R., Rachunok, B., Maia-Silva, D., Arbabzadeh, M., Nateghi, R., & Madani, K. (2021). The overlooked environmental footprint of increasing internet use. *Resources, Conservation and Recycling, 167*, 105389. https://doi.org/10.1016/j.resconrec.2020.105389

Oo, Jonah, & Thin. (2023). A systematic review of the pros and cons of digital pollution and its impact on the environment. *Journal of Sustainability and Environmental Management, 2*(1), 61–73.

Perino, G., & Requate, T. (2012). Does more stringent environmental regulation induce or reduce technology adoption? When the rate of technology adoption is inverted U-shaped. *Journal of Environmental Economics and Management, 64*(3), 456–467.

Pickering, J., Hickmann, T., Bäckstrand, K., Kalfagianni, A., Bloomfield, M., Mert, A., Ransan-Cooper, H., & Lo, A. Y. (2022). Democratising sustainability transformations: Assessing the transformative potential of democratic practices in environmental governance. *Earth System Governance, 11*. https://doi.org/10.1016/j.esg.2021.100131

Rolnick, D. et al. (2022). Tackling climate change with machine learning. *ACM Computing Surveys, 55*(2). https://dl.acm.org/doi/10.1145/3485128

Salahuddin, M., & Alam, K. (2016). Information and communication technology, electricity consumption and economic growth in OECD countries: A panel data analysis. *International Journal of Electrical Power and Energy Systems, 76*, 185–193.

Schlosberg, D., & Craven, L. (2019). *Sustainable materialism: Environmental practice and the politics of everyday life*. Oxford University Press.
Sen, A. (2001). *Development as freedom*. Oxford University Press.
Simpson, J. M., Dunlap, R. E., & Fullerton, A. S. (2019). The treadmill of information: Development of the information society and carbon dioxide emissions. *Sociology Faculty Publications., 2*.
Sparviero, S., & Ragnedda, M. (2021). Towards digital sustainability: The long journey to the sustainable development goals 2030. *Digital Policy, Regulation and Governance, 23*(3), 216–228.
Steg, L. (2016). Values, norms, and intrinsic motivation to act Proenvironmentally. *Annual Review of Environment and Resources, 41*, 277–292.
Strubell, E., Ganesh, A., & McCallum, A. (2019). Energy and policy considerations for deep learning in NLP. *Proceedings of the 57th Annual Meeting of the Association for Computational Linguistics*. https://doi.org/10.18653/v1/P19-1355.
Sutton, S. G., & Tobin, R. C. (2011). Constraints on community engagement with great barrier reef climate change reduction and mitigation. *Global Environtal Change, 21*(3), 894–905.
Tang, X., Yuan, J., & Zeng, X. (2023). Influencing factors of community residents' pro-environmental behavior in east Dongting Lake National Nature Reserve under the policy intervention. *Scientific Reports, 13*(6076). https://doi.org/10.1038/s41598-023-32553-0
Turken, N., Carrillo, J., & Verter, V. (2020). Strategic supply chain decisions under environmental regulations: When to invest in end-of-pipe and green technology. *European Journal of Operational Research, 283*(2), 601–613.
United Nations. (UN). (1995, March). *The Copenhagen declaration and programme of action: World summit for social development 6–12*. United Nations Department of Publications.
UN. (2022). *E-government survey 2022. The future of digital government*. Department of Economic and Social Affairs. https://publicadministration.un.org/en/publicadministration.un.org/egovkb/en-us/
Unicef. (2021). *Five tips for reducing your digital footprint. Digital pollution is the greenhouse gases that come from building and using digital technology*. https://www.unicef.org/armenia/en/stories/five-tips-reducing-your-digital-footprint
Wang, X., Pacho, F., Liu, J., & Kajungiro, R. (2019). Factors influencing organic food purchase intention in developing countries and the moderating role of knowledge. *Sustainability, 11*(209). https://doi.org/10.3390/su11010209
Watson, R. T., Boudreau, M.-C., & Chen, A. J. (2010). Information systems and environmentally sustainable development: Energy informatics and new directions for the community. *MIS Quarterly, 34*(1), 23–38.

Xu, J., She, S., & Liu, W. (2022). Role of digitalization in environment, social and governance, and sustainability: Review-based study for implications. *Frontiers in Psychology, 13*. https://doi.org/10.3389/fpsyg.2022.961057

Ye, Z., Yang, J., Zhong, N., Tu, X., Jia, J., & Wang, J. (2020). Tackling environmental challenges in pollution controls using artificial intelligence: A review. *Science of the Total Environment, 699*. https://doi.org/10.1016/j.scitotenv.2019.134279

Yi, M., Lu, Y., Wen, L., Luo, Y., Xu, S., & Zhang, T. (2022). Whether green technology innovation is conducive to haze emission reduction: Empirical evidence from China. *Environmental Science and Pollution Research, 29*(8), 12115–12127.

Young, J. C., Jordan, A., Searle, K. R., Butler, A., Chapman, D. S., Simmons, P., & Watt, A. D. (2013). Does stakeholder involvement really benefit biodiversity conservation? *Biological Conservation, 158*, 359–370.

Zawieska, J., Obracht-Prondzyńska H., Duda E., Uryga D., & Romanowska M. (2022). In search of innovative digital solutions enhancing social pro-environmental engagement. *Energies, 15*(14). https://doi.org/10.3390/en15145191

Zhang, M., Guo, S., Bai, C., & Wang, W. (2019). Study on the impact of haze pollution on residents' green consumption behavior: The case of Shandong Province. *Journal of Cleaner Production, 219*, 11–19.

CHAPTER 6

# A Bourdesian Approach to the Digital-Environmental Relationship

## 6.1 Introduction

The previous chapter referred to circumstantial determinants as a meso level that can be defined as a social space structured in fields in which social actors operate. This chapter adopts a Bourdesian approach to conceptualize the circumstantial level as an intersectional space where both agency and structure can mutually influence each other, leading to variations in what Bourdieu refers to as habitus. It is worth reflecting on the interplay between structural and individual determinants to understand the formation of what Ruiu et al. (2023) have defined as *Digital-Environmental Habitus.* Digital-environmental habitus, intended as an intersectional concept across the levels identified by the Digital-Environmental Poverty Framework (DEPF), can help comprehend the mechanisms at work at the circumstantial level and capture the connections between environmental and digital poverty.

This chapter delves into the Bourdesian concepts of field and (digital-environmental) habitus to understand how these concepts shed light on the variations in digital technology users' attitudes toward the environment. This chapter also draws from the literature on the "ecological habitus" (or "eco-habitus"), which forms the basis for the emergence of the digital-environmental habitus. Additionally, it considers the "digital



M. L. Ruiu, M. Ragnedda, *Digital-Environmental Poverty*, Palgrave Studies in Digital Inequalities,
https://doi.org/10.1007/978-3-031-56184-9_6

habitus," which encompasses digital dispositions influencing the digital experience (Adams, 2012; Eriksen, 2013; Haluza-DeLay, 2008; Kirby, 2017). The need to investigate the intersection between the digital and environmental habitus becomes even more pertinent within the context of multiple crises, including the COVID-19 pandemic, the climate crisis, and the economic crisis. These crises have produced an unprecedented digital acceleration while exacerbating inequalities. The chapter starts with the exploration of the circumstantial determinants through the lens of the Bourdesian concepts of field and habitus. Then it specifically refers to the intersection between environmental and digital poverty as reflected in the digital-environmental habitus. The final paragraph reflects on how the COVID-19 crisis has exposed the intersections of economic, environmental, and digital poverties. This crisis has not only added to the environmental crisis but, when combined with other contributing factors, has triggered a global social crisis.

## 6.2 Conceptualizing the Circumstantial Determinants Through the Lens of Field and Habitus

This paragraph delves deeper into the meso-level configuration of circumstantial determinants employing Bourdieu's concepts of fields and habitus. Chapter 5 applied Giddens' (1984) structuration theory to position digital and environmental behavior within a framework of shared social norms. The multiple facets of the DEPF have been framed through the lens of the "duality of structure," which simultaneously reproduces existing structures and enables change as both a determinant force and a result of human action. The meso level, represented by circumstantial determinants, can be viewed as a space where interactions and influences between agency and structure occur. It can be defined as the context where human agency manifests within the framework of social relationships. Drawing from Bourdieu's conceptual framework, this space could be also described as a social field where agents position themselves based on their relative influence or power. Bourdieu defines the field as the realm that embodies historical social memory and where habitus delineates the social position of the agents.

Bourdieu and Wacquant (1992, p. 97) define the field as:

> a network, or a configuration, of objective relations between positions objectively defined, in their existence and in the determinations they impose upon their occupants, agents of institutions, by their present and potential situation (situs) in the structure of the distribution of species of power (or capital) whose possession commands access to the specific profits that are at stake in the field, as well as by their objective relation to other positions. (domination, subordination, homology, etc.)

This definition underscores the multifaceted nature of the field in which agents occupy specific positions contingent on their power status, which, in turn, is shaped by their possession of social, economic, and cultural capital. These positions enable agents to pursue specific objectives and accumulate capital (Bourdieu, 1998) under the rules that shape the field. However, even though the configuration of the field will be influenced by structural factors and pre-existing possession of capital, it can be relatively autonomous from the social space depending on the relational structure established among the different positions (Bourdieu, 1985). This suggests that the most powerful agents in the field can establish their capital as the symbolic capital of the field (Singh, 2022). Several studies have characterized the digital domain as a field where agents (users) assume distinct positions and possess various forms of capital that empower them to engage with the Internet (Ignatow & Robinson, 2017). Some authors have proposed integrating a digital form of capital into the traditional forms of capital outlined by Bourdieu (Ragnedda & Ruiu, 2020; Ragnedda et al., 2019; Ragnedda et al., 2022). Others refer to the notion of technocultural capital, which encompasses the tools needed to navigate a digitally and technologically mediated social sphere more broadly (Gambetti, 2020).

Applying these considerations to the DEPF's circumstantial level, circumstances objectify the field as a result of both individual traits and structural configuration. These circumstances define the field in which routinized actions, dependent on the availability of capital, can produce consequences (Giddens, 1984) and different forms of power (see Fig. 5.1), which can also be unintended. These circumstances contribute to the available digital infrastructure, which is influenced by socio-economic, cultural, and environmental factors, as well as specific policies designed to enhance digital and environmental efficiency. We have also emphasized that these circumstances can influence individuals' motivation to use digital tools in an environmentally friendly manner, thereby alleviating their environmental poverty to some degree. They can also affect environmental dispositions due to the relational nature of the field that creates hierarchies but also horizontal types of exchange (which can also affect the pre-existing digital and environmental dispositions). As a result, such circumstances influence and are influenced by the positions of the various competing agents based on their capitals. We acknowledged that some authors have discussed the importance of including digital capital as a positioning element in the digital field. However, due to the interplay between environment and digital fields, environmental capital can also play a role at this level. Karol and Gale (2004, pp. 5–6) define environmental capital as the ways of understanding:

> the interdependence of all life on Earth, and an awareness of the complicity that individuals possess in contributing to both positive and negative environmental consequences. Environmental capital also entails an understanding of the interconnectedness of the social, cultural, political, technological and economic systems and the effects these have on the environment.

Despite acknowledging the intersectionality between systems, this definition appears to limit the meaning of this capital to environmental knowledge and the possession of certain skills that facilitate such understanding. However, we suggest that this definition should also include an individual's capacity to reduce their ecological footprint. The ecological footprint represents the quantity of natural resources appropriated and consumed by individuals or communities, as well as the proportion of waste reintroduced into the ecosystem (Nautiyal & Goel, 2021). It has also been specifically defined as "the area of land (and water) that would be required to sustain indefinitely a human population defined in terms of providing all energy/material resources consumed and absorbing all waste discharged" (Wackernagel & Rees, 1996). This component is crucial for understanding the position of social actors in the environmental field and their ability to prevent its degradation, thereby enhancing their well-being.

Therefore, we refer to the circumstantial level as the field where Bourdieu's habitus (Bourdieu, 1977, 1990; Bourdieu & Wacquant, 1992) can transform. In this specific structuration, it should be labeled as a digital-environmental field in which the digital-environmental habitus operates. The following paragraph provides a more in-depth exploration of the concept of digital-environmental habitus and its contribution to understanding the intersection of digital and environmental poverty.

## 6.3 Digital-Environmental Habitus

The previous chapters introduced some similarities between the duality of structure and Bourdieu's conception of habitus (Bourdieu, 1977). Chapter 5 introduced the idea that digital-environmental poverty is not isolated from the surrounding societal context but is interconnected with a complex web of social norms and regulatory mechanisms. However, the societal structure simultaneously reproduces existing conditions and provides opportunities for change as it is influenced by human action and also influences it. Moreover, discussing how social practice and agentic power interact in consumption practices, Chap. 4 discussed the concept of taste (Bourdieu, 1984), which encompasses one's preferences, lifestyle, choices, consumption practices, and cultural and social interactions. We defined it as being shaped by both individuals' background influences and their personal experience of social fields. This concept is closely tied to habitus, which acts as a meta-construct that shapes an individual's preferences. Habitus can be defined as a set of perceptual patterns and expectations through which individuals interpret social reality (and act accordingly) (Elam, 2008; Piroddi, 2021). The present chapter also proposes that habitus aids in grasping the connection between structure and agency as a dialectical one rather than a pure oppositional relationship. If we interpret habitus as layered by the unconscious acquisition of cultural, economic, and social backgrounds from the early stages of life (Bourdieu, 1977), as well as the ongoing transformation/adaptation to new contexts (Abrahams & Ingram, 2013; Bourdieu, 2002; Di Maggio, 1979; Reay, 2004), it becomes a point of intersection between structure and agency. In this sense, habitus is a reflection of structural dispositions but is also capable of transforming those conditions. For instance, individuals' dispositions can be cultivated in various settings, including family, community, and educational environments, and they mirror the material conditions and social influences they encounter, thus playing a role in shaping the "class habitus." Therefore, structural conditions that contribute toward determining certain life circumstances will increase the chances of generating similar perceptions, behaviors, and attitudes among individuals who live in these conditions. At the same time, incorporating a specific "class habitus" does not automatically translate into predetermined actions. By contrast, habitus serves as a mediator between the determinism of structure and the flexibility of individual action (Allen & Anderson, 1994). In this regard, Ruiu et al. (2021) define habitus as a "bridging concept" that connects structural and agentic aspects. It is dynamic being both a process and a product of individual life experiences and the social world (Bourdieu, 1993; Bourdieu & Chartier, 2015; Bourdieu & Wacquant, 1992; Schmidt, 1997). It is an unconscious force (Bourdieu, 1977, 1990), largely influencing behavior and preferences, but also "conscious calculation" (Crossley, 2001), and it is field-dependent. Agents' habitus generates practices that depend on the different fields of action and the relation with the other agents in the same field (Singh, 2022). The operational circumstances can modify the original configuration of habitus (Bourdieu, 2002). At the same time, "depending upon the stimuli and structure of the field, the very same habitus will generate different, even opposite, outcomes" (Bourdieu & Wacquant, 1992, p. 135). The previous paragraph characterized the field as a "space of social forces and struggles" (Bourdieu & Wacquant, 1992), where the interplay between various forms of capitals, habitus, and circumstances situates the agents and influences their opportunities in the network. Habitus prompts responses and shapes perceptions within a specific field, but these dispositions can be applied in fields different from the ones where they were originally developed (Bourdieu, 1991). While the field refers to the configuration of agents in the social network, habitus pertains to how these positions affect the values, perceptions, and behavior of agents as they are internalized through social practice (Hughes & Paterson, 2017). Here, we conceptualize habitus as linking individual actions (which in turn are influenced by both individual creativity and collective history) to the field in which these actions take place (Brulle & Norgaard, 2019). It is crucial to emphasize that in our definition, the field-dependent nature of habitus does not restrict an individual's taste and everyday behavior to a fixed and unalterable "positional" habitus. It neither confines habitus to "a structured structure" that simply incorporates the field structure, as often criticized in the sociological debate (see, for example, Atkinson, 2010; Crossley, 2001). In contrast, we situate habitus within the duality of structure, which has the dual function of both perpetuating existing structures and enabling change as both a shaping force and an outcome of human action. Therefore, habitus exists within this duality, as it can both trigger and result from alterations in both circumstantial (relatively independent fields of action) and structural configuration (existing systems and norms that regulate the social space). However, given its capacity to transpose the skills acquired in a specific field, habitus is capable of flexibility, adaptation, and transformative power. Habitus is a continuous process of acquiring various types of capital and adapting to external fields (Di Maggio, 1979; Reay, 2004), but it is also layered across society (Sterne, 2003). As a result, habitus can be interpreted as an individual's ability to deal with specific circumstances, but it is also subject to shifts in attitude and practice produced by the fluidity of the field of action (Costa et al., 2019). This builds on Bourdieu's claim that, while habitus is quite durable, a significant change in the environment can result in an altered habitus (Bourdieu & Wacquant, 1992). As Singh (2022) suggests, the creative responses of the habitus to new experiences are embedded in the relational structure and the specificity of relations characterizing the specific field of action. Applied to the study of DEP, the constructs of habitus and field can be particularly useful in helping understand habitus' capability of transposing its accumulated capital between the digital and environmental fields. They also help understand how the relational structure of the field and pre-existing structural conditions can constrain or favor agents' capability to improve their life chances. The "chameleon" potential of habitus has been applied to either digital or environmental dispositions, separately. Some scholars more generally refer to technological habitus by broadly considering how technology uses are metabolized by habitus (Costa, 2014; Kvasny, 2005). More specifically, digital habitus has been defined as a continuous and intense experience of digital technology (Gambetti, 2020; Masoom, 2023; Papacharissi & Easton, 2013; Richardson, 2015; Zevenbergen, 2007), resulting from both the type of digital technology and users' pre-existing ability to benefit from its use (Czerniewicz & Brown, 2013; Marwick & Boyd, 2011; Romele & Rodighiero, 2020). Some authors have also defined it in terms of "informational habitus" (Robinson, 2009). It is more than just internalizing constant engagement with digital tools; it is also about living in the digital field (Richardson, 2015) and its relational structure that situates actors at different levels of power. This concept has been used successfully in higher education to explain the individual capacity to "evolve" as a result of the use of various types of technology and the individual's preexisting ability to benefit from their use (Czerniewicz & Brown, 2013).

On the other hand, the literature supports that environmental dispositions should be simultaneously interpreted as a product of existing backgrounds and a process of relational practices (Hochschild, 2016; Kennedy & Givens, 2019). Environmental dispositions have been defined in terms of ecological or eco-habitus (Adams, 2012; Eriksen, 2013; Haluza-DeLay, 2008; Kasper, 2009; Kirby, 2017). This concept refers to social and ecological practices that emerge from a sense of place and influence tastes, practices, and dispositions (Carfagna et al., 2016; Haluza-DeLay, 2008; Smith, 2001). Eco-habitus has been linked to a high level of cultural capital (Kirby, 2017), which becomes more relevant than economic capital (Schor et al., 2016) and distinguishes those who develop tastes or dispositions to protect the environment (Maguire, 2016) and engage in green consumption (Kennedy & Givens, 2019). As a result, it has been used to investigate environmental social movements (Haluza-DeLay, 2008; Kasper, 2009; Kirby, 2017; Adams, 2012) and communities (Kirby, 2018).

Drawing from these two notions, Ruiu et al. (2021) suggested the use of techno-environmental habitus to indicate the interaction of structural determinants (existing backgrounds) and the metabolized increased use of technologies in people's daily lives, which also encapsulates individual environmental predispositions. A nuance of the techno-environmental habitus is expressed by the digital-environmental habitus, which specifically refers to the use of digital technologies (Ruiu et al., 2023). The authors applied the concept to study how digital users are distributed in the digital field in relation to their dispositions toward the environment (Ruiu et al., 2021). The digital-environmental habitus is not completely defined by structural factors or by individual agency (Bourdieu, 1990; Crossley, 2002). As a result, digital-environmental habitus includes both individual perceptions (which also depend on a collective metabolized understanding) of the environmental impacts of digital technologies (digital carbon footprint) and behavioral responses.

Previous research on the connection between the use of digital technologies and environmental awareness/engagement has primarily focused on the relationship between the use of ICTs and specific aspects of environmental change, such as CC understanding, for example, focusing on social media discussions (see, for example, Carfagna et al., 2016; Diehl et al., 2021; Gladston & Wing, 2019; Mavrodieva et al., 2019; Pearce et al., 2019; Shah et al., 2021). Extensive research has been conducted on media products (primarily news media) as a predictor of environmental behavior and awareness (Arlt et al., 2011; Shah et al., 2021; Zhang & Skoric, 2018). However, Ruiu et al. (2023) have shown the value of connecting digital and environmental predispositions to develop a use of digital technologies that is environmentally conscious. This is especially true, as the following paragraph highlights, in the context of the COVID-19 pandemic, which demonstrated how the economic, digital, and environmental components of poverty are inextricably linked.

## 6.4 The Long-Term Sustainability of (Digital) Consumption-Based Capitalism in the Context of Ecological Degradation

The COVID-19 pandemic has shown strong interdependencies between natural and societal systems, by highlighting that biodiversity loss and intensive food systems can increase the probability of diseases. The expansion and spread of pandemics in recent times have been aided by large, urban agglomerations (Hang, 2020; Pinheiro & Luís, 2020; Reyes et al., 2013) and by globalization and international movement and trade (Bontempi, 2020). More specifically, the COVID-19 pandemic occurred in parallel to the climate change crisis and was responsible for unintended, short-term, positive consequences on environmental systems due to, for instance, decreased pollution from industries and vehicle emissions (European Environmental Agency, 2020). This has been possible thanks to the restrictive measures on people's movement. Therefore, the COVID-19 crisis has forced individuals to suddenly adapt to a new situation, with many limitations in terms of traveling, more distance working, and less or no socializing activities. Epidemics and pandemics have existed throughout history and impacted societal ways of life and their modes of consumption at different geographical levels (Hays, 2005). Therefore, pandemics have influenced how individuals interact, work, and live (Snowden, 2020). In turn, these changes represent a moment for a re-examination of individual-level practices regarding lifestyles and consumption as they relate to the impact on the environment and future generations. These changes have been accompanied by the pervasive use of technologies in people's everyday lives. Even though both positives and negatives have been identified in terms of the environmental impact of the COVID-19 crisis (for example, an increase in healthcare waste; see Rume & Islam, 2020), the shift to digital forms of learning, consumption, and social networking might have produced positives due to a routinized (digital) behavior (Kirby, 2017) that might consciously or unconsciously influence everyday practices even after the health alert. In this direction, the COVID-19 crisis and its social, environmental, and economic consequences have raised questions about the long-term sustainability of consumption-based capitalism in the context of ecological degradation (Hanafi, 2020; Ozili & Arun, 2020). A brief reflection on the meaning of crisis can help understand the multilayered character of poverty and the cascading effects that crises can trigger on multiple aspects of society.

Holton (1987) refers to crises as helpful for challenging the *status quo* and producing social change. Different approaches to social crises have highlighted a multitude of specific characteristics. However, one common trait relates to the cascading detrimental effects (see, for example, the work by Walby, 2015 in the investigation of the 2008 economic crisis) that a crisis can produce and its intersectionality (Bergman-Rosamond et al., 2022). Walby (2022) highlights that a theory of crisis requires the "identification of the institutional domains through which a crisis may cascade and the regimes of inequality that shape the social forces" (Walby, 2022, p. 502). Such a conceptualization suggests that a crisis affects the circumstances in which social agents operate. Several studies have explored the intersection between the COVID-19 pandemic and economic and digital poverty (Robinson et al., 2020), by showing how the most vulnerable have experienced the worst consequences at multiple levels (see, for example, Francis & Weller, 2022).

The COVID-19 crisis, among its multiplicity of effects on widening socio-economic disparities, imposed a sudden acceleration in terms of moving many aspects of daily life online. While disrupting the routine, the COVID-19 crisis changed society by introducing an unprecedented level of digitalization of social practice, which has continued even after the restrictions imposed by the lockdown were lifted, by consolidating digital as the new normal. Digital acceleration is also relevant to social behaviors and organizations concerned with environmental protection. This suggests that structural conditions of the environment and individual understanding of environmental matter create the conditions for social understanding to rise, also considering that the proliferation of digital in multiple sectors has been shown to contribute to affecting the environment (Elavarasan & Pugazhendhi, 2020).

Digital technology is influencing how people see, contemplate, and interact with nature (Kahn, 2011). As we suggested in Chap. 4, depending on how it is used, digital technology has the potential to mitigate the anthropogenic factors contributing to environmental degradation. However, as Walby (2022) argues, a crisis can be both "real" (see Beck, 1992, 2009; physical harm, accidents, and disasters, see Perrow, 1999) and "socially constructed" (threat rather than actual physical harm, which, however, mobilize resources according to the perception of a threat; see Buzan et al., 1998). Climate and environmental changes fall into this duality since the extent of the harm can be debated and contested, often influenced by *discursive power* (see Chap. 5) and the use of politicized narratives (Urry, 2011). The combination of structural and individual changes during crises shows that breaking the routinized social practice might become an opportunity for both individual and collective reflexivity (Shove, 2004) and consciously or unconsciously metabolize new environmental attitudes (Alcock et al., 2017) as well as digital/technological routines. This is, for example, supported by the fact that citizens around the world cited climate action as important for COVID-19 recovery (UN, 2020). From a sociological standpoint, the digital acceleration due to the COVID-19 pandemic can be defined as a "sociocultural shock" between the cemented capitalist habitus and the experience of a new digital-dependent field. Therefore, the experience of a sudden digital acceleration can be interpreted as a "dialectical confrontation" (Bourdieu, 2002, p. 31) between the existing sedimented habitus and the new values and behaviors "altered" by the new field of action (Bourdieu & Wacquant, 1992), which in turn can give rise to a renovated digital-environmental habitus. Two main approaches can be identified in the sociological exploration of green behaviors, which focus either on individual choices (see Shove, 2010) and social desirability (Elliott, 2013; Sexton & Sexton, 2011) or on structural determinism (see Shove, 2004). On the one hand, interpreting green-oriented solutions as independent from structural constraints (Beck, 1992), and solely reliant on individual choices and self-identity (Giddens, 1990), might not be sufficient to tackle environmental issues. On the other hand, viewing digital behavior as entirely context-dependent might not provide a complete explanation for the interaction between societal dynamics and technologies.

Following the Bourdesian approach adopted by Laidley (2013), the combination of structural forces (related to class membership) and rational choices (dependent on the agent) are associated with different solutions to climate change, such as structural solutions to climate change, or more individual market-based and technological approaches. On the one hand, digital economy research has shown that digital skills empower consumers to make green choices (Gazzola et al., 2017); on the other hand, it does not consider the preference for using digital technologies (rather than, for example, materially accessing a service) as a reflexive choice to limit the physical impact on the environment with regard to certain activities. At the same time, as this chapter has tried to argue, the two levels (structural and agentic) appear to be connected through a relationship that shows the "duality of structure" as described by Giddens (1984). In this sense, the structural conditions for digital technologies to proliferate are simultaneously a trigger and an outcome of digital agency and evolution. Therefore, some intermediate approaches (Shove, 2004; Spaargaren, 2011) connect pro-environmental behaviors to a shift "in routine habits and practices" (Shove & Warde, 2002, p. 13) and context-dependent reflexivity (Pedersen, 2000). Following this approach, individual determinants interact with the structure and context of action (Diamantopoulosa et al., 2003). The COVID-19 crisis shows how ontological security (Giddens, 1990) is compromised by an excessively individualistic approach to environmental issues. It made clear a necessity to reflect on how structural and individual orientations on the problem can be effectively integrated. The COVID-19 crisis, coupled with the environmental crisis and its increasing media coverage, might represent the appropriate moment to activate processes of context-dependent reflexivity (Pedersen, 2000; Shove, 2004). On the one hand, the confluence of multiple crises may have created contextual alternatives (for example, for working, socializing, and entertaining from home) and increased individuals' opportunities to reflect on the fact that maintaining some digital components and behaviors in their daily lives does not affect their comfort while benefiting the environment. On the other hand, the lack of policy directions on how to avoid the perpetuation of environmentally damaging digital practices makes it difficult to alter the habitus of digital consumers. As suggested by Shulla et al. (2021), post-COVID intervention needs to be based on poverty reduction and capacity building, which encourages acting environmentally responsibly, as integral to green recovery. Furthermore, even though the pandemic has accelerated some green renovation processes among businesses, sustainable business models are still not mainstreamed. The resulting fragmentation of experiences may result in a rejection of either the original or new habitus (Wentworth & Peterson, 2001) or a chameleon transformative capacity. In this direction, Pappas et al. (2018) suggest that digital transformation aimed at creating sustainable societies must be based on an understanding of interactions and interrelations between different actors and levels that lead to knowledge, innovation, and value creation. Some studies have shown that synergies between digital and environmental dimensions can work in the direction of developing a sustainable digital-environmental habitus, such as the case presented by Agasisti et al. (2020). Their study shows how digital readiness, cultural openness, and strategic orientation represent relevant facilitators of the digital innovation process toward sustainability in higher education in Italy. Additional positive synergies between digital and environmental goals have been identified in other contexts in perpetuating telework even after the COVID-19 restrictions were lifted (Raghavan et al., 2021).

We have previously referred to the field as a space of competition. This implies that in the presence of opposing forces, a constellation of new habitus configurations may be generated, which may be difficult to reorient toward an environmentally friendly use of digital technologies once they have become consolidated. Therefore, the post-COVID crisis opens up an opportunity to reconcile socio-economic poverty with both environmental poverty and digital poverty. The COVID-19 recovery, followed by the Ukraine-Russia and the Middle East war crises, which in turn triggered a global energy crisis, still represents an opportunity to orient the digital-environmental habitus toward a sustainable principle.

## 6.5 Conclusion

This chapter focused on the meso level of the digital-environmental poverty framework by employing Bourdieu's concepts of fields and habitus along with Giddens' duality of structure. The goal was to shed light on how structural and individual determinants interact within the specific circumstances characterizing the field of action. We argued that the structural and agentic/individual determinants are intricately connected, illustrating the "duality of structure" as outlined by Giddens. Consequently, the structural conditions for the proliferation of digital technologies both influence and are influenced by digital agency and digital evolution, but also by environmental agency and structure. Digital-environmental habitus should be seen as a conceptual tool that can enhance understanding of the links between the different levels of the DEPF. Its intersecting nature encapsulates the convergence of determinants at all levels (structural, circumstantial, and individual). Throughout our discussion, we have emphasized that at the circumstantial level, habitus can transform due to the duality of interaction between structure and agency converging at this level. However, we have also highlighted how, despite the relative autonomy of the field and its rules, structural determinants continue to influence the position of the agents and their power in the social network configuring the field. This influence is a result of the structural distribution of capitals which unconsciously influence the evolution of habitus. We have also integrated the concepts of digital and environmental capital to illustrate how these new constructs can help us observe how agents position themselves in the digital and environmental fields. At the same time, we have referred to the capacity of habitus to acquire a novel taste based on the experiences and the relational structure of the fields in which it operates. Consequently, depending on the interplay between structural and agentic determinants, different circumstances may be generated that either enhance or constrain life chances. Therefore, we positioned the digital-environmental field at the circumstantial level in which the digital-environmental habitus operates and can simultaneously affect the "rules of the game" but also undergo transformation. The digital-environmental habitus, intended as the metabolized digital experience that also reflects environmental dispositions, differentiates agents in the digital field. In this direction, we suggested that digital-environmental habitus encompasses both individual perceptions, which in turn depend on a collective metabolized understanding of the environmental impacts of digital technologies, and behavioral responses.

Finally, we have suggested that the recent digital acceleration due to the COVID-19 pandemic has triggered a "dialectical confrontation" between the established, ingrained habitus and new values and behaviors influenced by the evolving field of action. This can, in turn, reshape the digital-environmental habitus, given the impact of digital technology on people's interaction with nature. The amalgamation of structural and individual changes during crises creates an opportunity for both individual and collective reflections. This, in turn, may lead to the conscious or unconscious assimilation of new environmental attitudes and technological routines. Conversely, the absence of clear policy guidance on how to mitigate environmentally harmful digital practices makes it challenging to alter the habitus of digital consumers. Additionally, although the pandemic has accelerated some environmentally friendly practices among businesses, sustainable models are not yet mainstream. Consequently, the fragmentation of experiences may result in unintended consequences of the habitus, which may result in a rejection of either the original or new habitus or may lead to a chameleon-like capacity for transformation.

The next chapter provides examples per each level of the digital-environmental poverty model described in Chap. 5. They serve to explore existing and potential ways of merging digital-environmental strategies in a comprehensive definition of digital-environmental poverty.

## References

Abrahams, J., & Ingram, N. (2013). The chameleon habitus: Exploring local students' negotiations of multiple fields. *Sociological Research Online, 18*(4), 21–34.

Adams, M. (2012). A social engagement: How Ecopsychology can benefit from dialogue with the social sciences. *Ecopsychology, 4*(3), 216–222.

Agasisti, T., Frattini, F., & Soncin, M. (2020). Digital innovation in times of emergency: Reactions from a School of Management in Italy. *Sustainability, 12*, 10312. https://doi.org/10.3390/su122410312

Alcock, I., White, M. P., Taylor, T., et al. (2017). 'Green' on the ground but not in the air: Pro-environmental attitudes are related to household behaviours but not discretionary air travel. *Global Environmental Change, 42*, 136–147.

Allen, D. E., & Anderson, P. F. (1994). Consumption and social stratification: Bourdieu's distinction. In C. T. Allen & D. R. John (Eds.), *Advances in consumer research volume 21* (pp. 70–74). Association for Consumer Research.

Arlt, D., Hoppe, I., & Wolling, J. (2011). Climate change and media usage: Effects on problem awareness and behavioural intentions. *International Communication Gazette, 73*(1–2), 45–63.

Atkinson, W. (2010). Phenomenological addition to Bourdieusian tool box: Two problems for Bourdieu, two solutions from Schutz. *Sociological Theory, 28*(1), 1–19.

Beck, U. (1992). *Risk society: Towards a new modernity.* Sage.

Beck, U. (2009). *World at risk.* Polity.

Bergman-Rosamond, A., Gammeltoft-Hansen, T., Hamza, M., Hearn, J., Ramasar, V., & Rydstrom, H. (2022). The case for interdisciplinary crisis studies. *Global Discourse, 12*(3–4), 465–486.

Bontempi, E. (2020). Commercial exchanges instead of air pollution as a possible origin of COVID-19 initial diffusion phase in Italy: More efforts are necessary to address interdisciplinary research. *Environmental Resources, 188.* https://doi.org/10.1016/j.envres.2020.109775

Bourdieu, P. (1977). *Outline of a theory of practice.* Cambridge University Press.

Bourdieu, P. (1984). *Distinction: A social critique o/the judgement o/taste.* Routledge.

Bourdieu, P. (1985). The social space and the genesis of groups. *Theory and Society, 14*(6), 723–744.

Bourdieu, P. (1990). *The logic of practice. Stanford.* Stanford University Press.

Bourdieu, P. (1991). *Language and symbolic power.* Harvard University Press.

Bourdieu, P. (1993). *Sociology in question.* Sage.

Bourdieu, P. (1998). *Practical reason: On the theory of action.* Polity Press.

Bourdieu, P. (2002). Habitus. In J. Hillierand & E. Rooksby (Eds.), *Habitus: A sense of place* (pp. 27–34). Ashgate.

Bourdieu, P., & Chartier, R. (2015). *The sociologist and the historian.* Polity Press.

Bourdieu, P., & Wacquant, L. J. D. (1992). *An invitation to reflexive sociology.* University of Chicago Press.

Brulle, R. J., & Norgaard, K. M. (2019). Avoiding cultural trauma: Climate change and social inertia. *Environmental Politics, 28*(5), 886–908.

Buzan, B., Wæver, O., & de Wilde, J. (1998). *Security: A new framework for analysis.* Lynne Rienner.

Carfagna, L. B., Dubois Poteat, E., Fitzmaurice, C., Ouimette, M. Y., Schor, J. B., Willis, M., Connor, P., Harris, E., Guy, S., et al. (2016). Interpersonal communication about climate change: How messages change when communicated through simulated online social networks. *Climatic Change, 136*(3–4), 463–476.

Costa, C. (2014). The habitus of digital scholars. *Research in Learning Technology, 21*(2013), 21274. https://doi.org/10.3402/rlt.v21i0.21274

Costa, C., Burke, B., & Murphy, M. (2019). Capturing habitus: Theory, method and reflexivity. *International Journal of Research & Method in Education, 42*(1), 19–32.

Crossley, N. (2001). The phenomenological habitus and its construction. *Theory and Society, 30*(1), 81–120.

Crossley, N. (2002). *Making sense of social movements.* Open University Press.

Czerniewicz, L., & Brown, C. (2013). The habitus of digital 'strangers' in higher education. *British Journal of Educational Technology, 44*(1), 44–53.

Di Maggio, P. (1979). Review essay on Pierre Bourdieu. *American Journal of Sociology, 84*, 1460–1474.

Diamantopoulosa, A., Schlegelmilch, B. B., Sinkovicsd, R. R., & Bohlen, G. M. (2003). Can socio-demographics still play a role in profiling green consumers? A review of the evidence and an empirical investigation. *Journal of Business Research, 56*, 465–480.

Diehl, T., Huber, B., de Zúñiga, H. G., et al. (2021). Social media and beliefs about climate change: A cross-national analysis of news use, political ideology, and trust in science. *International Journal of Public Opinion Research, 33*(2), 197–213.

Elam, A. B. (2008). *Gender and entrepreneurship: A multilevel theory and analysis.* Edward Elgar Publishing.

Elavarasan, R. M., & Pugazhendhi, R. (2020). Restructured society and environment: A review on potential technological strategies to control the COVID-19 pandemic. *Science of the Total Environment, 725*, 138858. https://doi.org/10.1016/j.scitotenv.2020.138858

Elliott, R. (2013). The taste for green: The possibilities and dynamics of status differentiation through "green" consumption. *Poetics, 41*(3), 294–322.

Eriksen, K. G. (2013). Why education for sustainable development needs early childhood education: The case of Norway. *Journal of Teacher Education for Sustainability, 15*(1), 107–120.

European Environmental Agency. (2020). *COVID-19 measures have mixed impacts ontheenvironment.*https://www.eea.europa.eu/highlights/impact-of-Covid-19-lockdown

Francis, D. V., & Weller, C. E. (2022). Economic inequality, the digital divide, and remote learning during COVID-19. *The Review of Black Political Economy, 49*(1), 41–60.

Gambetti, R. (2020). Netnography, digital habitus, and Technocultural capital. In R. V. Kozinets & R. Gambetti (Eds.), *Netnography unlimited*. Routledge.

Gazzola, P., Colombo, G., Pezzetti, R., & Nicolescu, L. (2017). Consumer empowerment in the digital economy: Availing sustainable purchasing decisions. *Sustainability, 9*(5), 693–712.

Giddens, A. (1984). *The constitution of society. Outline of the theory of structuration*. University of California Press.

Giddens, A. (1990). *The consequences of modernity*. Cambridge.

Gladston, I., & Wing, T. (2019). *Social media and public polarization over climate change in the United States*. A Climate Institute Publication.

Haluza-DeLay, R. (2008). A theory of practice for social movements: Environmentalism and ecological habitus. *Mobilization: The. International Quarterly, 13*(2), 205–218.

Hanafi, S. (2020). Toward a post-COVID-19 sociology. *Revue du MAUSS permanente*, 4. https://journaldumauss.net/?Toward-a-post-COVID-19-Sociology

Hang, M. (2020). *Preparing cities for epidemics: Lessons from the COVID-19 outbreak*. IJUUR. https://www.ijurr.org/the-urban-now/preparing-cities-for-epidemics/

Hays, J. N. (2005). *Epidemics and pandemics. Their impacts on human history*. ABC-CLIO.

Hochschild, A. R. (2016). *Strangers in their own land: Anger and mourning on the American right*. New Press.

Holton, R. J. (1987). The idea of crisis in modern society. *The British Journal of Sociology, 38*(4), 502–520.

Hughes, H. R., & Paterson, M. (2017). Narrowing the climate field: The symbolic power of authors in the IPCC's assessment of mitigation. *Review of Policy Research, 34*(6), 744–766.

Ignatow, G., & Robinson, L. (2017). Pierre Bourdieu: Theorizing the digital. *Information, Communication and Society, 20*(7), 950–966.

Kahn, P. (2011). *Technological nature: Adaptation and the future of human life*. The MIT Press.

Karol, J., & Gale, T. (2004). *What is 'environmental capital'? Bourdieu's social theory and sustainability* [Conference presentation]. Australian Association for Research in Education (AARE) International Conference.

Kasper, D. V. S. (2009). Ecological habitus: Toward a better understanding of socioecological relations. *Organization & Environment, 22*(3), 311–326.

Kennedy, E., & Givens, J. E. (2019). Eco-habitus or eco-powerlessness? Examining environmental concern across social class. *Sociological Perspectives, 62*(5), 646–667.

Kirby, J. (2017). Fleshing out an ecological habitus: Field and capitals of radical environmental movements. *Nature and Culture, 12*(2), 89–114.

Kirby, J. (2018). Grounding and comparing ecological habitus in environmental communities. *International Journal of Urban Sustainable Development, 10*(2), 154–169.

Kvasny, L. (2005). The role of the habitus in shaping discourses about the digital divide. *Journal of Computer-Mediated Communication, 10*(2). https://doi.org/10.1111/j.1083-6101.2005.tb00242.x

Laidley, T. M. (2013). Climate, class and culture: Political issues as cultural signifiers in the US. *The Sociological Review, 61*, 153–171.

Maguire, J. S. (2016). Introduction: Looking at food practices and taste across the class divide. *Food, Culture & Society, 19*(1), 11–18.

Marwick, A. E., & Boyd, D. (2011). I tweet honestly, I tweet passionately: Twitter users, context collapse, and the imagined audience. *New Media & Society, 13*(1), 114–133.

Masoom, M. R. (2023). The digital habitus of the unwedded emerging adults: A sociological interpretation of male-female differences in Facebook behaviour. *Global Knowledge, Memory and Communication, 72*(1/2), 24–43.

Mavrodieva, A. V., Rachman, O. K., Harahap, V. B., et al. (2019). Role of social media as a soft power tool in raising public awareness and engagement in addressing climate change. *Climate, 7*(10), 122.

Nautiyal, H., & Goel, V. (2021). Sustainability assessment: Metrics and methods. In J. Ren (Ed.), *Methods in sustainability science* (pp. 27–46). Elsevier.

Ozili, P. K., & Arun, T. (2020). *Economic effects of coronavirus outbreak.* http://hdl.handle.net/20.500.12323/4497

Papacharissi, Z., & Easton, E. (2013). In the habitus of the new: Structure, agency, and the social media habitus. In J. Hartley, J. Burgess, & A. Bruns (Eds.), *A companion to new media dynamics* (pp. 171–184). Blackwell.

Pappas, I. O., Mikalef, P., Giannakos, M. N., et al. (2018). Big data and business analytics ecosystems: Paving the way towards digital transformation and sustainable societies. *Information Systems and e-Business Management, 16*, 479–491.

Pearce, W., Niederer, S., Özkula, S. M., et al. (2019). The social media life of climate change: Platforms, publics, and future imaginaries. *WIREs Climate Change, 10*(2), e569. https://doi.org/10.1002/wcc.569

Pedersen, L. H. (2000). The dynamics of green consumption: A matter of visibility? *Journal of Environmental Policy and Planning, 2*(3), 193–210.

Perrow, C. (1999). *Normal accidents: Living with high-risk technologies.* Princeton University Press.

Pinheiro, M. D., & Luís, N. C. (2020). COVID-19 could leverage a sustainable built environment. *Sustainability, 12*(4). https://doi.org/10.3390/su12145863

Piroddi, C. (2021). Hope, habitus and social recognition: A Bourdieusian proposal. *The Theory of Social Behaviour, 51*(4), 619–635.

Raghavan, A., Demircioglu, M. A., & Orazgaliyev, S. (2021). COVID-19 and the new Normal of organizations and employees: An overview. *Sustainability, 13*(21), 11942. https://doi.org/10.3390/su132111942

Ragnedda, M., & Ruiu, M. L. (2020). *Digital Capital. A Bourdieusian approach to Digital Divide.* Emeralds Publishing.

Ragnedda, M., Ruiu, M. L., & Addeo, F. (2019). Measuring digital capital: An empirical investigation. *New Media and Society, 22*(5), 1–24.

Ragnedda, M., Ruiu, M. L., & Addeo, F. (2022). How offline backgrounds interact with digital capital. *New Media and Society.* https://doi.org/10.1177/14614448221082649

Reay, D. (2004). 'It's all becoming a habitus': Beyond the habitual use of habitus in educational research. *British Journal of Sociology of Education, 25*(4), 431–444.

Reyes, R., Ahn, R., Thurber, K., & Burke, T. F. (2013). Urbanization and infectious diseases: General principles, historical perspectives, and contemporary challenges. In I. Fong (Ed.), *Challenges in infectious diseases. Emerging infectious diseases of the 21st century* (pp. 123–146). Springer.

Richardson, J. M. (2015). Live theatre in the age of digital technology: "Digital habitus" and the youth live theatre audience. *Participation Journal of Audience and Reception Studies, 12*(1), 206–219.

Robinson, L. (2009). A taste for the necessary. A Bourdieuian approach to digital inequality. *Information. Communication & Society, 12*(4), 488–507.

Robinson, L., Schulz, J., Khilnani, A. et al. (2020). Digital inequalities in time of pandemic: COVID-19 exposure risk profiles and new forms of vulnerability. *First Monday, 25*(7). https://firstmonday.org/ojs/index.php/fm/article/view/10845/9563

Romele, A., & Rodighiero, D. (2020). Digital habitus or personalization without personality. *HUMANA.MENTE. Journal of Philosophical Studies, 13*(37), 98–126.

Ruiu, M. L., Ruiu, G., & Ragnedda, M. (2021). Conceptualizing techno-environmental habitus. *First Monday, 26*(11). https://doi.org/10.5210/fm.v26i11.12353

Ruiu, M. L., Ruiu, G., & Ragnedda, M. (2023). Digital–environmental habitus of families in England in times of pandemic. *New Media & Society.* https://doi.org/10.1177/14614448221146716

Rume, T., & Islam, S. M. D. (2020). Environmental effects of COVID-19 pandemic and potential strategies of sustainability. *Heliyon, 6*(9). https://doi.org/10.1016/j.heliyon.2020.e04965

Schmidt, M. (1997). Habitus revisited. *The American Behavioural Scientist, 40*(4), 444–453.

Schor, J. B., Fitzmaurice, C., Carfagna, L. B., Attwood-Charles, W., & Dubois Poteat, E. (2016). Paradoxes of openness and distinction in the sharing economy. *Poetics, 54*, 66–81.

Sexton, S. E., & Sexton, A. L. (2011). *Conspicuous conservation: The Prius halo and willingness to pay for environmental Bona fides.* UC Center for Energy and Environmental Economics.

Shah, Z., Wei, L., & Ghani, U. (2021). The use of social networking sites and pro-environmental behaviours: A mediation and moderation model. *International Journal of Environmental Research and Public Health, 18*(4), 1085.

Shove, E. (2004). Efficiency and consumption: Technology and practice. *Energy & Environment, 15*(6), 1053–1065.

Shove, E. (2010). Beyond the ABC: Climate change policy and theories of social change. *Environment and Planning A, 42*, 1273–1285.

Shove, E., & Warde, A. (2002). Inconspicuous consumption: The sociology of consumption, lifestyles and the environment. In R. Dunlap, F. Buttel, P. Dickens, & A. Gijswijt (Eds.), *Sociological theory & the environment: Classical foundations, contemporary insights.* Lanham MA.

Shulla, K., Voigt, B. F., Cibian, S., et al. (2021). Effects of COVID-19 on the sustainable development goals (SDGs). *Discover Sustainability, 2*(15). https://doi.org/10.1007/s43621-021-00026-x

Singh, S. (2022). Can habitus explain individual particularities? Critically appreciating the operationalization of relational logic in field theory. *Sociological Theory, 40*(1), 28–50.

Smith, M. (2001). *An ethics of place: Radical ecology, postmodernity, and social theory.* State University of New York Press.

Snowden, F. (2020). *Epidemics and society: From the black death to the present.* Yale University Press.

Spaargaren, G. (2011). Theories of practices: Agency, technology, and culture: Exploring the relevance of practice theories for the governance of sustainable consumption practices in the new world-order. *Global Environmental Change, 21*(3), 813–822.

Sterne, J. (2003). Bourdieu, technique and technology. *Cultural Studies, 17*(3–4), 367–389.

United Nations. (2020). *UN75: The future we want, the UN we need.* https://www.un.org/en/un75/presskit

Urry, J. (2011). *Climate change and society.* Polity Press.

Wackernagel, M., & Rees, W. (1996). *Our ecological footprint: Reducing human impact on the earth.* New Society Publishers.

Walby, S. (2015). *Crisis.* Polity Press.

Walby, S. (2022). Crisis and society: Developing the theory of crisis in the context of COVID-19. *Global Discourse, 12*(3–4), 498–516.

Wentworth, P., & Peterson, B. (2001). Crossing the line: Case studies of identity development in first-generation college women. *Journal of Adult Development, 8*, 9–21.

Zevenbergen, R. (2007). Digital natives come to preschool: Implications for early childhood practice. *Contemporary Issues in Early Childhood, 8*(1), 19–29.

Zhang, N., & Skoric, M. M. (2018). Media use and environmental engagement: Examining differential gains from news media and social media *International Journal of Communication, 12.* https://ijoc.org/index.php/ijoc/article/view/7650

CHAPTER 7

# Combining Digital, Post-pandemic Recovery, and Environmental Benefits: Examples at the Macro, Meso, and Micro at Tackling Digital and Environmental Poverty

## 7.1 Introduction

This chapter considers some practices in which digital, social, and environmental aspects intersect to shape a particular habitus. These practices can have both positive and negative implications for addressing digital-environmental poverty at different levels (micro, meso, and macro). As we explore these topics, we initially focus on (digital) nudging, a concept rooted in behavioral economics to indicate any aspect of the "choice architecture" that subtly influences people's choices without eliminating alternative options (Thaler & Sunstein, 2008). Research within the field of Green Information Systems has suggested that digital nudging can partially motivate users to adopt eco-friendly behaviors. In doing so, this chapter reviews the effects produced by different strategies of nudging in motivating digital pro-environmental behaviors. However, it also highlights that even though some positive effects of nudging have been identified by the literature, environmental choices in the long term still highly depend on personal orientations and social influences.

At the meso level, we assess the strengths and limitations of some initiatives such as the Single.Earth and Alipay Ant Forest projects, considering



M. L. Ruiu, M. Ragnedda, *Digital-Environmental Poverty*, Palgrave Studies in Digital Inequalities,
https://doi.org/10.1007/978-3-031-56184-9_7

their impact on the circumstantial factors associated with digital and environmental poverty. The chapter shows that these initiatives need to be contextualized in a wider set of political, economic, and environmental infrastructures, as well as consider the degree of participation of digital users, which can either increase or limit their chances of success.

At the structural level, we explore the eco-civilization project that permeates laws and regulations in China to implement a "green financial system" and recognizes the natural environment as a structural determinant of human existence. Since the 1980s, the Chinese approach has incorporated some elements of neoliberal reasoning; however, the Communist Party has a powerful role in combining both neoliberal and socialist strategies (Jeffreys & Sigley, 2009) by setting standards and regulations (Flynn et al., 2019). Therefore, despite some openings to decentralization in influencing market relations most non-governmental organizations are supported and encouraged by the state (Flynn et al., 2019). The Chinese conceptualization of ecological civilization is embedded in such a complex dynamic and shows both strengths and weaknesses. On the one hand, it has increasingly adopted a combined approach to the digital economy and the green economy, but through authoritarian environmentalism, which can both contribute toward the success of environmental regulations, but also harm some marginalized groups that might not benefit from changes. We emphasize how this example supports the need for integrated approaches to environmental poverty and other types of poverty, which otherwise can generate some degrees of exclusion. Moreover, some concerns remain regarding the effects of increasing uses of ICTs, in terms of byproducts, increased consumption, demand for energy, and carbon emissions. Concerns also remain on the use of digital tools as surveillance and disciplinary tools to control social actors' behaviors. However, the eco-civilization project shows that the regulative apparatus becomes a key for creating opportunities to simultaneously tackle environmental and digital challenges and can promote eco-innovation by supporting successful ideas, such as Alipay Ant Forest, and, in turn, create opportunities for citizens to contribute to the transition.

## 7.2 Individual Level: Nudging as a Case Study

We have so far described how, at the individual level, the impact of digitalization on pro-environmental behavior and, vice versa, the impact of environmental predispositions on digital behavior, is a complex interplay of factors, reflecting the multifaceted nature of digital-environmental poverty. Environmental issues are complex and depend on multiple variables and levels (from macro to micro dimensions) connecting rational goals (for example, economic interests), with natural targets (for example, environmental sustainability), and altruistic orientation (for example, social needs) (Henkel & Kranz, 2018).

At this level, research highlights how the digitalization of society has produced conflicting results in terms of enhancing an environmentally friendly lifestyle. Some studies have emphasized the positives deriving from shifting consumer practice online by, for example, reducing or controlling energy consumption (Wilson et al., 2020). Moreover, focusing on low-carbon digital innovations across mobility, food, and homes, a survey in the UK investigated the impacts of COVID-19 on the acquisition of innovations considering environmental concerns before and during the pandemic (Vrain et al., 2022). While some forms of shared mobility (for example, BlaBlaCar) have lost attractiveness during the pandemic due to the increasing use of private transport, more individuals started using e-bikes. The use of food boxes (for example, Hello Fresh) and food and home apps (for example, heating and lighting smart systems) has been increasingly adopted. The pandemic also negatively impacted the types and amount of face-to-face social contacts but increased the interaction online through, for instance, social media (Andrews & Wilson, 2021; Vrain et al., 2022). On the other side, we have already highlighted some adverse effects associated with the use of digital devices, such as energy consumption, associated infrastructure, digital pollution, and e-waste production. Vrain et al. (2022) argue that the positives of digital consumption might be overshadowed by several existing inequalities related, for example, to digital access and skills necessary to both protect users' privacy and security and make the best of the digital experience by getting benefits. Such limitations also restrict the diffusion of good practices within specific niches despite their pro-environmental potential. While digital innovations offer consumers the possibility of developing a digital-environmental habitus oriented to sustainable principles, its potential also depends on control, choice/motivation, interconnectedness, and integration with systems. However, these individual choices will simultaneously depend on personal experience of both environmental and digital poverty, and circumstantial and structural determinants, which in turn impact the individual space of maneuver. Therefore, as aforementioned when discussing the individual determinants of digital-environmental poverty, at the individual level the lack of a subject's ability to do something with transformative power can be considered a factor constituting poverty. The fact that users might not know that their digital behavior impacts the environment, but also their lack of engagement and motivation in implementing pro-environmental behaviors represents indicators of environmental poverty at the individual level. This combined with a lack of individual opportunities to access (also depending on the financial personal situation) and acquire digital skills and receive support in using digital tools makes challenging poverty a complex web of intersecting factors.

Earlier on, Chap. 5 proposed a revision of the DPF in light of incorporating, at the individual level, additional determinants related to personal awareness, engagement, motivation, and support to act pro-environmentally as complementary predictors of digital-environmental poverty at this level. Research in Green Information Systems has increasingly highlighted the need to focus on how to motivate users to adopt eco-friendly behaviors recently focusing on the concept of digital nudging (Weinmann et al., 2016), which shows the potential to empower individuals to act. Digital nudging for changing environmental dispositions has been applied in many different fields ranging from psychology to marketing and environmental studies (see Zimmerman et al., 2021 for a review). It refers to the use of "user-interface design elements to guide people's behavior" (Weinmann et al., 2016) in a digital environment. For example, one strategy of nudging transposes the traditional priming strategies (based on exposure to content) (for a review, see McCombs, 2004; Scheufele, 2000) of mainstream media online. Another strategy is represented by setting a default option, referred to as "status quo bias" by Henkel et al. (2019). This bias is based on individuals' tendency to accept the default setting to avoid potential discomfort associated with change. For instance, digital nudging to promote digital pro-environmental choices could involve e-commerce platforms (for example, Amazon) listing and ranking their products by default based on their sustainability. This might incentivize users to buy green products because they are more visible than the non-eco-friendly choices. In this direction, positive effects of nudging on pro-environmental behavior were shown via "green defaults" (Pichert & Katsikopoulos, 2008), for example, setting a default option for online shopping (Taube & Vetter, 2019) or setting a default option with higher carbon-offset payments on online flight-booking platforms (see Székely et al., 2016). However, even in the presence of "default effects" or AI-powered virtual assistants offering green recommendations, the literature suggests that environmental choices are highly influenced by factors such as personal orientations (He et al., 2022) and social influences (Gifford & Nilsson, 2014). These factors, especially in motivating users to sustain sustainable behaviors over the long term (see, for example, Milfont & Sibley, 2012; Kaida & Kaida, 2019; Kesenheimer & Greitemeyer, 2021; Terrier et al., 2016), emphasize the importance of considering environmental awareness, motivation for pro-environmental actions, and the influence of social networks when approaching certain forms of digital consumption. While these manipulative strategies might be effective in promoting eco-friendly consumers' behaviors in a precise moment, their reliance on existing predispositions implies that their influence might be limited in terms of altering individuals' convictions, motivation, and engagement (beyond the immediate effect of nudging). Moreover, this reinforces that only users with high-level digital skills may have an advantage in making informed decisions, as exemplified by the case of default effect, by consciously choosing not to change the default option. By contrast, for those who are unconsciously induced to choose the eco-friendly option, their degree of personal environmental poverty (in terms of awareness, engagement, motivation, and values) might remain unchanged.

Moreover, a study conducted by He et al. (2022), on the value of AI-powered virtual assistant recommendations in supporting decision-making for energy saving, suggests that those who are educated and digitally advantaged (because of their opportunity to access and take advantage of sophisticated technologies) will have more chances to increase their awareness, engagement, and motivation to act pro-environmentally. In general, some studies have found that virtual assistants might be able to influence customers' preferences (Klaus & Zaichkowsky, 2020) more effectively than online consumer reviews (Flavián et al., 2023). It is also interesting to note that in these examples the AI assistant somehow substitutes social networks' functions in terms of offering advice and models of behavior. This is further supported by a study by Jin and Zhang (2023) that shows that people perceive AI recommendations as more competent than human recommendations for material products (but not for experiential products). At the same time, Logg et al. (2019) found that lay people tend to trust an algorithm's advice more than a person's advice compared to experienced professionals. Therefore, high levels of skills (including digital awareness and competencies) are needed to recognize the risks, for example, associated with algorithmic biases, privacy breaches, security management, and overreliance on AI for decision-making (Atzori et al., 2010; Van Deursen & Mossberger, 2018). Digital literacy becomes a key factor in improving people's ability to interact with environmental issues. In Sect. I, we examined the three levels of the digital divide and found that, in addition to having access to cutting-edge technologies, people also need to be competent in navigating digital platforms to take more informed and environmentally friendly actions that benefit society, the environment, and themselves. Digitally empowered individuals have the competencies and skills to understand, and somehow control, how their preferences and decisions may be influenced by AI-powered virtual assistants, as well as how they are aware of these "neutral" recommendations. In this vein, digitally literate individuals perceive and utilize virtual assistants to influence their consumer behavior toward more sustainable options in areas other than energy conservation, such as product purchases and lifestyle choices. Instead, citizens who are digitally and environmentally impoverished might find themselves uncritically driven by digital technologies, following predetermined paths that may not be advantageous for them or the environment. These channels might, indeed, serve the interests of those who control digital technologies and their narratives. This, somehow, aligns with the ToP, as discussed in Chap. 4. ToP characterizes capitalist economies as necessitating continuous economic growth, ultimately benefiting influential companies as they extract natural resources and generate waste and pollution in the pursuit of profits (Hooks et al., 2021; Schnaiberg & Gould, 1994). This paradigm of perpetual growth stands in opposition to both environmental quality and societal well-being, as these are interconnected aspects of the same challenge. However, these businesses possess not only *material power*, grounded in wealth and physical resources, but also *discursive power*, which enables them to shape the discourse and craft a persuasive narrative (Galvin, 2020). In this sense, controlling the narrative surrounding the ostensibly "neutral" recommendations generated by AI may prioritize certain specific interests over the welfare of individuals and the environment.

In addition to considering the potential social ramifications of individuals turning to AI instead of social networks for guidance and role models, academics and policymakers must also consider how AI and algorithms are part of a larger sociocultural framework that promotes and supports an ostensibly rational model of society based on productivity, competition, calculation, and neutrality (Beer, 2017). Ultimately, the interaction between environmental poverty and digital poverty can result in positive or negative feedback loops that either break or strengthen current disparities in the digital, social, and environmental spheres. Policies that support fair access to digital technologies and digital literacy—more specifically, those that support the responsible development and application of AI systems for the good of society as a whole—need to be at the center of the analysis conducted by both academics and policymakers.

The effects produced by nudging in motivating pro-environmental behaviors are contrasting, especially in the case of simple exposure to content (priming) (Henkel et al., 2019). Some experimental studies have shown the ineffectiveness of nudging in promoting energy saving (Henkel et al., 2019) and sometimes only specific forms of nudging have been proven effective, for example, through the use of positive framing to increase consumers' pro-environmental engagement (Bimonte et al., 2019). The uncertain results of nudging depend on multiple factors that, as highlighted throughout these chapters, also depend on macro and circumstantial levels and multiple variables (Zimmerman et al., 2021). In fact, being pro-environmental requires planning, rationality, and reflective capacity around the consequences of actions and knowledge (Keller et al., 2020). By contrast, nudging works unconsciously and it might conflict with the "convenience" associated with certain behaviors (for example, cheaper versus sustainable products).

## 7.3 Meso Level: The Case of Single.Earth and Alipay Ant Forest

Defining the DEPF we have referred to a meso level in which opportunities to engage with the environment and participate in decision making can be created to increase citizens' power (Arnstein, 2007). At this level, the health of ecosystems is part of the circumstances that can influence the field in which social actors operate by affecting the regulatory apparatus, but also the societal understanding of environmental-related issues. Additionally, the opportunities citizens have to participate in responding to environmental degradation are also circumstances that can increase their level of knowledge and engagement. Such a meso level is an interactive space between agency and structure that generates conditions under which human agency exists as a social relationship. This section used the Bourdieusian concept of the social field in which agents are positioned according to their power. This is, therefore, a space in which citizens' and communities' participation can be incentivized through both private and public initiatives relevant to addressing the combination of environmental and digital poverty. Many companies invest in presenting themselves as socially and environmentally oriented to attract consensus from consumers and governments (Bahta et al., 2020) and this creates additional opportunities for citizens to make informed choices and engage in environmentally friendly behaviors. Therefore, exploring this intermediate level we refer to some examples that show how organizations can potentially create the circumstances for digital-environmental habitus to become eco-friendly with the contribution of political drivers, such as Single.Earth (https://www.single.earth/) and the Alipay Ant Forest project. While many initiatives are emerging in terms of supporting businesses and trades that are oriented to nature-based solutions through, for example, tokenization (see, for example, Regen Network, Toucan Protocol, and KlimaDao), both initiatives trigger reflections due to their purposes of conditioning circumstantial determinants of DEP.

The Alipay Ant Forest project is embedded in a wider plan of the Chinese government to implement policies that aim to encourage both organizations and individuals to reduce their environmental impact (Zhang et al., 2020; Zhang et al., 2018).

Single.Earth is a blockchain-based company that proposes an alternative vision of nature, as traditionally monetized as raw material to be exploited, which is based on valuing nature for its intactness rather than disruption. Single.Earth creates a "digital twin" of nature which is "a constantly updated model, representing an accurate simulation of the physical world it symbolizes" (Single Earth, 2022, p. 5). The aim is that of creating a digital copy of nature, using AI and big data, to constantly monitor its state including indicators related to carbon removal and storage and biodiversity status. Therefore, it tries to create conditions for businesses, communities, and citizens to make environmentally informed economic decisions. Single.Earth prioritizes forests to incentivize landowners at multiple levels (individuals, local communities, corporations) to maximize ecosystem services, and it is based on a system in which landowners receive tokens (MERITs) for as long as they keep their land or any other natural resource intact. The carbon sequestration process is constantly under evaluation thanks to geospatial engineering and machine learning. The newly created blockchain-based green currency, MERIT, attaches to carbon sequestration and biodiversity a digital value (1 MERIT costs 3 euros and corresponds to 100 kg of $CO_2$ captured). This can be used in exchange for goods or services, but the value of these goods is attached to the protection of nature. Those who do not directly own land can buy the green token to contribute to the value of the digital currency. The amount of MERIT available depends on nature's healthiness. In addition to forests, the company is currently developing systems and datasets to evaluate other ecosystems. Even though this project is still in its early stages, it shows how the combination of digital and environmental knowledge can create some circumstances for developing nature-based economic solutions. However, despite the recognition of the benefits that nature-based solutions can offer at the environmental and societal level (European Commission, 2015), several studies have identified multiple barriers to the expansion of these solutions due to the lack of collaborative governance between private and public bodies, as well as the scarcity of public funding and unattractiveness of private investments given the limited monetary value in return (Mayor et al., 2021). Single.Earth tries to overcome such barriers through the parceling of investments through the tokenization of natural assets. This, therefore, makes investments more attractive given the potential trading of MERITs. At the same time, private initiatives are operating in unregulated carbon finance, which can be potentially risky in terms of prioritizing economic stakes rather than the public interest. This risk has been, for example, highlighted in the context of the unregulated carbon market, in which private actors financialize carbon and become carbon credit certifiers of businesses' commitment to carbon reduction that might also not exist in reality (Morgan, 2021). In this context, an investigation conducted by *the Guardian*, *Die Zeit*, and SourceMaterial has suggested that 90% of the rainforest offset credits, certified by a world leader carbon certifier, do not result in real carbon reductions (Greenfield, 2023). This is also because the global carbon certifier certified offsets for protecting forestland that might not have been at risk of deforestation in the first place. Despite controversies in measuring the impacts of deforestation intervention and overstatements of impacts on avoided deforestation (West et al., 2022), there is a general recognition of the positive impact of reducing emissions from deforestation and forest degradation projects (Guizar-Coutiño et al., 2022). On the one hand, studies have shown the importance of paying households to reduce deforestation (see, for example, Jayachandran et al., 2017); on the other hand, in some cases, forestry corporations have joined the market because "they could get paid to keep doing what they'd been doing already" (Chapman & Masie, 2023), without any real reduction of deforestation and degradation. Therefore, the lack of supervision of such voluntary initiatives might result in unpredictable consequences, which necessitate monitoring and negotiation by policymakers at multiple levels. In the case of Single.Earth, the digital component of the project helps monitor the real benefits of protecting certain lands. It has developed a risk assessment tool to be integrated into the digital twin copy of nature that assesses when the forest is approaching harvesting time, as well as its conservation status, and the topography of the specific plot, which determines the cutting risk. On this basis, MERIT tokens are generated on the estimation of the ecological value of the land. Single.Earth has been defining a strategy to profit from the management of natural resources that could present both socio-environmental advantages and disadvantages. For example, the blockchain-based approach can contribute to making the process transparent to both regulators and participants and the automatization of data acquisition and monitoring can help produce real-time information (Golding et al., 2022). At the same time, it can have negative consequences by promoting speculation and the commodification of selected elements of nature (while neglecting others potentially less economically valuable). This reduction of the intricate complexity of ecosystems into minimal purchasable units redirects the focus away from holistic environmental protection efforts. Furthermore, it can disfavor communities living in vulnerable circumstances by depriving them of local resources for the sake of market profit. Finally, further investigation is required into the energy consumption of minting MERITs. This underscores the need for integrated approaches that combine private and public interests in overseeing the digital transformation of natural resources management and commodification, including the regulation of what should and should not be tokenized.

While Single.Earth is still in its early stages, Alipay, a Chinese mobile payment platform, which is part of the Ant Group (and in turn of Alibaba Group), started the Alipay Ant Forest game application in 2016, which is embedded in Alipay and rewards with "green energy points" those behaviors that reduce individual emissions (for example, biking, going paperless, and buying sustainable products). China's environmental protection has been traditionally carried out under the government's initiative. For example, in 1982, the State Council fixed the National Voluntary Tree Planting Campaign in national legal form, which is still underway and has become a green project with the longest duration and the largest number of participants and has produced both positive ecological and social effects (Zhou, 2021). Moreover, since the 1990s, China has launched reforestation programs that produced positive effects on forest recovery, mitigation of soil erosion, desertification, and flood risks (Downing et al., 2021; Feng et al., 2013). However, the business sector is an integral part of the implementation of the project and the Ant Forest initiative is directly connected to the ecological civilization project (Huang & Westman, 2021).

Alipay is an online payment platform which is used by more than a billion people for everyday purchases. A private environmental foundation, SEE Foundation, provided funding to Alipay for 1.6 million real trees in 2016 (Liu, 2022). Alipay Ant Forest aims to use digital technologies to encourage a low-carbon lifestyle by collecting "green points" which transform users' sustainable behaviors (for example, sharing bikes, or paying for public transportation via the Alipay system) into "virtual green energy." Users can decide to spend their points to grow a virtual tree or protect an area, which Alipay matches by planting a real tree or protecting an ecosystem (UNCC, 2019). The app attracted over 600 million users between 2016 and 2021 and planted 326 million real trees (Shen, 2021). In 2019 the UNCC also reported that Alipay Ant Forest protected a total area of 12,000 hectares of conservation land. Alipay Ant Forest gave birth to the largest private-sector tree-planting initiative in China (AntGroup, 2019). Moreover, Ant Forest contributed to creating around 730,000 green jobs, developing organic agricultural products, and connecting them with e-commerce platforms (Liu, 2022). It also received a Champions of the Earth award from the United Nations Environment Programme in 2019 (UN, 2019).

It should be noted that users must engage with the app to collect green energy manually before it expires, which requires an intentional implementation of pro-environmental behavior, as well as time and effort. Moreover, Ant Forest is a game-based app that allows users to interact with their friends and play with them by, for example, supporting their collection of green energy (Zhang et al., 2020). Users can, for example, engage with the game by using their energy points to take care of their virtual tree and exchange energy with other users. When the tree is fully grown, then a real tree or an area is protected by NGOs that work in partnership with AliPay, as a reward for individuals' pro-environmental behaviors (Chen et al., 2020). The app was also inspirational for similar initiatives in other countries, such as in the Philippines, where GCash Forest was created, in collaboration with the Ministry of Environment and Natural Resources and an environmental charity organization, and attracted immediate attention from digital users (Liu, 2022).

This initiative has shown some potential to mitigate the top-down approach followed by the Chinese government in implementing environmental policies and allowing citizens to actively participate. This is particularly relevant considering that in 2017 more than 90% of respondents to a survey conducted by the China Climate Communication Project Center believed that climate change was happening, but only 27.5% were willing to pay for their carbon emissions (Liu, 2022).

Even if on limited samples, some studies showed that a combination of intrinsic triggers (enjoyment, social interaction, fulfillment, altruism) and extrinsic triggers (external rewards, competition) motivates Alipay users to join the Ant Forest project (Wang et al., 2022). Satisfaction with the app, which is also increased by a reward system (for example, virtual medals) (Wang & Yao, 2020), was shown to influence users' intention to continue using Ant Forest (Zhang et al., 2020). Environmental awareness was also found to support long-term motivation to use the app whereas intention to social networking to support short-term entertainment goals (Chen et al., 2020). In general, the results of these studies suggest that environmental knowledge and awareness moderate the effects of attitude on continuance intention (Ashfaq et al., 2021, 2022; Chen et al., 2020). The main barriers to using the Alipay app were connected to privacy concerns, usage barriers, and green skepticism, which in turn connect environmental engagement to digital skills and competencies (Ashfaq et al., 2021).

The scientific debate around the benefits of reforestation, as promoted by Ant Forest, is controversial (see Weins et al., 2023, for a review), especially when social, economic, and operational constraints are taken into account beyond the biophysical suitability of the land (Zeng et al., 2020). However, what is clear is that a collaborative approach, which combines government commitment, policies based on science, and financial support from private businesses, can effectively address potential challenges by, for example, combining climate mitigation, with food security and local livelihoods (Zeng et al., 2020). Therefore, initiatives such as Alipay Ant Forest and Single.Earth, even though driven by a profit goal, show some potential to involve and engage citizens in pro-environmental behaviors (both online and offline). For example, Zhang et al. (2021) found that the Ant Forest initiatives have produced land restoration, carbon reduction, and socio-economic improvement in northern China. It also contributed to enhancing social responsibility, modifying users' way of life, and increasing their environmental awareness. Liu (2022) reports that by the end of 2020, Ant Forest has created partnerships with different bodies including non-profit organizations, research institutions and universities, local governments, and additional private companies, to define common environmental targets. Moreover, the company is also studying potential strategies to alleviate economic poverty in certain areas. An example is represented by the Pingwu County pilot, which is a rural cooperative in West China that has produced honey under environmentally friendly standards since 2018. In addition to providing the possibility of protecting land through the green points system, Alipay Ant Forest supports local farmers selling honey through Taobao, an e-commerce Marketplace (Data-Pop Alliance, Green Digital Finance Alliance, UNEP Inquiry, 2020).

Even though such a networking approach has the potential to improve both the monitoring and the implementation of pro-environmental behaviors (for example, through data sharing across the apps), it also raises concerns about the use of such a huge amount of personal data by for-profit private bodies (Liu, 2022). This suggests that these initiatives also need to be contextualized in a wider set of circumstances that make these efforts successful and minimize the drawbacks. This also shows the necessity to reflect on the connection between structural aspects related to political, economic, and environmental infrastructures and individual efforts, as mediated by circumstantial determinants that create favorable conditions for concerted approaches toward digital-environmental sustainability. Therefore, the meso level can be interpreted as resulting from the interaction of macro and micro levels that include "environmentally friendly technology and green economic indicators, good government decision-making, environmental nomocracy, and social welfare, as well as extensive public participation, and green culture" (Zhou, 2021, p. 86). Such interaction is translated into circumstances that define the rules of the field in which social agents position themselves in relation to their power. Therefore, the existence of certain circumstances can empower digital users to be environmentally responsible citizens thanks to their active involvement in the decisional process. Participation of digital users is also essential to the success of such pro-environmental schemes in both directions, upscaling structural changes to accommodate a process of change toward sustainability and increasing individual awareness, motivation, and engagement in digital behaviors that are eco-friendly. Having the tools, access, and capabilities to engage in digital pro-environmental behaviors, but also motivation, understanding, and engagement in using digital tools to protect the environment, are components of such a process.

## 7.4 Structural Level: The Case of Ecological Civilization as a Structuring Force

This paragraph explores China's ecological civilization as an example of structural interconnections between environmental and digital poverty, highlighting both its strengths and weaknesses. The crisis of civilization is constantly presented by science, especially in the face of climate change (Foster, 2017). Drawing on the Marxist conceptualization of social structure, the Communist Party of China adopted a "Five-in-One" approach to promoting civilization including ecological civilization (in addition to material, spiritual, political, and social civilization) (Zhou, 2021). Ecological civilization embraces both social and natural infrastructures as two faces of the same coin and requires structural adjustments to achieve green socio-economic transformation toward a pro-environmental paradigm.

The Ecological Civilization paradigm has attracted attention in the field of environmental sociology, especially for its departure from the Western worldview. It was originally introduced by Iring Fetscher in 1978, later incorporated into Soviet Union Marxist philosophy, and increasingly associated with China (Weins et al., 2023). Ecological civilization was incorporated into the Communist Party of China's Central Commission Report to its 17th Convention in 2007, thanks to President Hu's interest in promoting ecological orientations (Gare, 2009). In 2015, the government released the "Central Document No.12: Opinions of the Central Committee of the Communist Party of China and the State Council on Further Promoting the Development of Ecological Civilization." Despite not being legally binding, the document made the term ecological civilization appear in numerous subsequent policies, progressively shaping its implementation. The document also set targets and strategies for the Chinese economy and society for reconciling economic development and ecosystem conservation (Geal & Ely, 2018). Indeed, between 2015 and 2016 several policies were issued such as "Opinions on Accelerating the Construction of Ecological Civilization," the "Overall Plan for the Reform of Ecological Civilization System," and the "Measures for Evaluating and Assessing the Objectives of Ecological Civilization Construction," which further define objectives, tasks, and institutional arrangements for the implementation of ecological civilization (Huang & Westman, 2021). In 2018, ecological civilization became part of the Chinese Constitution (Huang & Westman, 2021).

Ecological civilization has been described as a state-driven framework that combines cultural and moral virtues to build a cultural and national continuity based on sustainability and become a driver for the global future (Hansen et al., 2018). Beyond, instrumental uses of the paradigm (also considering that China is one of the biggest polluters globally with 11.5 billion tons of $CO_2$ produced annually and the most carbon dependent—see Our World in Data, 2022), the concept has been adopted by the Chinese government to instill a direction (at least as a guiding principle) as opposed to capitalist civilization (Foster, 2017). Moreover, Chinese reforestation projects have received contrasting scientific evaluations in terms of benefits, methods of implementation, and effects on the protection of biodiversity. However, analyzing the principles at the basis of ecological civilization, Weins et al. (2023) emphasize the structural determinant of laws and regulations that are needed at both local and global levels to go in that direction. The success of such regulation can be favored through the creation of circumstances that encourage participation, as emphasized in the previous section. The harmonious coexistence of humans and nature can only happen through a structured approach that recognizes the natural environment as a structural determinant of human existence. In this direction, Weins et al. (2023) interpret forestry projects as an expression of ecological engineering that requires governance based on the interpretation of the environment as an infrastructure. China is the first country to develop a clear national policy to implement a "green financial system." At the same time, China has created an appealing environment for leading innovation in green financial technologies (fintech), as the example of Alipay Forest has suggested in the previous section (Data-Pop Alliance, Green Digital Finance Alliance, UNEP Inquiry, 2020). China has been promoting a fusion between the country's economy and digital economy by investing in both industrial digitalization and digital industrialization (Zhang et al., 2022). Some studies have suggested that the digital economy has been helpful in China in advancing the green economy (Song et al., 2022b; Zhang et al., 2022), especially thanks to the control of the whole process from production to consumption that can improve the efficiency of the green economy (Li, 2019). Moreover, studies in China have shown how digital finance, when coupled with technological innovation, rationalization, and government support (Du et al., 2022), can mitigate environmental pollution, drive economic growth, and improve people's living standards (Song et al., 2022a). Analyzing panel data of heavily polluting industries in China from 2008 to 2020, Zhao et al. (2023) found that environmental regulation positively influences green technology innovation through financial penalties and incentive policies. However, this effect is mediated by corporate social responsibility. In turn, both the relationship between corporate social responsibility and green technology innovation and the indirect effect of environmental regulation on green technology innovation through corporate social responsibility are moderated by public attention. This multilevel interplay suggests a need for combined joint approaches for the creation of favorable circumstances at the enterprise level.

However, some studies have also emphasized the drawbacks of authoritarian environmentalism on vulnerable communities, potentially nullifying the positive outcomes of efforts to increase citizens' environmental responsibility. This is the case, for example, of those communities that are highly dependent on their extractive activities and have experienced severe socio-economic impacts due to some eco-civilization projects (Lo, 2020). Moreover, some studies showed that strict environmental control can increase production costs while reducing competitiveness and, therefore, space for the green economy to emerge (Wang et al., 2021). On the other hand, Filiou et al. (2023) found that when digital policies that promote AI and the IoT are implemented in cities characterized by strict environmental policies, the production of green patents increases, limiting the negative impacts of increasing costs for businesses and increasing investments in eco-innovations. Finally, Huang and Westman (2021) emphasize that the Chinese state is not separated from society from a cultural perspective, and the relationship between agents at different levels is more complex than simply authoritarian impositions.

Therefore, while the Chinese conceptualization of ecological civilization is appealing, it shows both strengths and weaknesses. In terms of weaknesses, even though this approach is slowly shaping society through a pro-environmental structuration, it does not create the conditions for a participatory approach to emerge, given the centrality of the government to drive these initiatives. While authoritarian environmentalism can contribute toward the success of environmental regulations, it can also be harmful if it marginalizes vulnerable groups that are highly dependent on the exploitation of natural resources (Li & Shapiro, 2020). This further reinforces the need for tackling environmental poverty in conjunction with other types of poverty that otherwise can create a vicious circle.

In this direction, Filiou et al. (2023) argue that there is a need for mixed and more comprehensive approaches that simultaneously promote digital technological development and environmental protection/valorization. To overcome the challenges imposed by the scarcity of reliable environmental data and the fragmentation in the implementation of environmental regulations (a responsibility of local authorities), the government has promoted the implementation of digital-environmental governance, also to empower citizens (for example, through environmental microblogs, WeChat accounts, and reporting platforms) in the surveillance of polluters and provide information directly to the government. Moreover, the 2016 Law on Air Pollution Prevention and Control imposes on major polluters to install air pollution monitoring systems (Monjon & René, 2021).

At the same time, as discussed in Chap. 4, there remain concerns about the potentially detrimental effects of the growing use of ICTs, which can produce damaging byproducts and increase consumption, energy demand, and carbon emissions. For example, in 2020, the power consumption of China's data centers exceeded 200 billion kWh (2.7% of total power consumption) (Zhang et al., 2022). On the other hand, a positive relationship has been shown between the digital economy and the green economy (Filiou et al., 2023; Song et al., 2022; Wang et al., 2022). These studies suggest that investments in the digital economy, the construction of digital infrastructure, and research would accelerate the passage to a green economy. It has also shown the role of the government in building platforms for industries to network, providing digital infrastructures, and promoting the digital economy and market-oriented reforms with a long-term vision. Digital infrastructures can also create favorable conditions for citizens to participate in interacting with the government and access data on air and water quality (Monjon & René, 2021).

Concerns remain on how technologies can be used as a surveillance and disciplinary tool to evaluate social actors not only in relation to their compliance with regulations but also to their "morality" (as interpreted by the government) (Monjon & René, 2021). This is in line with China's Social Credit System, developed by the government, which is a system of evaluating the "reliability" of actors (from citizens to businesses) in society in all sectors (for example, finance, social, environmental, and political) (Liang et al., 2018).

To sum up, the Chinese government's conceptualization of the environment helps us understand how the digital and environmental aspects of everyday life should be considered two interlinked components. The structural configuration of society also includes the intersection between digital and environmental regulatory frameworks to foster transitions toward eco-civilization, and the regulative apparatus becomes a key for creating opportunities based on democratic principles. This is also supported by those studies that analyzed the effects of complementary policies based on the combination of environmental and digital challenges. For example, ICTs can serve to monitor and push alignment with regulations (Schlæger & Zhou, 2019) or facilitate forecasting of air pollution concentration (Liu et al., 2021). They can also facilitate eco-innovation, for example, favoring the emergence of successful ideas such as Alipay Ant Forest, and, in turn, create the conditions for citizens to actively contribute to the transition.

## 7.5 Conclusions

This chapter provided some examples, which can be located at each level of the DEPF framework, showing the interconnections between macro-meso and micro dimensions of digital-environmental poverty. These examples also showed the interconnected nature of social, environmental, and digital inequalities within the construct of digital poverty, where these disparities tend to reinforce each other. This exploration revealed the potential of digital nudging to motivate individuals to make pro-environmental choices in the short term. However, we have also emphasized the persistence of factors related to personal and social network orientations, motivation, and habits in influencing long-term behavior. This highlights the importance of considering environmental awareness, pre-existing engagement, motivation for pro-environmental actions, and the influence of social networks in addressing the sustainable orientation of digital behaviors and consumption. Proficiency in navigating digital platforms influences an individual's ability to make informed and ecologically responsible choices that benefit society, the environment, and oneself. Digitally empowered individuals possess the knowledge and skills to critically evaluate algorithm-driven recommendations and to understand how their choices and preferences can be impacted by AI-powered virtual assistants. Digitally literate people actively participate in the critical understanding and sustainable use of digital technologies. This supports the inclusion of these variables when considering digital-environmental poverty at the individual level. However, this micro perspective needs to be interpreted in combination with the other determinants of digital-environmental poverty at a meso and macro level of analysis. Such interconnection is further supported by initiatives like the Single.Earth and Alipay Ant Forest projects. Their success is indeed tied to a broader socio-political, economic, digital, and environmental infrastructure. At the same time, the participation and support of users is pivotal in determining the impacts of these initiatives. Specifically, despite criticalities, the case of Alipay provided valuable insights into how an application can serve as an arena for interaction among government, business, and citizens' interests. It also establishes circumstances that encourage citizens to become involved in environmental matters, particularly in a context heavily affected by environmental degradation such as China. On the other hand, the Single.Earth project suggested that creating participatory spaces cannot be exclusively relegated to private initiatives. This is because the absence of government overseeing and lack of regulations might create power imbalances between participants with the risk that only the most powerful actors in the network might benefit from the monetization of the environment at the expense of those who rely on those resources for livelihood. Moreover, these examples also show that challenging digital-environmental poverty requires combining both circumstances that favor the acquisition of digital skills that can help users engage with these experiences profitably, but also develop environmental awareness, motivation, social network, and engagement with the environment. Participation in digital-environmental decision-making necessitates both the availability of suitable spaces for this interaction and relevant digital-environmental competencies. These considerations directly link with the structural level of digital-environmental poverty, which intersects the political, cultural, economic, social, and environmental configuration of society.

Analyzing the eco-civilization project as an intricate initiative that amalgamates aspects of neoliberalism and authoritarian environmentalism, we stressed the need for integrated approaches that consider both environmental and digital challenges to avoid exclusion and ensure sustainable development. This is because, while the eco-civilization principle permeates decision-making, it does not foster active citizen participation, mainly limited to reporting to the government. In conclusion, the fight against digital-environmental poverty should be seen as a multi-dimensional challenge that requires the coordinated efforts of various stakeholders, including governments, private businesses, and the elite/local community.

## References

Andrews, B., & Wilson, C. (2021). *The impact of coronavirus on digital consumer innovations for climate change. SILCI.* https://silci.org/impacts-of-Covid-19-on-digital-low-carbon-innovations/

AntGroup. (2019). *Alipay gallery: Ant forest tree-planting spring 2019.* https://medium.com/alipay-and-the-world/alipay-gallery-ant-forest-tree-planting-spring-2019-dc4e0578cc7c

Arnstein, S. R. (2007). A ladder of citizen participation. *Journal of the American Institute of Planners, 35*(4), 216–224.

Ashfaq, M., Zhang, Q., Ali, F., Waheed, A., & Nawaz, S. (2021). You plant a virtual tree, we'll plant a real tree: Understanding users' adoption of the Ant Forest mobile gaming application from a behavioural reasoning theory perspective. *Journal of Cleaner Production, 310*, 127394. https://doi.org/10.1016/j.jclepro.2021.127394

Ashfaq, M., Zhang, Q., Zafar, M. M., & Waheed, A. (2022). Understanding Ant Forest continuance: Effects of user experience, personal attributes and motivational factors. *Industrial Management & Data Systems, 122*(2), 471–498.

Atzori, L., Iera, A., & Morabito, G. (2010). The Internet of things: A survey. *Computer Networks, 54*(15), 2787–2805.

Bahta, D., Yun, J., Islam, M. R., & Ashfaq, M. (2020). Corporate social responsibility, innovation capability and firm performance: Evidence from SME. *Social Responsibility Journal.*

Beer, D. (2017). The social power of algorithms. *Information, Communication and Society, 20*(1), 1–13.

Bimonte, S., Bosco, L., & Stabile, A. (2019). Nudging pro-environmental behaviour: Evidence from a web experiment on priming and WTP. *Journal of Environmental Planning and Management, 63*(4). https://doi.org/10.1080/09640568.2019.1603364

Chapman, A., & Masie, D. (2023). Are carbon offsets all they're cracked up to be? We tracked one from Kenya to England to find out. *Vox.* https://www.vox.com/23817575/carbon-offsets-credits-financialization-ecologi-solutions-scam

Chen, B., Feng, Y., Sun, J., & Yan, J. (2020). Motivation analysis of online green users: Evidence from Chinese "Ant Forest". *Frontiers in Psychology, 11*, 1335. https://doi.org/10.3389/fpsyg.2020.01335

Data-Pop Alliance, Green Digital Finance Alliance, UNEP Inquiry. (2020). *Digital technology shaping green and sustainable lifestyles: Exploring Alipay Ant Forest.* https://datapopalliance.org/publications/publicacion-sin-categorizar/

Downing, A. S., Wong, G. Y., Dyer, M., Aguiar, A. P., Selomane, O., & Aceituno, A. J. (2021). When the whole is less than the sum of all parts – Tracking global-level impacts of national sustainability initiatives. *Global Environmental Change, 69.* https://doi.org/10.1016/j.gloenvcha.2021.102306

Du, M., Hou, Y., Zhou, Q., et al. (2022). Going green in China: How does digital finance affect environmental pollution? Mechanism discussion and empirical test. *Environmental Science and Pollution Research, 29*, 89996–90010.

European Commission. (2015). *Directorate General for research and innovation. Towards an EU research and innovation policy agenda for nature-based solutions & re-naturing cities: Final report of the Horizon 2020 expert group on 'Nature Based Solutions and Re-Naturing Cities'*. Publications Office of the European Union.

Feng, X., Fu, B., Lu, N., Zeng, Y., & Wu, B. (2013). How ecological restoration alters ecosystem services: An analysis of carbon sequestration in China's Loess Plateau. *Scientific Reports, 3*, 3–7.

Filiou, D., Kesidou, E., & Wu, L. (2023). Are smart cities green? The role of environmental and digital policies for Eco-innovation in China. *World Development, 165*, 106212.

Flavián, C., Akdim, K., & Casaló, L. V. (2023). Effects of voice assistant recommendations on consumer behaviour. *Psychology and Marketing, 40*(2), 328–346.

Flynn, A., Hacking, N., & Xie, L. (2019). Governance of the circular economy: A comparative examination of the use of standards by China and the United Kingdom. *Environmental Innovation and Societal Transitions, 33*, 282–300.

Foster, J. B. (2017). The Earth-system crisis and ecological civilization: A Marxian view. *International Critical Thought, 7*(4), 439–458.

Galvin, R. (2020). Power, evil and resistance in social structure: A sociology for energy research in a climate emergency. *Energy Research & Social Science, 61*. https://doi.org/10.1016/j.erss.2019.101361

Gare, A. (2009). Toward an ecological civilization: The science, ethics, and politics of eco-poiesis. *Process Studies, 39*(1), 5–38.

Geal, S., & Ely, A. (2018). Narratives and pathways towards an ecological civilization in contemporary China. *The China Quarterly, 236*, 1175–1196.

Gifford, R., & Nilsson, A. (2014). Personal and social factors that influence pro-environmental concern and behaviour: A review. *International Journal of Psychology, 49*, 141–157.

Golding, O., Yu, G., Lu, Q., & Xu, X. (2022, May 2–5). *Carboncoin: Blockchain tokenization of carbon emissions with ESG-based reputation*. Conference presentation, IEEE International Conference on Blockchain and Cryptocurrency (ICBC), Shanghai, China. https://doi.org/10.1109/ICBC54727.2022.9805516

Greenfield, P. (2023, January 18). Revealed: More than 90% of rainforest carbon offsets by biggest certifier are worthless, analysis shows. *The Guardian*. https://www.theguardian.com/environment/2023/jan/18/revealed-forest-carbon-offsets-biggest-provider-worthless-verra-aoe.

Guizar-Coutiño, A., Jones, J. P. G., Balmford, A., Carmenta, R., & Coomes, D. A. (2022). A global evaluation of the effectiveness of voluntary REDD+

projects at reducing deforestation and degradation in the moist tropics. *Conservation Biology, 36*(6). https://doi.org/10.1111/cobi.13970

Hansen, M. H., Li, H., & Svarverud, R. (2018). Ecological civilization: Interpreting the Chinese past, projecting the global future. *Global Environmental Change, 53*, 195–203.

He, T., Jazizadeh, F., & Arpan, L. (2022). AI-powered virtual assistants nudging occupants for energy saving: Proactive-smart speakers for HVAC control. *Building Research and Information, 50*(4), 394–409.

Henkel, C., & Kranz, J. (2018, December 13–16). *Pro-environmental behaviour and green information systems research – Review, synthesis and directions for future research.* Conference presentation, 39th International Conference on Information Systems (ICIS), San Francisco, USA.

Henkel, C., Seidler, A.-R., Kranz, J., & Fiedler, M. (2019, June 8–14). *How to nudge pro-environmental behaviour: An experimental study.* Conference presentation, 27th European Conference on Information Systems (ECIS), Stockholm and Uppsala, Sweden.

Hooks, G., Lengefeld, M., & Smith, C. L. (2021). Recasting the treadmills of production and destruction: New theoretical directions. *Sociology of Development, 7*(1), 52–76.

Huang, P., & Westman, L. (2021). China's imaginary of ecological civilization: A resonance between the state-led discourse and sociocultural dynamics. *Energy Research & Social Science, 81*. https://doi.org/10.1016/j.erss.2021.102253

Jayachandran, S., de Laat, J., Lambin, E. F., Stanton, C. Y., Audy, R., & Thomas, N. E. (2017). Cash for carbon: A randomized trial of payments for ecosystem services to reduce deforestation. *Science, 357*, 267–273.

Jeffreys, E., & Sigley, G. (2009). Governmentality, governance and China. In E. Jeffreys (Ed.), *China's governmentalities: Governing change, changing government* (pp. 1–23). Routledge.

Jin, F., & Zhang, X. (2023). Artificial intelligence or human: When and why consumers prefer AI recommendations. *Information Technology & People*. https://doi.org/10.1108/ITP-01-2023-0022

Kaida, N., & Kaida, K. (2019). Positive associations of optimism–pessimism orientation with pro-environmental behaviour and subjective well-being: A longitudinal study on quality of life and everyday behaviour. *Quality of Life Research, 28*, 3323–3332.

Keller, L., Gollwitzer, P. M., & Sheeran, P. (2020). Changing behaviour using the model of action phases. In M. S. Hagger, L. D. Cameron, K. Hamilton, N. Hankonen, & T. Lintunen (Eds.), *The handbook of behaviour change* (pp. 77–88). Cambridge University Press.

Kesenheimer, J. S., & Greitemeyer, T. (2021). Going green (and not being just more pro-social): Do attitude and personality specifically influence pro-environmental behaviour? *Sustainability, 13*, 3560. https://doi.org/10.3390/su13063560

Klaus, P., & Zaichkowsky, J. (2020). AI voice bots: A services marketing research agenda. *Journal of Services Marketing, 34*(3), 389–398.

Li, X. H. (2019). New features and the formation mechanism of new growth drivers of digital economy. *Journal of Reform, 11*, 40–51.

Li, Y., & Shapiro, J. (2020). *China goes green*. Polity Press.

Liang, F., Das, V., Kostyuk, N., & Hussain, M. M. (2018). Constructing a data-driven society: China's social credit system as a state surveillance infrastructure. *Policy & Internet, 10*(4). https://doi.org/10.1002/poi3.183

Liu, B., Yu, X., Chen, J., & Wang, Q. (2021). Air pollution concentration forecasting based on wavelet transform and combined weighting forecasting model. *Atmospheric Pollution Research, 12*(8), 101144. https://doi.org/10.1016/j.apr.2021.101144

Liu, S. (2022). *Ant Forest: Using financial technologies to advance climate solutions in China*. Lincoln Institute of Land Policy.

Lo, K. (2020). Ecological civilization, authoritarian environmentalism, and the eco-politics of extractive governance in China. *The Extractive Industries and Society, 7*(3), 1029–1035.

Logg, J. M., Minson, J. A., & Moore, D. A. (2019). Algorithm appreciation: People prefer algorithmic to human judgment. *Organizational Behaviour and Human Decision Processes, 151*, 90–103.

Mayor, B., Toxopeus, H., McQuaid, S., Croci, E., Lucchitta, B., Reddy, S. E., Egusquiza, A., et al. (2021). State of the art and latest Advances in exploring business models for nature-based solutions. *Sustainability, 13*(13), 7413.

McCombs, M. E. (2004). *Setting the agenda: The mass media and public opinion*. Blackwell.

Milfont, T. L., & Sibley, C. G. (2012). The big five personality traits and environmental engagement: Associations at the individual and societal level. *Journal of Environmental Psychology, 32*(2), 187–195.

Monjon, S., & René, É. (2021). The new tools of environmental governance in China: Top down control and environmental credit. https://geopolitique.eu/en/

Morgan, J. (2021, September 22). Why carbon offsetting doesn't cut it. *World Economic Forum*. https://www.weforum.org/agenda/2021/09/greenpeace-international-carbon-offsetting-net-zero-pledges-climate-change-action

Our World in Data. (2022). *China: What are the country's annual CO2 emissions?* https://ourworldindata.org/co2/country/china?country=~CHN#what-are-the-country-s-annual-co2-emissions

Pichert, D., & Katsikopoulos, K. V. (2008). Green defaults: Information presentation and pro-environmental behaviour. *Journal of Environmental Psychology, 28*(1), 63–73.

Scheufele, D. A. (2000). Agenda-setting, priming, and framing revisited: Another look at cognitive effects of political communication. *Mass Communication and Society, 3*, 297–316.

Schlæger, J., & Zhou, J. (2019). Digital environmental monitoring in Urban China. In J. Delman, Y. Ren, O. Luova, M. Burell, & O. Almén (Eds.), *Greening China's urban governance* (*ARI – Springer Asia Series*) (Vol. 7, pp. 131–149). Springer.

Schnaiberg, A., & Gould, K. (1994). *Environment and society: The enduring conflict.* Blackburn Press.

Shen, L. (2021). *Over 600 million people planted more than 326 million trees via Alipay Ant Forest in five years.* https://www.businesswire.com/news/home/20210825005340/en/Over-600-Million-People-Planted-More-Than-326-Million-Trees-via-Alipay-Ant-Forest-in-Five-Years

Single Earth. (2022). *The scientific background behind the MERIT.* https://www.single.earth/our-approach

Song, M., Zheng, C., & Wang, J. (2022a). The role of digital economy in China's sustainable development in a post-pandemic environment. *Journal of Enterprise Information Management, 35*(1), 58–77.

Song, X., Tian, Z., Ding, C., Liu, C., Wang, W., Zhao, R., & Xing, Y. (2022b). Digital economy, environmental regulation, and ecological well-being performance: A provincial panel data analysis from China. *International Journal of Environmental Research and Public Health, 19*, 11801. https://doi.org/10.3390/ijerph191811801

Székely, N., Weinmann, M., & vom Brocke, J. (2016, June 12–15). *Nudging people to pay CO2 offsets – The effect of anchors in flight booking processes.* Conference presentation, Proceedings of the 24th European Conference on Information Systems (ECIS), Istanbul, Turkey

Taube, O., & Vetter, M. (2019). How green defaults promote environmentally friendly decisions: Attitude-conditional default acceptance but attitude-unconditional effects on actual choices. *Journal of Applied Social Psychology, 49*(11), 721–732.

Terrier, L., Kim, S., & Fernandez, S. (2016). Who are the good organizational citizens for the environment? An examination of the predictive validity of personality traits. *Journal of Environmental Psychology, 48*, 185–190.

Thaler, R., & Sunstein, C. (2008). *Nudge: Improving decisions about health, wealth, and happiness.* Penguin Books.

UN. (2019). *Chinese initiative Ant Forest wins UN Champions of the Earth award.* https://www.unep.org/news-and-stories/press-release/chinese-initiative-ant-forest-wins-un-champions-earth-award.

UNCC. (2019). *Alipay Ant Forest: Using digital technologies to scale up climate action.* https://unfccc.int/climate-action/momentum-for-change/planetary-health/alipay-ant-forest

Van Deursen, A. J. A. M., & Mossberger, K. (2018). Any thing for anyone? A new digital divide in Internet-of-Things skills. *Policy and Internet, 10*(2), 122–140.
Vrain, E., Wilson, C., Kerr, L., & Wilson, M. (2022). Social influence in the adoption of digital consumer innovations for climate change. *Energy Policy, 162*, 112800.
Wang, S., Ibrahiem, M. H., & Li, M. (2022). Motivations influencing Alipay users to participate in the Ant Forest campaign: An empirical study. *International Journal of Environmental Research and Public Health, 19*(24), 17034.
Wang, S., Sun, X., & Song, M. (2021). Environmental regulation, resource misallocation, and ecological efficiency. *Emerging Markets Finance and Trade, 57*(3), 410–429.
Wang, X., & Yao, X. (2020). Fueling pro-environmental behaviours with gamification design: Identifying key elements in Ant Forest with the Kano model. *Sustainability, 12*, 2213. https://doi.org/10.3390/su12062213
Weinmann, M., Schneider, C., & Vom Brocke, J. (2016). Digital nudging. *Business & Information Systems Engineering, 58*(6), 433–436.
Weins, N. W., Zhu, A. L., Qian, J., Seleguim, F. B., & da Costa Ferreira, L. (2023). Ecological civilization in the making: The 'construction' of China's climate-forestry nexus. *Environmental Sociology, 9*(1), 6–19.
West, T. A., Börner, J., Sills, E. O., & Kontoleon, A. (2022). Overstated carbon emission reductions from voluntary REDD+ projects in the Brazilian Amazon. *PNAS, 117*(39), 24188–24194.
Wilson, C., Kerr, L., Sprei, F., Vrain, E., & Wilson, M. (2020). Potential climate benefits of digital consumer innovations. *Annual Review of Environment and Resources, 45*, 13.1–13.32.
Zeng, Y., Sarira, T. V., Carrasco, L. R., Chong, K. Y., Friess, D. A., Lee, J. S. H., Koh, L. P., Worthington, T. A., Zhang, Y., & Koh, L. P. (2020). Economic and social constraints on reforestation for climate mitigation in Southeast Asia. *Nature Climate Change, 10*(9), 842–844.
Zhang, Y., Jiayin, C., Han, Y., Qian, M., Guo, X., Chen, R., Xu, D., & Chen, Y. (2021). The contribution of Fintech to sustainable development in the digital age: Ant Forest and land restoration in China. *Land Use Policy, 103*. https://doi.org/10.1016/j.landusepol.2021.105306
Zhang, Y., Wei, Y., & Zhou, G. (2018). Promoting firms' energy-saving behaviour: The role of institutional pressures, top management support and financial slack. *Energy Policy, 115*, 230–238.
Zhang, Y., Xiao, S., & Zhou, G. (2020). User continuance of a green behaviour mobile application in China: An empirical study of Ant Forest. *Journal of Cleaner Production, 242*, 118497.
Zhang, Z., Fu, W. K., & Ma, L. (2022). The impact of digital economy on green development in China. *Frontiers in Environmental Science, 10*. https://doi.org/10.1016/j.igd.2023.100094

Zhao, Y., Huang, Y., Hu, S., & Sun, J. (2023). How tripartite stakeholders promote green technology innovation of China's heavily polluting enterprises? *Sustainability, 15*(12), 9650. https://doi.org/10.3390/su15129650
Zhou, X. (2021). Ecological civilization in China: Challenges and strategies. *Capitalism Nature Socializm, 32*(3), 84–99.
Zimmerman, S., Hein, A., Schultz, T., & Gewald, H. (2021, July 12). *Digital nudging toward pro-environmental behaviour: A literature review*. Conference presentation, Twenty-Fifth Pacific Asia Conference on Information Systems, Dubai, UAE.

PART III

# Case Study and Policy Recommendations

CHAPTER 8

# Digital Policy Analysis and Connections Between Digital Poverty and Environmental Poverty in the UK

## 8.1 Introduction

This chapter provides an overview of some major digital and environmental strategies designed by the UK government to tackle digital and environmental vulnerabilities, which also reflects how the country conceptualizes the interconnections between these issues. This enables us to comprehend how effective merging environmental and digital strategies may be in the fight against a more all-encompassing definition of poverty that also includes digital and environmental dimensions in a time of environmental crisis and digital acceleration.

The Coalition for Digital and Environmental Sustainability (CODES, 2022) highlights that "the future of humanity and the health of planet Earth depend to a large extent on how we undergo this digital transformation." However, the direction of digital development mainly depends on policy intervention that aims to reduce the negative impacts and progress environmentally and socially sustainable development through digitalization processes. Focusing on digital sustainability inventions in the period between 2001 and 2018, the European Commission (Jindra & Leusin, 2022) suggested some recommendations to achieve a comprehensive approach to digital sustainability technologies. The report highlights that digital sustainability inventions mainly originate from digital-related



M. L. Ruiu, M. Ragnedda, *Digital-Environmental Poverty*, Palgrave Studies in Digital Inequalities,
https://doi.org/10.1007/978-3-031-56184-9_8

companies adopting sustainable technologies and emphasizes the importance of promoting the twin transition to digital and green technologies. The UK emerges as a relevant context to study, given that it appears among the top 15 countries investing in these technologies.

This chapter provides an overview of the macro approaches proposed by the UK to tackle digital and environmental poverty. Both the academic and political debate around digital poverty emphasizes that a lack of consensus on what constitutes digital poverty has made it difficult to implement effective policies (Donaghy, 2021). As highlighted in previous chapters, this book extends the definition of digital poverty to incorporate the environmental dimension. It highlights the need to consider this phenomenon as multidimensional and multilevel, showing the challenges faced by policy intervention in adopting a comprehensive approach. As already underlined in the first section, digital-environmental poverty cannot be merely attributed to a lack of access to digital devices. In some cases, the overabundance of access to digital devices has, by contrast, been identified as negatively affecting social interactions and family relationships. This suggests that mere access is not beneficial itself, but it can impoverish users by affecting their well-being (Agrawal, 2021). Instead, digital-environmental poverty emerges from a complex web that includes access (or lack of) to technology, digital competencies, and the advantages and benefits derived from accessing and using digital technologies (both online and offline, including social and environmental aspects). Additionally, digital-environmental poverty is also influenced by an individual's ability to manage and cope with the potential negative consequences (social, individual, and environmental) that may arise from the use of digital technologies. Therefore, digital-environmental poverty can be considered the outcome of many intersected aspects that include the different levels of digital, social, and environmental exclusion. Digital-environmental poverty exacerbates and is exacerbated by other socioeconomic (Allman, 2022) and environmental inequalities (Gould et al., 2008).

Tackling digital poverty and different forms of digital inequalities has been at the center of policy interventions since the very beginning of the new digital era in the UK. The UK framed the fight against digital poverty as an opportunity to provide socially vulnerable individuals with the tools they need to interact with the digital world and, as a result, get advantages and improve their socioeconomic conditions (Davies et al., 2017). However, with a few exceptions, most initiatives in this direction have only partially achieved their intended goal. This is also due to the instability deriving from the lack of any consistent political design to combat digital poverty, which by contrast highly depends on partisan orientations. Specifically, in the UK, we can observe how these policies are intertwined with the arising complexities of the different levels of the digital divide. The policies' initial intent was, indeed, primarily to close the first level of the digital divide by seeking to address disparities in Internet access. To prevent a society of digital "haves and have-nots" many of these early government initiatives concentrated on enhancing public access to the Internet and digital devices. At that point, decision-makers began to put new policies into place to close the second level of the digital divide after seeing that users were developing disparities in how they used digital technologies due to different expertise levels and competencies.

The chapter starts by examining the New Labour Initiatives (1997–2010) overarching strategy on the information society "*Our Information Age*" that focus on issues relating to the first and some degree, the second level of the digital divide, trying to prevent the emergence of a society with information haves and have-nots (Central Office for Information, 1998). Such intervention reflected the need for bringing citizens online as the digital choices were still limited in number and typology. It then refers to the steps made by the conservative Government Digital Inclusion Strategy—2014 (Cabinet Office, 2014), which confirms the direction of partnerships between public, private, and voluntary sectors to implement a unified strategy. Moreover, it considers the UK Digital Strategy—2017 (DCMS, 2017) aimed to provide free digital skills training to adults. Working within the parameters set out within this legislation, certain Internet Service Providers (ISPs) provide a social tariff for people conventionally defined as disadvantaged (claimants of benefits), acting as a discount for broadband and mobile connectivity. Despite the innovative character of this policy, the minimum standards need to be updated in line with the increasing requirement of speed and data to benefit from the Internet. Some steps in this direction have been made by the Levelling Up Agenda—2022 (Gov.UK, 2022a) delivered by Johnson's government, which mainly addresses the issue of improving connectivity via the upgrading of infrastructure according to regional requirements.

In parallel, this chapter considers the environmental legislation of the UK, which has been the lead long-term legislation on climate change since the Climate Change Act of 2008, and the definition of a Net Zero Strategy by 2050 adopted in 2021, after the UK departed from the European Union. However, it also highlights some criticalities in meeting the expected emissions cuts due to the lack of clear guidance in achieving the target of net zero emissions by 2050 (Harvey, 2023).

Finally, the chapter concludes by examining the points of interconnections between the digital and environmental policy realms. It highlights how the development of policies tends to focus on each component independently. Despite efforts to incorporate the digital dimension into green development and some overlaps acknowledged by the government, a comprehensive strategy that views environmental, social, and digital poverty as elements of the same challenge is still to be defined.

## 8.2 UK Digital Policy Context Evolution Over Time: The New Labour Initiatives (1997–2010)

A green paper published in 1996 grounded opportunities to provide services that could be more accessible, more convenient, easier to use, quicker, and less costly to both citizens and businesses in the use of information technology, thanks to collaborations between governments and the private sector. The same paper mentioned that at that point, the UK had the highest ratio of personal computers to pupils in schools in the world thanks to the funding provided by the government (for example, in 1995, the government launched a £10 million program, Superhighways in Education, to increase the use of technology in education) (Chancellor of the Duchy of Lancaster, 1996).

The primary focus of New Labour Initiatives (1997–2010) was predominantly on addressing the first level of the digital divide (refer to Chap. 3 for a definition). This emphasis aimed at thwarting the development of a society characterized by disparities between information haves and have-nots (Central Office for Information, 1998). These policies adopted a dichotomous approach that underpinned the discussion of access and expanding infrastructure. In this first attempt, the New Labour government, led by Tony Blair, interpreted digital poverty as connected to access and possession of digital tools that could align with a new globalized digital system (Cole, 1998). Setting the program to modernize the government, the Labour approach aimed to be comprehensive by simultaneously innovating education, libraries, and the health service, and encouraging the growth of electronic commerce and digital broadcasting (Blair & Cunningham, 1999). Several policies were developed in this direction over time, such as the National Grid for Learning (1998–2006), which was implemented in the context of education to connect all schools to the Internet by 2002. It adopted Giddens' third-way approach (Blair, 1998), establishing synergies between public and private bodies in education to integrate ICTs into the educational setting (Selwyn, 2000). This was done to provide the necessary infrastructure for schools to become connected via the provision of broadband connectivity and/or computers.

The National Grid for Learning site and its connected partners offered thousands of pages of content. In the same direction, the government agency, namely, the British Educational Communications and Technology Agency (BECTA), was established in 1998 to lead the effective introduction of technology in education in the UK. Moreover, funding for teacher training supported the inclusion of ICTs into lesson planning and a learning portal served to share relevant content via educational websites. According to the 2005 BECTA Review, 76% of schools and colleges made progress in using ICTs in their work, with an emphasis on increasing teachers' confidence and competencies and improving students' results (Hunt et al., 2005). However, it also shows that for every school that embraced technology in education and administration, two others lagged far behind in terms of ICT use.

The grid's closure in 2006 cast doubt on the initiative's goal of achieving such personalized education, which was initially framed as a game-changing initiative that would result in a more tailored learning experience for students. The failure has been attributed in part to the private sector's role, which shifted the focus from ICTs' skill mentoring to simply being a conduit for the proliferation of ICTs and infrastructure (Eason, 2006).

Another attempt was made to address digital challenges through "Harnessing Technology: Next Generation Learning" (2008–2014) to provide personalized learning through the use of ICT adoption, which, due to the mode of delivery, required existing digital skills. This attempt reinforces a political approach that sees the incorporation of digital technologies into all levels of education as having two effects: increasing educational attainment and providing individuals with the skills needed to compete in the globalized (digital) economy. When it was published, this policy served as the blueprint for how ICT integration in educational settings, specifically incorporation into teaching, would be managed. The policy paper's main objectives were to narrow the gap and increase educational attainment; improve the health and well-being of children/young people; increase the number of young people on the path to success; improve the skills of the population throughout their working lives; build social and community cohesion; strengthen the Further and Higher Education systems. It specifically refers to enabling access and use of technology effectively, safely, and purposefully in support of learning thanks to collaborative approaches that consult bodies and partners operating at the local level. This paper also refers to the need to implement a use of technology that is simultaneously environmentally sustainable (BECTA, 2008a). The sustainability of technology is interpreted in both terms, affordability in the long run and reduced impact on the natural environment. The impact of technologies on the environment is mainly attributed to their dependence on electricity. Therefore, the program also includes guidance on saving power and recycling components. BECTA also sets the intention to collaborate with the technology industry to develop components that can be more easily recycled and technology infrastructures that allow users to make efficient use of devices and encourage the development of "smart buildings" with heating, lighting, and water systems controlled via ICTs.

This second stage of addressing digital inequalities includes some interventions on the second level of the digital divide by acknowledging the existence of imbalances in the possession of digital skills among certain groups engaged in education, which also affect educational outcomes. This intervention reflected the findings of several studies conducted to investigate how digital skill gaps affect society, focusing on more traditional components of social stratification and the factors that contribute to the formation of societal inequalities (Van Dijk & Hacker, 2003; Wilhelm, 2006; Mossberger et al., 2007). This specific outline for ICT integration in the educational setting was intended to form the contextual framework up to 2014 when it was to be reviewed. However, public funding for BECTA was withdrawn after the election of the Lib-Dem/Conservative coalition in 2010, which led to a decrease in public spending that year, resulting in the non-departmental organization's functions being liquidated the following year (Arthur, 2010).

The Extending Opportunity Final Report was released in 2008 by the Minister's Taskforce on Home Access to Technology and refers to the importance of promoting home access to technology for educational, economic, and wider societal benefits. However, it also estimates that around 35% of families still do not have access to the Internet mainly due to low incomes (BECTA, 2008b). The report attributes educational benefits to giving students more options for how, where, and when they study, particularly when a student's close contacts (for example, parents) can participate actively in their child's education. It also emphasizes the need to focus on maximizing the benefits of home access by all, increasing the perceived value by parents, and removing the barriers of cost for families with low incomes. The report also refers to its commitment to challenging the exclusion of around 17 million adults from the digital world by, for instance, signing the Riga Declaration on e-Inclusion, to halve the digital divide by 2010 (BECTA, 2008b). However, accessing content from home is seen as a supplementary channel for content delivery that allows students to take an active role in achieving their educational goals outside of designated school hours. The study links higher educational attainment to home access, but the majority of recommendations are drawn on the first level of the digital divide, for instance, by referring to 1.4 million students with no Internet access at home at the time of publication. However, the report discusses how structural conditions create circumstances (primarily the implementation of support programs for learners and their families, schools, and local governments) that affect access and how students use these technologies from their homes for remote learning. In this direction, studies show that parents with high levels of digital capital can leverage their acquired knowledge to benefit their children, particularly in the realm of education (Ragnedda & Ruiu, 2020). However, the transmission of digital skills and knowledge from one generation can perpetuate and fortify the existing social structure and inequalities. Children born into households where digital devices are used and digital competencies are rooted can leverage this advantage to excel academically and, in the long run, in their professional lives. Conversely, those born into environments where there is a lack of digital devices and digital skills may find themselves at a disadvantaged position. This process not only reinforces social stratification but also amplifies the disparities between different socioeconomic groups.

Such a strategy was also supported by complementary intervention in increasing digitalization processes. In "Putting the Frontline First: Action Plan," the government focuses on some macro areas such as citizen participation, access to public services, and streamlining the center of government, saving money through sharper delivery (HM Government, 2009). The efficiency in these fields is thought to be improved by improving access, skills, and technological infrastructures. Therefore, to address digital inequities, the New Labour approach prioritized an education-centered strategy that put children (and their parents) at the center of the solution. These New Labour initiatives, with a strong emphasis on access (and to some extent, the acquisition of digital skills), set a course for contemporary policy direction.

## 8.3 UK Digital Policy Context Evolution Over Time: Digital Inclusion Strategies 2014–2022

Following these first attempts to understand and tackle the digital divide, the Government Digital Inclusion Strategy—2014 seeks to consolidate the efforts of the public, private, and voluntary sectors in creating an equitable Internet by planning to reduce the number of people with no basic digital skills and capabilities by a quarter in two years (and bring every citizen online by 2020). Since it acknowledges the idea of digital poverty, although, in terms of digital exclusion, one may argue that this policy is among the most significant for conversations about it. In this direction, the paper defines digital exclusion as the result of three digital determinants (digital skills, connectivity, and accessibility). An individual is considered digitally excluded when one of these issues interferes with their ability to obtain benefits from Internet use. Digital exclusion is caused by factors that are primarily determined by larger structural forces that reproduce inequalities; however, some complementary factors can be attributed to individuals' dispositions. These are linked to motivation and trust (safety concerns), which may prevent an individual from appreciating the societal benefits of Internet use. While motivation is explicitly mentioned as a prerequisite for access in van Dijk's resource appropriation theory (Van Dijk, 2005), the inclusion of the trust factor is nebulous, given its connection with "fear," for example, in relation to potentially becoming victims of online crime, or not being able to recognize credible services available. In this sense, it might be associated with motivational determinants, given that the presence of online crime may demotivate a user to engage. These determinants (digital skills, connectivity, accessibility, and motivation) are also present in the Digital Poverty Framework (DPF), however, with the inclusion of further supplementary factors such as support. The strategy also refers to the need for integrating digital aspects into the main governmental programs to provide users with the digital skills necessary to access certain services. Individuals and groups at risk of digital exclusion in this strategy follow the more traditional components of social inequalities. This strategy targets groups and individuals across the entire spectrum of society, tracing a departure from New Labour's digital policies, which placed a strong emphasis on ICTs in the educational setting. The strategy reflects the conservative party orientation and the concept of Cameron's Big Society. In this conceptualization, "civil society becomes the third sector formed of a modernized and more competitive voluntary sector—one that has a more market-based approach to delivering services—associated with the newly created social enterprises, which are private companies whose business is to deliver a social service" (Espiet-Kilty, 2016). The reinforcement of private-public collaboration is seen with the consolidation of the partnership with *GO ON UK*, which includes ten of the UK's leading private and public sector organizations, to coordinate a nationwide effort in digital exclusion reduction. To highlight the Big Society ethos of sectoral interrelationship delivering market-based solutions, this network included Age UK, Argos, BBC, Big Lottery, E.ON, EE, Lloyds Banking Group, Post Office, Sage, and TalkTalk (Age UK, 2015).

Initial success in meeting its goals was seen from 2014 to 2016; however, analysis of this policy's effectiveness shows that between 2017 and 2020, the target of reducing the number of people offline by 25% every 2 years, with all those able to become digitally included expected to have done so by 2020, was not achieved in any region except for the South West (Taylor, 2021). In continuity with this plan, the UK Digital Strategy—2017 served as both a review of the outcomes achieved by the magnitude of digital initiatives implemented till that moment and ultimately informing the direction of future policy implementation.

The focus on shifting services and governmental support online has produced contradictory results by also contributing toward increasing the social and economic exclusion of vulnerable groups, who cannot access online basic services (Allman, 2022). For this reason, the Department of Education published the Essential Digital Skills Framework in 2018 and supported initiatives to provide citizens with free digital skills training through a new Digital Skills Partnership. This was essentially the retrofitting of *GO ON UK*, which had relinquished its direct governmental responsibilities the year before the publication of the paper. It should be noted that this specific policy paper has been criticized for being limited in its actual application since its publication in 2017 (Vecciolini, 2019).

The introduction of a Universal Service Obligation (USO; effective in 2018), which was intended to be ratified as legal legislation by 2020, is one of the most significant contributions in governance aimed at reducing digital poverty. The Universal Service Obligation (USO)—2017 replaces previous obligations in the provision of universal Internet access. The legislation specifically requires ISPs to provide a minimum for their operation, such as download speeds of 10 Mbps and upload speeds of 1 Mbps, effective voice calls (representative of the required Mbps), a contention ratio of 50:1 (meaning 50 households can use one network node); data usage of 100 gigabytes a month, and affordability (defined as an average of £45 a month). Moreover, USO provides the right to anyone without a connection meeting the above criteria to request an upgrade, with subsidization of the costs up to £3400 per household. Working within the parameters set out within this legislation, certain ISPs provide a social tariff for citizens who claim benefits, acting as a discount for broadband and mobile connectivity. Criticisms of this proposed safety "net" explicitly highlight the fact that both download and upload speeds are extremely slow, implying that this minimum standard would become obsolete over time. The policy's designers recognize this as an obvious fact, so they included a clause stating that once super-high-speed Internet is available in 75% of the UK, this basic provision will be reviewed.

The conservative approach is also reflected in the Levelling Up Agenda—2022, which defines the principles identified as responsible for tackling inequalities and encourages private sector investment across the UK. However, in comparison to the digital strategy (2017), references to digital poverty are vague, as this white paper focuses on improving connectivity in the UK through infrastructure upgrades. The issue of digital connectivity is framed as a by-product of existing regional disparities and suggests that the digital divide can be tackled by improving the infrastructural capabilities of rural regions. The only mention of a digital skills initiative is the Local Digital Skills Partnership from 2018, which is a reimagining of the Digital Skills Partnership conceived in 2014, but with a decidedly more regional approach. Decentralization is a recurrent theme of this white paper, characterized by the commitment by 2030, to involve any English region in a deal that grants the highest level of devolution, which would reduce the barriers of bureaucracy for future fiscal procurement, and the implementation of initiatives that address digital exclusion from a bottom-up perspective.

The UK Digital Strategy—2022 (DCMS, 2022) is developed on six areas represented by Digital Foundations (including infrastructure, data availability, regulation, and security), Ideas and Intellectual Property, Skills and Talent, Finance and Investment, Levelling up, and "Enhancing the UK's place in the world." Within the first pillar, the strategy sets targets such as ensuring that the majority of the population will have access to a 5G signal by 2027, simplification of the UK General Data Protection Regulation and enabling secure digital identities, simplification of the regulatory approach to tech innovation, enhancing online safety and security through, for instance, the introduction of the Online Safety Bill (Gov.UK, 2022b), and the online media literacy strategy (DCMS, 2021a). The Online Safety Bill also aims to combat misinformation and disinformation. Moreover, pillar three directly refers to skills and talent needed by the workforce and estimates that the digital gaps cost the UK economy £63 billion per year (DCMS, 2022). This area of intervention only considers high-skill demand by the market to be addressed through education in schools and qualifications through programs (for example, Skills Bootcamps and free courses for jobs). Among the innovations introduced by the strategy is the institution of the Digital Skills Council, which is built with a focus on the private-public partnership model to address the digital skills shortage among the workforce. In this direction, many of the programs mentioned by the strategy are provided by private companies (such as Amazon, Google, and Microsoft), which are emphasized as key players in upskilling the digital force. However, the document does not consider how to address the lack of basic skills outside the educational setting. It also does not mention how the circulation of such information on the availability of these opportunities will be enhanced. At the same time, it recognizes that some regions of the UK, such as the North East, Yorkshire and the Humber, and Northern Ireland are the most affected by digital exclusion. It predicts positive outcomes through the Local Digital Skills Partnership to develop educational programs based on regional needs. Local Digital Skills Partnerships bring together partners from the public, private, and third sectors to advance digital inclusion and improve the workforce's digital skills (DCMS, 2021b). Such an approach has shown some benefits at the local levels of intervention (see, for example, the Leicester and Leicestershire Enterprise Partnership with a strong focus on educating, reskilling, and upskilling the workforce [LLEP, 2022]).

Moreover, in addition to government strategies, local councils and third-sector entities have devised a wealth of resources centered on digital inclusion activities, strategies, and projects. For example, the Digital Inclusion Evaluation Toolkit, initiated by Croydon and Leeds councils, stands as an independent and exhaustive repository of advice and information on digital inclusion specifically tailored for local councils (Digital Inclusion Toolkit, 2023). It compiles a multitude of resources aimed at supporting organizations in evaluating the impact of their digital inclusion projects. In addition, it functions as a dedicated hub for the latest digital inclusion developments spanning the UK, hosting regular roundtable discussions for councils to facilitate the exchange of best practices and drive progress in council-led digital inclusion efforts. The primary objective of this toolkit is to enable teams to substantiate the success of their projects in driving change and offer insights on how to enhance or iterate these projects to amplify their impact.

Finally, it is worth exploring the approach taken by the UK government to regulate AI and its impact on everyday life. In March 2023, the UK government released an AI White Paper, "A pro-innovation approach to AI regulation" (Gov.UK, 2023g), which outlines five guiding principles to shape AI legislation based on safety, security and robustness, transparency and explainability, fairness, accountability and governance, contestability, and redress (Gov.UK, 2023h). Differently from the precautionary approach guiding the EU AI regulation process, the paper aims to provide flexibility and distribute responsibility for translating these principles into concrete guidance and for AI governance across existing regulators to facilitate context-specific approaches. This is in line with the Science and Technology Framework and the UK's International Technology Strategy papers earlier published in 2023. They all aim to make the UK a global science and technology superpower by 2030, supported by consistent investments in infrastructures and technology skills. The paper refers to shared responsibilities without the institution of a central regulator, which might simplify the adaptability to an evolving technological context. At the same time, it might make it difficult to coordinate the fragmented approaches across sectors and produce deregulation to favor industrial development. The plan states that the central government will, however, provide guidance to regulators on how to apply these principles to specific problematic contexts and will monitor and evaluate the effectiveness of the framework provided. At the same time, it does not provide information on resourcing, management, and accountability mechanisms. It also does not provide an evaluation of challenging and potential tensions with existing regulatory frameworks (Charlesworth et al., 2023). Moreover, the plan refers to an education-based approach, but it does not clarify what entity will be responsible for it. The plan has been criticized for its "innovation-first" approach that reiterates the market-based orientation of conservative strategies, which sidelines the public. This is further supported by recent findings by *the Guardian* investigation (Stacey, 2023) that revealed how government officials use complex algorithms to help decisions around several issues including welfare, immigration, and criminal justice. However, such an approach has been already shown to be discriminatory in several contexts (for example, the Netherlands). The "algorithmic transparency reporting standard" launched by the government is a voluntary tool for public sector bodies to report on how algorithms are used to support decision-making (Gov.UK, 2023i).

To summarize, the goal of this policy review was to review some relevant current and past policies that are related in some way to the concept of digital poverty. In the New Labour years, the understanding of policy aimed at the level of wider society began to take shape by intervening at the educational level. Since Labour's definition of the digital approach in terms of collaboration between private and public bodies, this relationship has been shifted to the market side by displaying a neoliberal orientation that favors market-led responses to digital exclusion. Following Holmess and Burgess (2022), this is reinforced by a report by the House of Lords Select Committee on COVID-19 (Covid-19 Committee, 2021a), which stated that there was no need for tariff regulation because the market regulated the provision of affordable tariffs and that the Internet was available in libraries for those who could not access broadband at home (Covid-19 Committee, 2021b).

Even though digital exclusion is often associated with pre-existing disadvantages, a common denominator of the initiatives examined in this section is the focus on specific aspects such as digital infrastructure, users' skills, and access to the digital realm. This suggests that the operational pathway differs from the conceptualization of digital exclusion, which is treated independently from other policies that address inequalities (Holmess & Burgess, 2022).

Given the ongoing cost of living crisis, which is exacerbating the existence of this phenomenon rooted in social inequalities, any future policy will have to address the concept of digital poverty, which, as mentioned throughout the book, goes beyond the mere lack of possession of digital devices, access to the Internet, and acquisition of basic digital skills. It is also important to ensure that AI technologies are developed and implemented in a way that prioritizes fairness, safety, and public welfare, rather than solely focusing on innovation and market-driven strategies. As previously mentioned, the AI White Paper "A Pro-innovation Approach to AI Regulation" takes positive steps by emphasizing some essential principles. These principles are aimed at promoting innovation and decentralizing the responsibility for AI governance among existing regulators. However, as noticed, this approach does not involve the establishment of a central regulator, whose absence potentially enhances adaptability, but at the same time carries the risk of fragmenting and deregulating practices, which could, in turn, prioritize industrial interests over public welfare. It is, therefore, vital to ensure that the regulation of AI will prevent digital poverty and inequalities stemming from AI implementation.

Provision of those specific policies aimed at empowering citizens with digital skills can almost be seen as the first step toward reducing digital poverty, with later policies aimed at infrastructural upgrades and standardization of minimum provisions for ISPs tackling another area related to digital poverty. In the upcoming paragraph, we explore the UK's environmental policies to better understand the steps taken to secure and preserve the environment. Similar to digital inclusion policies, which aim to improve individuals' well-being by reducing the risks of digital exclusion, environmental policies are implemented with the intent to enhance individuals' well-being by preventing environmental degradation and impoverishment.

## 8.4 UK Environmental Policy Context Evolution Over Time

The UK represents a relevant case study among Western countries given its long history of environmental advocacy and protection. Up until 2022, it ranked among the top performers internationally for its environmental policies (SGI, 2022). Since the late 1980s, the UK has gained high visibility and accountability on environmental matters thanks to its environmental legislation (OECD, 2022). The green orientation of its legislation has been built since the Climate Change Act of 2008, which inspired the Net Zero Strategy adopted in 2021. Such a strategy is built on several plans such as the 2020 Ten Point Plan for a Green Industrial Revolution, the 2021 Industrial Decarbonisation Strategy, Transport Decarbonisation Plan and Hydrogen Strategy, the 2021 Plan to Build Back Better, Net Zero Strategy to Build Back Greener and the Fairer, and Greener Scotland Programme for Government 2021–2022 (OECD, 2022). The UK is the first country to adopt long-term legislation on climate change (which legally binds the country to reduce greenhouse gas emissions) (HM Government, 2023a). The Climate Change Act introduced legally binding "carbon budgets," which set a cap on the amount of greenhouse gases emitted in the UK over five years (CCC, 2022). This amount was first set at an 80% reduction and in 2019, under the advice of the Climate Change Committee (CCC; an independent body established under the Climate

Change Act of 2008), increased to 100% on 1990 levels by 2050. In 2012 the first carbon budget was met (2008–2012) with a reduction of carbon emissions by 25% of 1990 levels. Also, the second carbon budget (2013–2017) was successfully met, and in 2017 the government introduced the Clean Growth Strategy, which sets out a range of measures and proposals to combine economic growth and reduction of emissions through investments in low-carbon innovation. The CCC observed that the UK was on track to meet the third carbon budget (2018–2022), but it is still uncertain if the target was met, due to the publication of the Progress Report in 2024. However, between 1990 and 2021, UK emissions fell by 48%. Six carbon budgets have been set to date (2008–2037), but the CCC has also warned that the UK is behind in meeting the targets of future carbon budgets, and more stringent measures are needed to meet the Net Zero Target (CCC, 2022).

The climate change mitigation strategy includes measures related to transport (phasing out the sale of new petrol and diesel vehicles first set by 2040 and then brought forward to 2030 by the Johnson government), buildings (upgrading the energy efficiency of homes by 2035), power (low-carbon electricity generation to provide 85% of UK generation in 2032), industry (improving business energy efficiency at least 20% by 2032), and innovation (including greenhouse gas removal technologies). However, the preliminary report released by the CCC in 2018 emphasized that there was a gap between the announced measures and meeting the fourth and fifth carbon budgets. The CCC encouraged a further step from ambitions to action, by emphasizing a need for clear policies to be implemented with predicted outcomes (CCC, 2018). In the same year, the UK government published its 25-Year Environment Plan (A Green Future: Our 25-Year Plan) (HM Government, 2018), which sets 47 strategies to assess environmental problems in England.

Following its departure from the European Union, the UK was forced to replace environmental regulations with a new Environment Act. The Environment Act of 2021 includes a net zero carbon emissions target by 2050, with an emissions reduction of 78% by 2035 compared to 1990 levels.

The plan establishes five principles that aim to advance the goals of the 25-year Environment Plan (integration of environmental protection into policymaking, prevention, rectification at source, polluter pays, and precautionary approach), as well as the requirement for all government ministers to consider them when making policy. It also institutes the Office for

Environmental Protection (OEP) as an independent environmental watchdog to report on progress. The OEP released an independent assessment in 2022 on the government's progress in the delivery of the 25-Year Environment Plan, suggesting that "environmental laws and government strategy and policy have not yet proved successful in significantly slowing down, halting or reversing biodiversity decline or the unsustainable use of resources or the pollution of the environment" (OEP, 2022). In January 2023, the OEP (2023a) published another report relative to 2021/2022 that found that the government's progress in delivering the 25-Year Environment Plan was far from achieving the expected outcomes in terms of environmental improvements.

Across the UK, resource efficiency and a circular economy have been supported, and private sector initiatives contributed to reducing waste and increasing circularity. However, in 2022, Friends of the Earth, ClientEarth, and the Good Law Project took legal action because the government's climate change strategy failed to include the policies it needed to meet the expected emissions cuts (Gayle, 2022). The strategy, published in October, committed the country to end the sales of new fossil fuel cars by 2030 and gas boilers by 2035. However, it did not provide any indications about how this could be achieved and its impact on cuts in emissions. The high court ruled that the government's strategy did not provide sufficient details to understand how the country will meet its legally binding target of net zero emissions by 2050 and ordered a new plan to reach carbon neutrality by March 2023 (Harvey, 2023). In its 2023 Report to Parliament, the CCC states that the UK is unprepared to adapt to climate change and that there is no evidence that the UK is reducing its vulnerability to climate change in areas including food and water security, natural habitats, health, energy, transport, and urban adaptation. Therefore, on 30 March 2023, the government published a Carbon Budget Delivery Plan (Gov.UK, 2023a) that still raises questions about how the UK will meet the targets for 2030 under the Paris Agreement (Dunne et al., 2023). After consideration of the new plan, the CCC (2023b) declared that its confidence in the UK government to meet its targets from 2030 onward was "markedly less than it was" in the previous assessment. Lawyers for Friends of the Earth, ClientEarth, and Good Law Project found breaches to the Climate Change Act and decided to bring the government back to court (Good Law Project, 2023a). This is because the plan does not provide any information on the government's assessment of the risk connected to the proposals and does not provide sufficient support for how policies can meet legally binding climate targets. The uncertainty is mainly related to the reliance on emergent technologies, which are still in their early stages of development (for example, hydrogen, carbon capture and storage, and low-carbon aviation fuel) (ClientEarth, 2023). This is further supported by the Energy Act 2023, which introduces a licensing framework for carbon transport and storage with an investment of £20 billion in carbon capture technology (Coutinho, 2023).

On 30 March, the government also released a "Net zero growth plan" paper for its net zero target, responding to an independent review of the government's approach to delivering its net zero targets (Skidmore, 2023). Such a plan includes responses to 129 recommendations that emerged from roundtables across the industry, government, and civil society (Gov.UK, 2023b). However, the plan does not include a specific timeline for emissions reductions in each sector postponing the publication of the timescale in the future. Some recommendations emerge in this plan, which connects the environmental strategy to digitalization processes and digital technologies.

Recommendation 89 refers to the promotion of digital technologies (including AI, robotics, digital twins, and autonomous systems) to ensure the industry's energy efficiency and for a wider decarbonization process. The government references the Made Smarter program, which aims to develop and reinforce technology solutions including AI, robotics, and digital twins in the manufacturing sector. The program is also mentioned in the Digital Strategy 2022, which refers to £147 million already invested in driving the development of digital solutions for manufacturing and ensuring continuous support for the next three years. This reinforces the goals of the Smart Grid Vision and Routemap already published in 2014 by the Department of Energy and Climate Change, which envisages reductions in energy waste, lower carbon emissions, and more efficiency of the energy system thanks to smart grids. Smart grids use, in fact, digital technology by connecting smart meters, monitoring devices, and computers (IoT) to manage energy distribution more efficiently.

Recommendation 90 refers to the digitization process as a strategy for the Department for Business, Energy and Industrial Strategy to enhance energy efficiency and emissions projections.

There is also a mention of digitalization processes in recommendation 99 for accelerating planning. While these government responses are connected to creating the digital infrastructure for businesses and decision-making, recommendation 102 refers to supporting consumers' choices through the creation of a carbon calculator (https://www.gov.uk/guidance/carbon-calculator) to make informed decisions. The government refers to the launch of an online advice service in 2022 that provides consumers with information on how to improve home energy performance. The "It All Adds Up" campaign is also mentioned, which provides advice on actions that households can take to cut energy use. While the idea of a carbon calculator can be appealing, in its current form the interface of the calculator is not user-friendly and needs training to be used. It consists of 30 interactive graphs, maps, and flow diagrams to show the impact of decision-making on carbon emissions. However, it is primarily for education purposes (Royal Geographical Society, 2022). This suggests that users need skills and competencies before accessing and properly using the tool. Moreover, there is no mention of how to use ICTs sustainably.

Finally, in September 2023, the prime minister, Rishi Sunak, announced significant changes to the measures aimed at reaching net zero carbon emissions by 2050. These changes, aimed at limiting potential short-term economic drawbacks (Gov.UK, 2023d), involve delaying the deadline for discontinuing the sale of new petrol and diesel cars from 2030 to 2035. There is also a delay in the goal of phasing out the sale of gas boilers for residential use and the ban on off-grid oil boilers. Moreover, homeowners and landlords are granted more flexibility to invest in insulation upgrades. These come in addition to the approval of the first coal mine in 30 years in Cumbria in December 2022. Sunak also announced scrapping proposals for increasing recycling at home, taxes on meat or flights, and how many passengers a car can have (Horton, 2023). Friends of the Earth (2023) and the Good Law Project (2023b) wrote letters to both the Energy secretary and the government, seeking clarifications on the intentions of the government to meet the legally binding requirements of the "carbon budgets."

Despite contradictions and the government's mixed messages, the UK has an intention to adopt a market-oriented approach, supported by the UK Green Finance Strategy launched in 2019, which focuses on mobilizing and channeling private investments to support the transition to a low-carbon economy. The updated version released in March 2023 emphasizes the need for incorporating nature into green finance policy and channeling financial flows by recognizing that environmental degradation also represents a financial risk to be addressed and avoided (HM Government, 2023b).

The market-based approach has been reinforced by the publication of a Nature Markets Framework, which supports the creation of units or credits that can be bought and sold in the market (Gov.UK, 2023e). These approaches, defined as natural capital approaches, assign financial value to natural resources and employ market-based instruments to incentivize stakeholders to engage in environmental conservation (Sullivan, 2013, 2017). The UK government currently supports two projects, the UK Woodland Carbon and the UK Peatland Code, which have operated since 2017/2018 to generate carbon credits to sell into voluntary carbon markets. Two additional markets are emerging in terms of biodiversity net gain (to avoid loss of habitat in land development) and nutrient mitigation (designing development alongside suitable mitigation measures). Finally, an additional market related to marine net gain is likely to emerge, and the government expects the emergence of many more markets. The framework encourages firms to invest in the provision of ecosystem services and nature projects with the ambition of reaching at least £500 million in investment by 2027 and going over £1 billion by 2030. Even though the document sets standards on how the public and private sectors can work together, it does not provide a clear course of action and does not reassure smaller stakeholders, such as individual farmers and land managers, on market regulations. For example, Lyon and Burnett (2023) reported that despite farmers' willingness to act, there are concerns over the private sector payments for natural capital, how they complement the public sector programs, uncertainties related to business risks, and the standards governing both the payments (defining what farmers must do) and the effectiveness of the model (to prevent greenwashing). Moreover, many peer-reviewed voluntary standards exist in the carbon market, including those provided by organizations like Verra and ICROA (the International Carbon Reduction and Offset Alliance), which provide certificates of carbon sequestration. As highlighted in the previous chapter, some scandals related to "phantom credits," which might not reflect real reductions in carbon emissions, have affected the credibility of voluntary carbon markets as "greenwashing" strategies (Greenfield, 2023; Ehrenstein & Valiergue, 2021, 2023). As discussed in Chap. 7, when examining the MERIT case, it is evident that some additional weaknesses must be addressed in natural capital approaches. These concerns revolve around the commodification of natural resources (Fletcher et al., 2018) and the compensation mechanisms that encourage balancing harmful and preventive actions, rather than addressing the root causes of harm (Morgan, 2021; Stuart et al., 2017). Finally, voluntary carbon markets remain fragmented and challenging to completely understand in terms of their functioning mechanisms (Ehrenstein & Valiergue, 2023).

Despite this variegated policy landscape, a report published by the Environment Agency (Gov.UK, 2023c), a non-departmental public body, sponsored by the Department for Environment, Food & Rural Affairs, shows that air pollution is the most significant environmental threat to health in the UK. This concern is compounded by the growing challenge of treating infectious illnesses, as antimicrobial-resistant microbes increase due to contamination. Moreover, the report connects mental health to environmental damage due to the impact of pollution, flooding, and climate change. This document also mentions the unequal distribution of pollution and "natural capital" across society with deprived suffering from low-quality environments and lack of green space. The disadvantaged conditions of the poorer people also include living in the most polluted environments, which costs the National Health Service over £2 billion in treatment for health-related issues. It envisages equality of access to healthy environments, which could reduce healthcare costs and attribute responsibility to multiple stakeholders at multiple levels, including the government, regulators, businesses, and individuals. The 2023 Environmental Improvement Plan (EIP) engages with such environmental inequality across the country by setting the aim of ensuring that everyone in the UK lives no more than a 15-minute walk from a green or blue space (Gov.UK, 2023f). The EIP (Gov.UK, 2023f) reinforces the 10 targets already set by the 25-Year Environment Plan and outlines a 5-year plan to restore declining nature in the UK. The aims are preventing a decline in biodiversity, ensuring clean air and water, tackling the exposure to chemicals and pesticides that can affect land and water, minimizing waste production thanks to a circular economy and using resources sustainably, mitigating and adapting to climate change, improving defense and reducing the risk of harm from environmental hazards, ensuring biosecurity while tackling invasive species, and enhancing engagement with the natural environment. The OEP (2023b) has been gathering information from the central government to understand how to achieve the environmental targets, barriers, and enablers. They also launched a call for further evidence held by other parties as part of their scrutiny of the progress and opportunities for improvement.

While it is unpractical to conduct a comprehensive analysis of all policies in both the digital and environmental realms, the preceding two paragraphs only highlighted a few connections between environmental and digital inequalities that emerged in policymaking relative to these challenges. The next paragraph will delve into the intersection of these two crucial areas. This intersection is especially relevant, given the mandate established in the Environment Act of 2021, which compels ministers to consider environmental impacts when formulating policy decisions.

## 8.5 Environmental and Digital Realms: The Current State of the Art

As mentioned in the previous paragraph, the policy document published in 2018, "A Green Future: Our 25-Year Plan to Improve the Environment," shaped the government's long-term vision to improve the environment by setting some main goals in terms of clean air, water, and land, protection of wildlife, mitigation and adaptation to climate change, reduction of waste, and enhancing resource efficiency. To achieve these objectives, the plan recognizes that ICTs can play a pivotal role in improving efficiency in multiple sectors (for example, tracking waste) while limiting the environmental impact of economic activity. Therefore, it considers ICTs as a transversal tool that can help achieve environmental targets. However, this plan does not consider the direct interconnections between digital and environmental poverty and how they should be addressed. The same applies to the EIP 2023, which considers digital tools as complementary support to some environmental projects, such as in the case of improving digital services for homeowners to check for their flood risk, the implementation of forestry education through digital hubs, support to apprenticeships in digital occupations for a green economy, and other digital services.

Reviewing the policies that simultaneously address digital and environmental challenges, it is possible to identify some levels of overlapping in the digital-environmental policy landscape. Three main overlappings can be identified. The first relates to moving in-person activities and physical functions to the digital realm; the second involves the material dimension of ICTs that impacts the environment (for example, through types and efficiency of infrastructures, devices, and waste); the third involves the connection between private and public bodies that operate in the environmental and digital fields (Gov.UK, 2020). Despite the recognition of such overlaps, the government's commitment to addressing the interconnections between ICTs and the environment tends to focus primarily on government activities and functions or businesses and scarcely considers the environmental impact produced by citizens' use of ICTs.

In 2011 the UK government published the first Greening Government IT Strategy, which together with the Way We Work program, aimed to ensure greener digital technologies and sustainable working practices. After revisions and adaptation to the continuous digital evolution, the 2021–2025 Greening Government Commitments program superseded the Greening Government Commitments Framework for 2016–2020, by setting the targets from 2021 to 2025. It also includes a specific emphasis on ICT and digital services strategy 2020–2025 (Gov.UK, 2020). This strategy is based on some driving principles, already introduced by the Sustainable Technology Strategy 2018–2020, related to minimizing waste and embracing a circular economy; using resources more sustainably and efficiently; ensuring ICT sustainability in social, economic, and ethical terms; mitigating and adapting to climate change; analyzing the whole life costing; and seeking innovation opportunities (Gov.UK, 2018).

The new framework aims to reduce the energy consumption and carbon footprint of the government, promote the use of renewable energy, and improve the sustainable design of ICT products and services. It also aims to increase resilience, responsibility, transparency, collaboration, and accountability. The aim of increasing responsibility directly refers to the concept of digital citizenship. In this direction, the strategy includes self-led training programs on sustainable technology (for example, OneGreenGov, the Cross Whitehall Sustainability Group, Defra e-Sustainability Network, and MOD Sustainable Procurement Working Group) (Gov.UK, 2020). However, this training does not directly involve citizens but recognizes the role of digital technologies in reducing the government's carbon footprint while setting an example. It also establishes minimum business rules for achieving net zero by 2050, implementing a circular economy, and meeting transparency and accountability commitments. The targets for 2025 impose ICT suppliers to show progress toward net zero and zero waste. The Greening Government Strategy also shows advances in setting the government as a driver for change and the use of ICTs in a more sustainable way. However, it does not include the direct involvement of citizens in the process and does not address how the interplay between environmental and digital aspects can widen social inequalities.

The second level of intersection between ICTs and the natural environment is linked to the tangible components of ICTs and their infrastructure. The UK is committed to transit to a circular economy, which aims to reduce waste and promote the reuse and recycling of materials (Kirchherr et al., 2017). This is evidenced by the Resources and Waste Strategy for England, Beyond Recycling for Wales, Making Things Last for Scotland, and the Northern Ireland Environmental Strategy, as part of the UK 25-Year Environment Plan for England to recycle and reuse materials (Gov.UK, 2020). While digital technology can support this goal (for example, through the tracking and tracing of materials and the sharing economy), it also represents part of the problem. In fact, ICT waste is part of the waste of electrical and electronic equipment (commonly defined as e-waste). The UK ranks as the second-largest producer of e-waste globally and first in per capita production, producing 23.9 kg of e-waste per capita in 2019 (Ali, 2023). Recycling of Waste Electrical and Electronic Equipment recycling (WEEE) was originally regulated by the WEEE Regulations 2006, which was subsequently replaced by the WEEE Regulations 2013, which became law on 1 January 2014 in line with Directive 2012/2019/EU on WEEE (Gov.Uk, 2021a). However, in 2019 only 17% of e-waste was collected for recycling while the inappropriate disposal of harmful materials of which electronic and electric equipment are made causes environmental contamination (for example, the production of carbon dioxide and sulfur dioxide) in addition to health and economic damage (Sundar et al., 2023). More specifically, between 2008 and 2022 IT and telecoms e-waste in the UK increased by 98% (Ali, 2023). Despite the introduction of some rules, such as right-to-repair guidelines that oblige manufacturers to provide repair manuals and spare parts to consumers who buy a specific range of electronic products (washing machines and washer-dryers, fridges, dishwashers, and electronic displays) (UK, 2021b), the lack of clear guidelines on e-waste still represents a criticality. The EIP 2023 mentions the introduction of a mandatory digital waste tracking service to gather data and inform policymaking. Sundar et al. (2023) emphasize that scarce financial support for the effective management of e-waste, as well as a lack of existing laws and effective guidance that support e-waste management (at the household level) in the direction of a circular economy, undermines attempts to reduce pollution deriving from e-waste.

In addition to e-waste, the digital infrastructure represents a relevant aspect for tackling the first level of the digital divide, and its status also depends on climate change and environmental degradation. Despite the recommendations provided by the Climate Change Committee in the 2023 review (CCC, 2023a) about the adaptation capacity of ICTs and telecommunications infrastructure, the recent growth plan proposed by the government in March 2023 only marginally considers this aspect. The report highlights that climate change will affect digital infrastructures through extreme weather events that put vulnerable groups who depend on digital technologies (for example, for health) at high risk. However, for the most part, the digital infrastructure is private, and it is difficult to get data and information on the advances in this area. The lack of data also makes it difficult to assess the risk for remote communities to be isolated during extreme weather, with the risk of a limited possibility of asking for help. Moreover, the interdependencies between infrastructures made the urgency for increasing digital infrastructure resilience even more essential.

This directly connects to the third level of overlapping regarding the interconnections between private and public bodies in addressing digital-environmental challenges. Some of the recent UK policies established long-term targets aimed at improving resource efficiency and moving toward a circular economy. However, as highlighted by the OECD review (2022), achieving these ambitions requires public and private efforts (also via domestic recycling, reusability, and recyclability of products). In this direction, the UK government has recently created the Government Digital Sustainability Alliance (GDSA) (Gov.UK, 2022c), which is a collaborative partnership with small, medium, and multinational enterprises that supply to the UK government. The GDSA was launched at COP27 to encourage the use of digital technologies to improve environmental sustainability, reduce emissions, and increase resource efficiency by focusing on areas such as transportation, sustainable food systems, responsible mineral supply chains, and the circular economy (Howes, 2022).

In the direction of using digital tools to improve efficiency through multistakeholders' partnerships, in 2018 the UK government committed to the UK's National Digital Twin Programme, which is a partnership between the UK government and the University of Cambridge, to develop a digital replica of the built environment (such as buildings, roads, railways, energy systems, and water networks). By supporting innovation in areas such as smart cities, mobility, and energy, the program represents an important step forward for the digital transformation agenda in line with sustainability goals. The principles upon which the program is founded connect multiple dimensions, such as social, economic, and environmental outcomes, with digital advances (Digital Twin Hub, 2023). These principles are embedded in the mission of the program that calls for the academic and education sector, industry, and governments to collaborate and share responsibilities to define a strategy that combines economic, social, and environmental benefits through the use of digital technologies. The program has generated several connected initiatives, such as the creation of the Digital Twin Hub in 2019, which serves as a web-enabled collaborative platform of exchange and dialogue among entrepreneurs, academics, and policymakers, at both national and international levels. However, the NDT is still under development and requires the collaboration of multiple bodies to produce the data necessary to create the digital replica of the built environment (Digital Twin Hub, 2022).

The commitment and policies described so far mainly adopt a governance approach that involves private and public bodies operating in certain fields and have an indirect impact on citizens (for example, in terms of facilitating the decision-making process that impacts them or by making the decision-making process more transparent and accessible). There are other policies aimed at reducing emissions via creating certain structural conditions for improving the efficiency of homes and businesses, but also investing in low-carbon energy innovation (for example, Energy Company Obligation delivers energy efficiency in homes). However, the costs of such policies are mainly sustained by households through their energy bills, which, following Owen and Barrett (2020), add 13% on average to household energy bills in the UK. Moreover, manufacturers do not have, for example, the infrastructure for the collection and disposal of e-waste (Sundar et al., 2023). To address the criticality of raising costs, the UK Energy Act 2023 incentivizes the installation of smart meters and provides the Office of Gas and Electricity Markets (Ofgem) with the capacity to regulate the increasing energy prices and improve quality of service (Gov. UK, 2023l).

A recent report published by the Environmental Agency on the connection between health, well-being, and the environment (Gov.UK, 2023b), introduced in the previous paragraph, refers to multidimensions that also include the natural environment as a determinant of health and well-being. However, this model does not mention the digital environment as part of such multidimensionality. Indirectly, the report refers to how environmental poverty increases inequalities, with the most deprived areas in England being affected by higher pollution and lack of green spaces. While recognizing the links between financial and environmental poverty and their effects on human health and well-being, there is no mention of the linkages between digital poverty and environmental and financial poverty, and how these, in turn, affect access to the health system. The need for concerted intervention in digital-environmental terms is emphasized by approaches that aim to reduce the environmental impacts of the healthcare system through digitalization. Net zero healthcare requires public and private sector involvement to develop a sustainable and efficient healthcare system. In this direction, leaders from across the healthcare system have formed at the 26th United Nations Climate Change Conference a Health Systems Task Force. This is a public-private partnership (AstraZeneca, GSK, Merck KGaA, Novo Nordisk, Roche, Samsung Biologics, Sanofi, Karolinska Institutet, National Health Service England, the Sustainable Healthcare Coalition, UNICEF, the University of Pavia, and the World Health Organization) that sets sustainability targets to accelerate net zero health systems by focusing on some priority areas, one of which is represented by Digital Innovation in Clinical Research (Sustainable Markets Initiative, 2021). The report "The Digital Solution for Sustainability in Clinical Research Trials," produced by the Health Systems Task Force (2021), recognizes the link between socioeconomic poverty, environmental degradation, and higher incidence of poor health conditions because populations living in low- and middle-income countries tend to be the most severely impacted by environmental problems (for example, pollution) and climate change (Beagley et al., 2021; Fuller et al., 2022; Lelieveld et al., 2018). It also highlights the need for increasing the digitalization of the trial process at multiple stages, from the drug discovery (through, for example, the implementation of AI to reduce energy consumption and accelerate the process), research stage (through, for example, remote data monitoring), manufacturing (through, for example, the automatization of the production), to the screening and patient care (through AI screening and disease management, and remote care). While the benefits of such transformation are expected to reduce energy consumption and resources, it not only requires upskilling employees and large investments in digital technologies, but also closing the digital divide to avoid further enlarging digital inequalities and in turn health inequalities. Moreover, the report also acknowledges the difficulties in harmonizing the interaction between digital platforms (for example, due to different ways of collecting data) and simultaneously responding to regulations of different bodies and countries' national regulatory authorities at the global level.

However, despite the recognition of the interconnection between the digital and environmental fields, and ad hoc, sparse, and fragmented attempts to link digital and environmental challenges, both concepts of environmental and digital poverty are still overshadowed in the UK policy landscape, and their interdependence is even more neglected.

## 8.6 Conclusion

This chapter examined some attempts to combine strategies aimed at addressing digital and environmental issues. Despite the effort to integrate the digital dimension into green development, and some overlaps recognized by the UK government, there is still a need to develop a holistic approach that considers digital, social, and environmental poverty as facets of the same problem. However, in recent years, we have observed a shift in policy focus that started acknowledging the intricate connections between digital and environmental dimensions. These combined approaches represent a crucial step forward in the understanding of the complex interdimensional nature of digital-environmental poverty and develop effective strategies that address these multifaceted challenges.

A report published by the British Academy (2022) emphasizes some key lessons from history for policymaking working in the environmental field represented by the importance of considering culture and society in environmental policymaking (because of cultural and political-economic factors that constrain strategies for responding to environmental issues); the challenge of meeting diverging stakeholder interests (local—including citizens—and non-local stakeholders); the understanding of the implications of short-term environmental protection policies; the need for a holistic and collaborative approach to policymaking (which combines environmental, societal, and economic pillars of sustainability); and the role of civil society organizations in actively contributing to the decision-making process. However, revising the 2021 Environment Act's approach concerning access to environmental information, participation, and public access to justice, as advocated by the Aarhus Convention (ClienthEarth, 2022), Lee (2023) has shown that participation in the development of the Bill was selective in its participants' inclusion, inconsistent, and missed the opportunity to establish a legal right to participate in environmental decision-making (Lee, 2023). The quality of consultation was mainly compromised by the selection of areas of consultation, lack of information and evidence to support the consultation, selective participation, and uncertain impacts of consultation on final decisions.

This chapter emphasized a need for a holistic approach that also considers digital factors in both exacerbating and alleviating environmental inequalities, while also enhancing opportunities for citizens to participate in the decision-making process. The UK example showed that there is still more to be done in terms of connecting and tackling both tangible and intangible components of digital-environmental poverty.

Both labor and conservative strategies to ensure digital inclusion underpin the aim of creating a globally connected society, as also explicitly signaled by Cameron's Big Society. Digital inclusion becomes an integral part of the wider government approach and programs. In this sense, the digitalization of multiple aspects of society becomes a pillar for society's development based on multistakeholders' partnerships. Chapter 9 will explore how certain structural conditions imposed by institutional directions interact with the individual dimension at a meso level. In so doing, it will shed light on how users metabolize external regulations to develop their digital-environmental habitus and will show how environmental, social, and technological aspects are intertwined.

## References


Age UK. (2015). *Go ON UK*. https://www.ageuk.org.uk/london/projects-campaigns/our-projects/info/go-on-uk/

Agrawal, S. R. (2021). Digital pollution and its impact on family and social interactions. *Journal of Family Issue, 42*(11), 2648–2678.

Ali, R. (2023). *Mobile emissions*. https://www.uswitch.com/mobiles/compare/sim-only-deals/mobile-emissions/#how-much-e-waste-is-generated-in-the-uk

Allman, K. (2022). *UK digital poverty evidence review 2022*. https://digitalpovertyalliance.org/wp-content/uploads/2022/06/UK-Digital-Poverty-Evidence-Review-2022-v1.0-compressed.pdf

Arthur, C. (2010, May 24). Government to close Becta. *The Guardian*. https://www.theguardian.com/technology/2010/may/24/becta-government-closure

Beagley, J., Scagliarini, M., & Husselby, K. (2021). *Health inequalities and climate change: Action for Global Health position paper*. Action for Global Health.

BECTA. (2008a). *Harnessing technology: Next generation learning*. https://dera.ioe.ac.uk/8287/2/A9R3172_Redacted.pdf

BECTA. (2008b). *Extending opportunity. Final report of the minister's taskforce on home access to technology*. https://dera.ioe.ac.uk/8285/7/home_access_report_Redacted.pdf

Blair, T. (1998). *The third way: New politics for the new century*. Fabian Society.

Blair, T., & Cunningham, J. (1999). *Modernising government*. https://ntouk.files.wordpress.com/2015/06/modgov.pdf

Cabinet Office. (2014). *'Government digital inclusion strategy' 2014*. https://www.gov.uk/government/publications/government-digital-inclusion-strategy/government-digital-inclusion-strategy#actions

CCC. (2018). *An independent assessment of the UK's Clean Growth Strategy—From ambition to action*. http://www.theccc.org.uk/publications/

CCC. (2022). *Progress in reducing emissions. 2022 Report to Parliament*. http://www.theccc.org.uk/publications/

CCC. (2023a). *Progress in adapting to climate change*. http://www.theccc.org.uk/publications/

CCC. (2023b). *Better transparency is no substitute for real delivery*. https://www.theccc.org.uk/2023/06/28/better-transparency-is-no-substitute-for-real-delivery/.

Central Office of Information. (1998). *Our information age: The government's vision*. COI.

Chancellor of the Duchy of Lancaster. (1996). *Government direct: A prospectus for the electronic delivery of government services*. The Stationery Office Books. https://archive.org/stream/b32224242/b32224242_djvu.txt

Charlesworth, A., Fotheringham, K., Gavaghan, C., Sanchez-Graells, A., & Torrible, C. (2023). What are the main shortcomings of the 'pro-innovation approach to AI regulation' white paper published by the UK Government in March 2023? *University of Bristol Law School Blog*. https://legalresearch.blogs.bris.ac.uk/2023/07/what-are-the-main-shortcomings-of-the-pro-innovation-approach-to-ai-regulation-white-paper-published-by-the-uk-government-in-march-2023/

ClientEarth. (2023). *UK Government faces fresh legal challenge over "unlawful" climate plans*. https://www.clientearth.org/latest/press-office/press/uk-government-faces-fresh-legal-challenge-over-unlawful-climate-plans/

ClienthEarth. (2022). *Public participation in environmental matters in the UK/England & Wales*. https://www.clientearth.org/media/ftxnaemc/draft-guidance-on-public-participation-9-february-2022-public.pdf

CODES. (2022, November 14). *Action plan for a sustainable planet in the digital age*. https://www.sparkblue.org/CODES

Cole, M. (1998). Globalisation, modernization and competitiveness: A critique of the new labour project in education. *International Studies in Sociology of Education*, *8*(3), 315–333.

Coutinho, C. (2023). *UK's carbon capture opportunities*. https://www.gov.uk/government/speeches/uks-carbon-capture-opportunities

Covid-19 Committee. (2021a). *House of lords select committee on Covid-19—Beyond digital: Planning for a hybrid world*. 1st report of session, 2019–21. Paper 263. https://publications.parliament.uk/pa/ld5801/ldselect/ldcvd19/263/26302.htm

Covid-19 Committee. (2021b). *House of lords select committee on Covid-19—Beyond digital: The government response.* 1st Report of Session, 2019–21. Paper 51. https://publications.parliament.uk/pa/ld5802/ldselect/ldcvd19/51/5102.htm

Davies, H., Eynon, R., & Wilkin, S. (2017). Neoliberal gremlins? How a scheme to help disadvantaged young people thrive online fell short of its ambitions. *Information, Communication & Society, 20*(6), 860–875.

DCMS. (2017). *UK digital strategy.* https://www.gov.uk/government/publications/uk-digital-strategy

DCMS. (2021a). *Online media literacy strategy.* https://assets.publishing.service.gov.uk/government/uploads/system/uploads/attachment_data/file/1004233/DCMS_Media_Literacy_Report_Roll_Out_Accessible_PDF.pdf

DCMS. (2021b). *Evaluation of the local digital skills partnerships.* https://assets.publishing.service.gov.uk/government/uploads/system/uploads/attachment_data/file/1021163/Evaluation_of_LDSP_final_report_270921.pdf

DCMS. (2022). *UK digital strategy.* https://www.gov.uk/government/publications/uks-digital-strategy/uk-digital-strategy.

Department of Energy and Climate Change. (2014). *Smart grid vision and Routemap.* http://www.gov.uk/decc

Digital Inclusion Toolkit. (2023). *Digital inclusion advice for councils, by councils.* https://digitalinclusionkit.org/.

Digital Twin Hub. (2022). *National Digital Twin programme to 2022.* https://digitaltwinhub.co.uk/archive/national-digital-twin-programme/

Digital Twin Hub. (2023). *Gemini papers.* https://digitaltwinhub.co.uk/about/the-gemini-papers/.

Donaghy, D. (2021). Defining digital capital and digital poverty. *ITNOW, 63*(1), 54–55.

Dunne, D., Dwyer, O., & Evans, S. (2023). *The UK's 'green day' avalanche of climate and energy announcements.* Carbon Brief. https://www.carbonbrief.org/in-depth-qa-the-uks-green-day-avalanche-of-climate-and-energy-announcements/

Eason, G. (2006). *Computer learning 'grid' scrapped.* http://news.bbc.co.uk/1/hi/education/5145882.stm

Ehrenstein, A., & Valiergue, V. (2023). Quality offsets? A commentary on the voluntary carbon markets. *Consumption Markets & Culture, 26*(4), 298–310.

Ehrenstein, V., & Valiergue, A. (2021). Studying a (contested/concerned) market in the making voluntary offsetting, from UN climate talks to corporate sustainability departments. *Economic Sociology, 22*(2), 4–9.

Espiet-Kilty, R. (2016). David Cameron, citizenship and the big society: A new social model? *Revue française de civilization britannique, 21*(1). https://doi.org/10.4000/rfcb.796

Fletcher, R., Dressler, W. H., Anderson, Z. R., & Büscher, B. (2018). Natural capital must be defended: green growth as neoliberal biopolitics. *The Journal of Peasant Studies, 46*(5), 1068–1095. https://doi.org/10.1080/03066150.2018.1428953

Friends of the Earth. (2023). *Clarification sought on impact of weakened climate policies.* The. https://friendsoftheearth.uk/climate/climate-friends-earth-writes-government-lawyers

Fuller, R., Landrigan, P. J., Balakrishnan, K., Bathan, G., Bose-O'Reilly, S., Brauer, M., Caravanos, J., Chiles, T., Cohen, A., Corra, L., Cropper, M., Ferraro, G., Hanna, J., Hanrahan, D., Hu, H., Hunter, D., Janata, J., Kupka, R., Lanphear, B., Lichtveld, M., Martin, K., Mustapha, A., Sanchez-Triana, E., Sandilya, K., Schaefli, L., Shaw, J., Seddon, J., Suk, W., Téllez-Rojo, M. M., & Yan, C. (2022). Pollution and health: A progress update. *The Lancet, 6*(6). https://www.thelancet.com/journals/lanplh/article/PIIS2542-5196(22)00090-0/fulltext

Gayle, D. (2022, July 18). Court orders UK government to explain how net zero policies will reach targets. *The Guardian.* https://www.theguardian.com/environment/2022/jul/18/court-orders-uk-government-to-explain-how-net-zero-policies-will-reach-targets

Good Law Project. (2023a). *Net Zero II: We are taking the Government back to court.* https://goodlawproject.org/case/net-zero-ii-we-are-taking-the-government-back-to-court/

Good Law Project. (2023b). *We're demanding answers from Government about howitcanstillexpecttohitnetzero.* https://goodlawproject.org/were-demanding-answers-from-government-about-how-it-can-still-expect-to-hit-net-zero/

Gould, K., Pellow, D. N., & Schnaiberg, A. (2008). *The treadmill of production.* Paradigm Publishing.

Gov.UK. (2018). *The greening government: sustainable technology strategy 2020—Sustainable technology for sustainable government.* Policy Paper. https://www.gov.uk/government/publications/greening-government-sustainable-technology-strategy-2020/the-greening-government-sustainable-technology-strategy-2020-sustainable-technology-for-sustainable-government

Gov.UK. (2020). *Greening government: ICT and digital services strategy 2020–2025.* Policy Paper. https://www.gov.uk/government/publications/greening-government-ict-and-digital-services-strategy-2020-2025/greening-government-ict-and-digital-services-strategy-2020-2025

Gov.UK. (2021a). *Regulations: Waste electrical and electronic equipment (WEEE).* https://www.gov.uk/guidance/regulations-waste-electrical-and-electronic-equipment

Gov.UK. (2021b). *Draft ecodesign and energy labelling regulations 2021.* https://www.gov.uk/government/consultations/draft-ecodesign-and-energy-labelling-regulations-2021

Gov.UK. (2022a). *Levelling up the United Kingdom*. https://assets.publishing.service.gov.uk/government/uploads/system/uploads/attachment_data/file/1052708/Levelling_up_the_UK_white_paper.pdf?forcedefault=true.
Gov.UK. (2022b). *World-first online safety laws introduced in Parliament*. https://www.gov.uk/government/news/world-first-online-safety-laws-introduced-in-parliament
Gov.UK. (2022c). *Leader's blog: Chris Howes—Why I'll be at COP27*. https://defradigital.blog.gov.uk/2022/11/04/leaders-blog-chris-howes-why-ill-be-at-cop27/
Gov.UK. (2023a). *Carbon budget delivery plan*. http://www.gov.uk/official-documents
Gov.UK. (2023b). *Responding to the Independent Review of Net Zero's Recommendations*. https://www.gov.uk/government/publications/independent-review-of-net-zero-government-response/responding-to-the-independent-review-of-net-zeros-recommendations
Gov.UK. (2023c). *State of the environment: Health, people and the environment*. https://www.gov.uk/government/publications/state-of-the-environment/state-of-the-environment-health-people-and-the-environment
Gov.UK. (2023d). *PM recommits UK to Net Zero by 2050 and pledges a "fairer" path to achieving target to ease the financial burden on British families*. https://www.gov.uk/government/news/pm-recommits-uk-to-net-zero-by-2050-and-pledges-a-fairer-path-to-achieving-target-to-ease-the-financial-burden-on-british-families#:~:text=Press%20release,PM%20recommits%20UK%20to%20Net%20Zero%20by%202050%20and%20pledges,approach%20to%20reaching%20net%20zero
Gov.UK. (2023e). *Nature markets: A framework for scaling up private investment in nature recovery and sustainable farming*. https://assets.publishing.service.gov.uk/government/uploads/system/uploads/attachment_data/file/1147397/nature-markets.pdf
Gov.UK. (2023f). *Environmental improvement plan 2023*. https://www.gov.uk/government/publications/environmental-improvement-plan
Gov.UK. (2023g). *A pro-innovation approach to AI regulation*. https://www.gov.uk/government/publications/ai-regulation-a-pro-innovation-approach/white-paper
Gov.UK. (2023h). *UK unveils world leading approach to innovation in first artificial intelligence white paper to turbocharge growth*. https://www.gov.uk/government/news/uk-unveils-world-leading-approach-to-innovation-in-first-artificial-intelligence-white-paper-to-turbocharge-growth
Gov.UK. (2023i). *Algorithmic transparency recording Standard—Guidance for public sector bodies*. https://www.gov.uk/government/publications/guidance-for-organisations-using-the-algorithmic-transparency-recording-standard/algorithmic-transparency-recording-standard-guidance-for-public-sector-bodies

Gov.UK. (2023l). *New laws passed to bolster energy security and deliver net zero.* https://www.gov.uk/government/news/new-laws-passed-to-bolster-energy-security-and-deliver-net-zero

Greenfield, P. (2023, January 18). Revealed: More than 90% of rainforest carbon offsets by biggest certifier are worthless, analysis shows. *The Guardian.* https://www.theguardian.com/environment/2023/jan/18/revealed-forest-carbon-offsets-biggest-provider-worthless-verra-aoe

Harvey, F. (2023, March 30). Hasty changes to Sunak's climate strategy reveal a warring Tory party. *The Guardian.* https://www.theguardian.com/environment/2023/mar/30/hasty-changes-to-rishi-sunak-climate-strategy-reveal-a-warring-tory-party

Health Systems Task Force. (2021). *The digital solution for sustainability in clinical research.* https://a.storyblok.com/f/109506/x/42119be232/smi-hstf-digital-health-whitepaper.pdf

HM Government. (2009). *Putting the frontline first: Smarter government.* The Stationery Office. https://ntouk.files.wordpress.com/2020/06/uk-government-government-ict-strategy_0.pdf

HM Government. (2018). *A green future: Our 25 year plan to improve the environment.* https://assets.publishing.service.gov.uk/government/uploads/system/uploads/attachment_data/file/693158/25-year-environment-plan.pdf

HM Government. (2023a). *Carbon budget delivery plan.* https://www.gov.uk/guidance/carbon-budgets

HM Government. (2023b). *Mobilising green investment, 2023 green finance strategy.* https://assets.publishing.service.gov.uk/government/uploads/system/uploads/attachment_data/file/1149690/mobilising-green-investment-2023-green-finance-strategy.pdf

Holmess, H., & Burgess, G. (2022). Digital exclusion and poverty in the UK: How structural inequality shapes experiences of getting online. *Digital Geography and Society, 3.* https://doi.org/10.1016/j.diggeo.2022.100041

Horton, H. (2023, September 23). UK net zero policies: what has Sunak scrapped and what do changes mean? *The Guardian.* https://www.theguardian.com/politics/2023/sep/20/uk-net-zero-policies-scrapped-what-do-changes-mean

Howes, C. (2022). *Leader's view: Reflections from COP27.* https://defradigital.blog.gov.uk/2022/11/25/leaders-view-reflections-from-cop27/

Hunt, M., Davies, S., & Pittard, V. (2005). *British Educational Communications and Technology Agency (BECTA), Becta Review 2005. Evidence on the progress of ICT in education.* https://mirandanet.ac.uk/wp-content/uploads/2019/06/becta_review_2005.pdf

Jindra, B., & Leusin, M. (2022). *The development of digital sustainability technologies by top R&D investors.* Publications Office of the European Union.

Kirchherr, J., Reike, D., & Hekkert, M. (2017). Conceptualizing the circular economy: An analysis of 114 definitions. *Resources, Conservation and Recycling, 127,* 221–232.

Lee, M. (2023). The Aarhus convention 1998 and the environment act 2021: Eroding public participation. *Modern Law Review, 86*(3), 756–784.

Lelieveld, J., Haines, A., & Pozzer, A. (2018). Age-dependent health risk from ambient air pollution: A modelling and data analysis of childhood mortality in middle-income and low-income countries. *The Lancet, 2*(7). https://www.thelancet.com/journals/lanplh/article/PIIS2542-5196(18)30147-5/fulltext

LLEP. (2022). *Digital skills partnership*. Report 2021–2022. https://llep.org.uk/app/uploads/2022/10/LLEP-Digital-Skills-Partnership-report-2021-22.pdf

Lyon, F., & Burnett, A. (2023). *Natural capital: What farmers and policy makers need to know*. https://ffcc.co.uk/publications/natural-capital-markets-report

Morgan, J. (2021, September 22). Why carbon offsetting doesn't cut it. *World Economic Forum*. https://www.weforum.org/agenda/2021/09/greenpeace-international-carbon-offsetting-net-zero-pledges-climate-change-action/

Mossberger, K., Tolbert, C. J., & McNeal, R. S. (2007). *Digital citizenship: The internet, society, and participation*. MIT Press.

OECD. (2022). *OECD environmental performance reviews: United Kingdom 2022*. https://www.oecd-ilibrary.org/sites/b6a2be87-en/index.html?itemId=/content/publication/b6a2be87-en

OEP. (2022). *Taking stock: Protecting, restoring and improving the environment in England*. https://www.theoep.org.uk/report/taking-stock-protecting-restoring-and-improving-environment-england

OEP. (2023a). *Progress in improving the natural environment in England, 2021/2022*. https://www.theoep.org.uk/progress-improving-natural-environment-england-20212022

OEP. (2023b). *OEP launches call for evidence on nature recovery*. https://www.theoep.org.uk/report/oep-launches-call-evidence-nature-recovery

Owen, A., & Barrett, J. (2020). Reducing inequality resulting from UK low-carbon policy. *Climate Policy, 20*(10), 1193–1208.

Ragnedda, M., & Ruiu, M. L. (2020). *Digital Capital. A Bourdieusian approach to Digital Divide*. Emeralds Publishing.

Royal Geographical Society. (2022). *The MacKay carbon calculator*. https://www.rgs.org/CMSPages/GetFile.aspx?nodeguid=3206391c-e848-4049-b40d-8eb10c7d402f&lang=en-GB

Selwyn, N. (2000). The discursive construction of the National Grid for learning. *Oxford Review of Education, 26*(1), 63–79.

SGI. (2022). *Environmental policies. United Kingdom*. https://www.sgi-network.org/2022/United_Kingdom/Environmental_Policies#:~:text=This%20includes%20a%20goal%20of,%2C%20biodiversity%2C%20water%20and%20waste

Skidmore, H. C. (2023). *Mission zero. Independent review of net zero*. https://assets.publishing.service.gov.uk/government/uploads/system/uploads/attachment_data/file/1128689/mission-zero-independent-review.pdf

Stacey, K. (2023, October). UK officials use AI to decide on issues from benefits to marriage licences. *The Guardian*. https://www.theguardian.com/technology/2023/oct/23/uk-officials-use-ai-to-decide-on-issues-from-benefits-to-marriage-licences

Stuart, D., Gunderson, R., & Petersen, B. (2017). Climate change and the Polanyian counter-movement: Carbon markets or degrowth? *New Political Economy, 24*(1), 89–102.

Sullivan, S. (2013). Banking nature? The spectacular Financialisation of environmental conservation. *Antipode, 45*(1), 198–217.

Sullivan, S. (2017). On 'NaturalCapital', 'fairy Tales' and ideology. *Development and Change, 48*(2), 397–423.

Sundar, D., Mathiyazhagan, K., Agarwal, V., Janardhanan, M., & Appolloni, A. (2023). From linear to a circular economy in the e-waste management sector: Experience from the transition barriers in the United Kingdom. *Business Strategy and the Environment*, 1–17. https://doi.org/10.1002/bse.3365

Sustainable Markets Initiative. (2021). *Health systems task force*. https://www.sustainable-markets.org/taskforces/health-systems-taskforce/

Taylor, S. (2021). *The great digital divide: Mapping the UK's internet non-users*. https://www.rouge-media.com/blog/the-great-digital-divide-mapping-the-uks-internet-non-users/

The British Academy. (2022). *Lessons from the history of UK environmental policy*. https://www.thebritishacademy.ac.uk/publications/lessons-from-the-history-of-uk-environmental-policy/

Van Dijk, J., & Hacker, K. (2003). The digital divide as a complex and dynamic phenomenon. *The Information Society, 19*(4), 315–326.

Van Dijk, J. A. G. M. (2005). *The Deepening Divide*. SAGE.

Vecciolini, C. (2019). *Gearing up for digital transformation: How the UK digital strategy can underpin productivity growth*. Kings College.

Wilhelm, A. G. (2006). *Digital nation: Toward an inclusive information society*. MIT Press.

CHAPTER 9

# Digital-Environmental Habitus in England: Families as Vulnerable Subjects at Risk of Digital Poverty

## 9.1 Introduction

This chapter focuses on the interaction between the macro and individual determinants at a meso level by exploring how users absorb external inputs to develop their digital-environmental habitus. Reviewing the literature, this chapter shows that, beyond regulating the rising use of technology in daily life, which is also associated with a sharp rise in environmental and socioeconomic degradation, it is crucial to focus on the advantages and effects users expect from their digital technology experience.

It is based on a specific case study represented by England. The English case study is relevant due to both its historical environmental advocacy, as described in Chap. 8, and the high percentage of Internet users who possess basic skills and connectivity (Hutton, 2021). This might lead to the assumption that digital poverty is not a prevalent concern in England.

Chapter 3 introduced digital poverty as both an independent and intersectional concept. Chapter 8 identified some policies in the digital and environmental realm implemented in the UK by concluding that further steps are needed to tackle digital and environmental poverty as two faces of the same challenge at the macro and individual levels. Continuing along this path, this chapter starts by considering digital poverty independently and then explores its interconnections with the environmental dimension at the individual level. This helps identify some aspects that contribute to



M. L. Ruiu, M. Ragnedda, *Digital-Environmental Poverty*, Palgrave Studies in Digital Inequalities,
https://doi.org/10.1007/978-3-031-56184-9_9

increasing the risk of becoming digitally poor even in those contexts characterized by some degree of digital access and use. Nonetheless, our case focused on a highly connected society to shed light on those individuals who, despite their access to the Internet and their digital skills, might be living on the edge of digital poverty due to the digital acceleration of recent times. Therefore, the next paragraph focuses on those who might be out of the radar of digital inclusion programs. This shift is primarily due to the rapid digital advancements driven by the pandemic, compounded by the economic repercussions stemming from lockdowns, Brexit, and geopolitical complexities.

This chapter highlights that digital poverty might not be exclusively triggered by economic poverty (Barrantes, 2007), but it can become the cause of economic and additional vulnerabilities. Vulnerable citizens have been commonly identified as disadvantaged in economic terms, age, disabilities, ethnic minorities, and vulnerable conditions (such as being single parents). Given that, due to COVID-19, many societal functions have shifted online, showing how limitations in accessing and effectively using ICTs have put some digital users at risk of being left behind, we are specifically focusing on the pandemic's digital consequences for English families. By moving education, work, socialization, and almost all aspects of their daily life online, some families might have, for the very first time, gone through poor Internet experiences due to the limited number of digital devices available for both their children's education and their work, unreliable Internet connections, limited digital skills to support their children and conduct their work online.

Not only do these households experience digital poverty but their level of digital poverty intersects with their environmental poverty. For instance, energy poverty has affected specific demographics (including families with children, pensioners, and disabled individuals) who become trapped in a vicious cycle of financial, digital, and environmental vulnerability. The limited availability of resources makes it difficult to invest in technological innovations that, in turn, could help them reduce their environmental footprint. Low-income households tend to allocate a larger portion of their income to cover energy expenses compared to higher-income households (Owen & Barrett, 2020). This, paradoxically, further contributes to their environmental poverty because they cannot afford to adopt more eco-friendly practices or technologies. This chapter uses a study conducted by the authors to reflect on the interconnections between environmental poverty and digital poverty to see how these affect the benefits that users can get from digital technologies, and specifically from the Internet, while limiting the negative outcomes (also in environmental terms). By looking at the specific digital-environmental habitus of parents in England, this chapter suggests that parents' education levels, gender, age, and income are interconnected with their awareness about the environmentally friendly use of technologies.

The concept of digital-environmental habitus is applied to study how families in England reacted to such a digital acceleration and how digital use in their everyday lives reflects their environmental habitus. In such assimilation, the environmental predispositions of the habitus play a role in influencing how users behave online. The first section of this book has highlighted the need to reflect on the individual level of poverty in both environmental and digital terms. This chapter further reflects on how the individual dimension intersects the structural determinants navigating the circumstantial level through the digital-environmental habitus.

## 9.2 Digital Poverty Case Study: Families as Subjects at Risk of Digital Poverty in England

This paragraph refers to the application of the Digital Poverty Alliance (DPA) framework to a specific context represented by England. Ruiu et al. (2023b) revised the Inequality Framework developed by the DPA (2022) to explore vulnerabilities in England by using an online randomized stratified sample of parents aged between 20 and 55 with children at school. The study focused on England, given the high Internet penetration (Hutton, 2021) and the number of digital users who possess basic skills (National Institute of Economic and Social Research, 2020). This choice was motivated by the assumption that some users may be excluded from digital inclusion programs due to some degree of digital access and literacy, but they may be living on the verge of digital poverty as a result of the pandemic's drastic digital acceleration.

Ruiu et al. (2023) approach considers digital poverty to be multidimensional, arguing that access to the Internet (the first level of the digital divide) does not guarantee a beneficial experience in the absence of digital skills/competencies (the second level of the digital divide) to make the most of Internet use or to cope with its negative outcomes (third level of the digital divide). According to this approach, digital poverty is linked to the three levels of the digital divide (access-skills-benefits) and goes far beyond economic and technological factors (see Chap. 3 for a definition of the digital divide and its different levels). During the pandemic, data from Ofcom (2020) revealed that 2% of households with children in the UK had no access to the Internet at all. In 2021, 11% of parents with primary school-age children and 3% with secondary-school-age children at home stated that their children "rarely" or "never" had access to an appropriate device for their schooling needs (Ofcom, 2022). Despite increases in digital ownership and educational initiatives, digital inequalities remain a societal challenge to social inclusion. While technology has enabled numerous activities that would have otherwise stopped during the pandemic lockdowns (for example, some job tasks), users who struggled with broadband access before the pandemic were affected by this issue more severely, which resulted in increased exclusion from social and professional activities.

Those who are highly exposed to the risk of poverty are not only more likely to be digitally poor but also impoverished from an environmental perspective. Families with children, pensioners, and disabled citizens are at a higher probability of being in energy poverty (Snell et al., 2014; Liddell & Morris, 2010). Households who experience energy poverty are also at high risk of poverty rates and do not have the possibility of mitigating climate change, because they cannot afford technological innovation and reduce their environmental impact. At the same time, low-income households tend to spend more on energy than high-income families (for example, according to Owen & Barrett, 2020, the lowest-income households spend 10% of their income on heating and powering their homes, while the highest spend less than 1.5%), meaning that if they need to spend more for satisfying basic energy needs, they need to save money on other basic goods (and digital technologies might not be a priory for them) (Streimikiene et al., 2020). Furthermore, vulnerable families, given their limited access to digital resources and digital literacy, may encounter greater challenges when attempting to use the Internet to seek cost-effective options for saving on their electricity bills. As a result, they might end up paying higher bills. Therefore, this triggers a detrimental circle that can be difficult to break if multilevel policies are not implemented.

Using the DPF, Ruiu et al. (2023) investigated the relationship between circumstantial determinants and individual determinants of digital poverty as phenomenological, assuming that parents may act following their assimilation of external determinants and circumstances through their individual characteristics. This study supports how the structuration theory (see Chap. 3) can be used to interpret digital poverty by arguing that social structure and human agency are intertwined and absorbed by individuals who act according to their assimilation of external structures (Greenhalgh & Stones, 2010; Stones, 2005) and develop what Bourdieu defines as habitus. This implies that the interaction of personal, social, and digital technological fields cannot be reduced to a simple dichotomy of users versus non-users (Neves et al., 2018). Therefore, the outcomes of the interaction between habitus and field of action need to be investigated in terms of both intended and unintended outcomes, which can include change, elaboration, reproduction, and preservation of both the structure (Stones, 2005, p. 84) and habitus. This implies that structural conditions in the digital realm can create either opportunities or barriers to users' intentions. Not surprisingly, almost all individual determinants were found to be affected by economic circumstances, with higher income levels associated with more efficient devices and connectivity, access, capabilities, and motivations. According to this research (Ruiu et al., 2023), lower-income families, households with a single parent, and families with three or more children were significantly impacted by the digital acceleration imposed by the pandemic and have been pushed to the edge of digital poverty. Affordability and the requirement to share devices are a few examples of the kinds of obstacles that made it difficult for some residents to engage fully with the online community during the pandemic. Given that some of these households were considered to be digitally included before the epidemic from a policy point of view, this emphasizes the need for policymakers to reconsider obsolete elementary indicators of digital poverty. However, while financial poverty is generally recognized to be a leading cause of digital exclusion (Mubarak et al., 2020), other studies show that income levels are not the only cause of digital inequalities. Having children with disabilities and additional socio-demographic traits (such as age and education), parental status, lifestyles, and digital behaviors also predict digital poverty (Ruiu et al., 2023). The study suggests that digital poverty can be explained by several variables, which can play a role in increasing the chances of becoming digitally poor. The following paragraph further develops the interconnection between individual digital poverty and environmental digital poverty by exploring how digital and environmental dispositions can combine in the definition of digital-environmental habitus.

## 9.3 Digital-Environmental Habitus in England

Chapter 6 defined and described the techno-environmental habitus, and more specifically the digital-environmental habitus in its ICT's specific focus, as a useful tool for studying the layered nature of techno/digital users' predispositions toward the environment (Ruiu et al., 2021). These concepts are valuable tools also for helping define recommendations for policies that simultaneously consider technology/digital use and environmental protection. Habitus conceptually encapsulates individuals' interpretation of social reality (and consequent actions) thanks to a set of perceptive patterns and expectations (Piroddi, 2021). Such a Bourdesian concept also incorporates social inequalities because it is stratified due to cultural, economic, and social backgrounds (structural determinants) from childhood (Bourdieu, 1977). However, it is not a fixed force that governs individuals' actions, but it follows a continuous process of transformation according to its operational fields and its capacity to transfer the acquired knowledge and skills from one field to another (Abrahams & Ingram, 2013; Bourdieu, 2002; Di Maggio, 1979; Reay, 2004). Therefore, although the notion is continuously under scrutiny and subject to debate, habitus is generally understood as not entirely determined by external determinants or individual agency (Bourdieu, 1990; Crossley, 2002). It is a combination of subjective and collective dimensions (Bourdieu & Wacquant, 1992; Ingram, 2011; Schmidt, 1997) that plays a bridging function between individual actions and their context (field) (Brulle & Norgaard, 2019; Ruiu et al., 2021). Chapter 6 referred to the circumstances in which agents operate as shaping the field in which Bourdieu's habitus (Bourdieu, 1977, 1990; Bourdieu & Wacquant, 1992) can undergo transformation. At the same time, the agentic power of habitus can affect the field configuration in response to the prevailing relational configuration within the field (Singh, 2022). In this sense, the field can be interpreted as the operational space of social actors, a "space of social forces and struggles" (Bourdieu & Wacquant, 1992) where different social actors' interests intersect. This struggle gives rise to specific networks of relationships, depending on the ability of actors to shape the circumstances. However, this capability is either limited or facilitated by pre-existing rules and resources characterizing the social world. Costa et al. (2019) also identify the Internet as one of the key contributors to the rapid transformation of society, which in turn imposes a continuous redefinition of an individual's habitus according to changing conditions of action.

Ruiu et al. (2023a) define digital-environmental habitus as "the combination of structural determinants […] and the metabolized increased use of digital technologies in people's everyday life that also reflects individual environmental attitudes." The authors emphasize the need for studying digital and environmental habitus as part of the same social challenge, given the tremendous acceleration in the digitalization of society, especially due to the COVID-19 pandemic, and its impact on the environment (Elavarasan & Pugazhendhi, 2020). In this sense, the digital acceleration deriving from lockdowns and restrictions imposed by the health crisis represents a moment of dialectical confrontation between "old" and "new" routines, which can enhance an alteration of the habitus (Bourdieu, 1977, 1990; Bourdieu & Wacquant, 1992) thanks to the capacity of habitus to unconsciously metabolize new stimuli. Therefore, the pandemic has shown an urgency to create the circumstances for promoting eco-friendly uses of digital technologies and simultaneously is an opportunity to create the infrastructures for a new sustainable global culture (Galvani et al., 2020) that can sediment green uses of digital instruments as the new normal. This is in line with the need to meet the Sustainable Development Goals by 2030, for which it is necessary to readdress the digital revolution in a more sustainable way (Sparviero & Ragnedda, 2021). Creating the conditions for metabolizing a routinized use of digital technologies that supports sustainable development can contribute toward advancing a sustainable future by challenging digital-environmental poverty at the same time. Following Sparviero and Ragnedda (2021), digital sustainable development recognizes that the success of digital technological interventions in achieving sustainability goals is based not only on technology itself but also on the individual capacity to engage with digital technologies effectively. Digital sustainability seeks to align the use of digital technologies with the core values of equality, harmony, and self-determination (Sparviero, 2021). Incorporated into these three foundational objectives, Sparviero and Ragnedda introduce "individuals" as an essential component of the definition of digital sustainable development. This approach underlines the interplay between digital literacy and the overarching objectives of sustainable development, as the effective use of digital technologies to foster economic, social, or environmental benefits relies upon individuals' digital (and environmental) literacy. This further emphasizes the need for comprehensive consideration of economic, social, environmental, and individual variables in the pursuit of a sustainable digital future. However, how access to digital tools and the possession of digital competencies interact with environmental engagement has been scarcely considered by the sociological literature. The scientific debate mainly focuses on how news media can affect environmental behavior (Östman, 2014) and awareness (Arlt et al., 2011; Shah et al., 2021; Zhang & Skorics, 2018). However, research into the digital economy has identified digital skills as influential in affecting consumers' green choices (Gazzola et al., 2017). Moreover, Chap. 7 referred to studies in the economics and psychology field that have focused on understanding the unconscious mechanisms behind ICT's influence on users' choices (for example, in the case of nudging). However, these examples mainly aim to unmask hidden mechanisms of influence but do not consider the preference for sustainably using digital technologies as a reflexive choice. The next paragraph provides some useful insights to contextualize the case study presented in this section by referring to how families with children coped with the digital shift in England.

## 9.4 An Empirical Application of the Digital-Environmental Habitus

The study conducted by Ruiu et al. (2023a) uses an online survey with parents of children attending school. As shown in the previous paragraphs, the focus on families with children derived from a need to analyze the effects of moving multiple aspects of everyday life online due to the pandemic. However, many essential activities remained predominantly or more quickly accessible online (for example, see the increasing digitalization of the health system also continuing in the post-pandemic, Gov.UK, 2022). The pandemic has increased digital inequalities by further excluding certain groups who already were socially and economically vulnerable. For example, in 2022, 1 in 20 UK households had no access to the Internet and 2 million households struggled to afford an Internet connection (Good Things Foundation, 2022). Secondly, the focus on families derived from studies that showed how this group tends to be more sensitive to environmental problems (Fornwagner & Hauser, 2021). The survey involved digital ICT users to investigate how the daily use of digital technologies (based on certain environmental predispositions) interacts with existing socioeconomic backgrounds.

The study was based on the assumption that the COVID-19 crisis might have created some conditions, resulting from the combination of structural/contextual determinants (such as opportunities to work from home, restrictive rules, and existing individuals' socio, cultural, and economic backgrounds) and individual traits (predisposition toward the environment and the adoption of digital technologies) for different digital behavioral patterns to emerge, as well as new habitus configurations, which might be more difficult to change in a green direction once they are consolidated. Therefore, the digital-environmental habitus was used as a tool to facilitate the identification of different patterns resulting from how the combination of environmental predispositions and digital capability is applied in the digital field.

This study showed that the digital-environmental habitus of parents is nuanced depending on different factors related to both structural orientations defined by the rules of the field (promotion of certain digital technologies' use contextualized in increasing environmental degradation) and individuals' expectations to get benefits from their actions (Bourdieu, 2002). For example, the study identified two components, which were extracted through a factorial analysis and described the digital uses of parents in England (see Ruiu et al., 2023a for methodological notes). The first group represents those parents who use digital technologies with, in mind, the aim of protecting the environment. This category falls into what consumption studies identified as environmentally conscious (Brochado et al., 2017; Roberts, 1996), which explains consumers' purchasing decisions as based on knowing the negative impacts of certain behaviors on the environment.

The second group includes environmentally friendly digital uses if additional practical benefits exist (for example, unsubscribing from automatically generated newsletters).

The study emphasizes how the identification of nuances in digital environmental orientations is relevant for multilevel policy approaches that aim to tackle complex problems, such as in the case of digital and environmental poverty. However, the macro-structural level also needs to understand individual orientations before creating economic, societal, and political circumstances that favor the gain of environmental benefits in the digital arena. The COVID-19 pandemic might have created such a window to reflect on how the use of digital technologies can produce benefits in everyday life without compromising the environment. In the case of parents in England, education levels, gender, age, and income influence awareness about the green use of digital technologies, which should be considered when developing mixed policy and educational initiatives (Ruiu et al., 2023a).

Van der Linden (2015) groups the predictors of risk perceptions into the Climate Change Risk Perception Model, which is organized into four categories: cognitive, experiential, socio-cultural, and socio-demographic. Such an approach takes into account not only individual psychological barriers to the perception of the climate problem but also socio-cultural and experiential determinants that are independent of individuals' demographics, motivation, emotions, and knowledge. In this direction, the socio-cultural component also includes the social understanding of risk and social norms, which socially contextualizes individuals' values, knowledge, and perspectives. This also suggests that the structural, circumstantial, and individual determinants all play fundamental roles in shaping the digital-environmental habitus of users. Moreover, the study by Ruiu et al. (2023a) showed that parents might be concerned about the environment in general, but not necessarily about specific aspects such as climate change. The perception of environmental and climate change-related problems might be influenced by different variables, such as those examined by van der Linden (2015), including, for example, certain direct experiences of the consequences of environmental degradation. Even though some studies have not found the experience of extreme weather events/natural disasters significantly contributing to the perception of environmental problems (for example, Marquart-Pyatt et al., 2014), a consistent amount of studies has shown how the direct experience of these events increases the perception of risk related to climate change (for example, Akerlof et al., 2013; Demski et al., 2017; Frondel et al., 2017; Lujala et al., 2015). In some cases, the experiential component is context dependent, and a plausible explanation might be that in certain contexts the routinized experience of certain weather events can have made individuals more resilient and decrease their perception of risk (see, for example, the case of Australia, Bradley et al., 2020). However, reviewing the literature on the experience of nature and pro-environmental awareness and behavior, Rosa and Collado (2019) found that also the opposite is true. When direct contact with a non-degraded environment persists, the attachment to (and a sense of protection) the natural environment and green behaviors are more likely to be developed.

However, some studies on consumer behavior (Kumar et al., 2021; Muranko et al., 2018; Shamsi et al., 2022) showed that environmental consciousness influences intentions and the perception of risks (such as in the case of consumption practices). At the same time, perceived benefits play a role in mediating the interaction between environmental consciousness and purchase intention (Shamsi et al., 2022). Barbu et al. (2022)

summarize the factors debated in the literature that can influence consumers' behaviors into social norms, natural environmental orientation, the company's perceived green image, green product characteristics, perceived risks and inconveniences of buying green products, perceived benefits of buying green products, institutional trust, socio-demographic characteristics, and consumer confidence. This implies that when making a decision, individuals/consumers/users are likely to be influenced not only by their original taste and knowledge (which are shaped by specific structural settings that determine society's actions regarding pro-environmental issues, business, and individual responses) but also by the circumstances (which are influenced by both individual orientations and structural configurations) that may socially construct and contribute to influencing the individual perception of benefits and risks. This is further supported by findings that show how the adoption of producers' and retailers' green policies is fundamental to orienting consumers' purchase intentions (for example, through the use of labels and logos that inform decisions) (De Canio et al., 2021). Moreover, green purchase intention is shown to be mediated by additional stimuli, such as institutional trust (either in governments or businesses) (Ricci et al., 2018), government support (Al-Kumaim et al., 2022), and governmental and NGO initiatives (Kumar et al., 2019). Therefore, new circumstances might trigger certain reactions by the habitus, which can either reject the original habitus or adapt to the new techno-digital context in light of environmental consciousness.

However, policymaking oriented to digital and environmental poverty should consider that some individual characteristics that are traditionally associated with digital poverty (such as education, gender, age, and income) are also relevant in the classification of environmental awareness and engagement of digital users. However, the policy intervention that aims to increase access and connectivity, which addresses the first level of the digital divide, as in the case of most of the policy interventions described in Chap. 8, might not be sufficient to tackle both digital and environmental individual levels of poverty. Tackling digital poverty means simultaneously intervening on the three levels of the digital divide by providing the conditions for accessing, exploiting all the potential of the Internet, and benefiting from it, while coping with the negative outcomes. However, the environmental consciousness attached to this process (access-use-benefit) must also be taken into account, for example, acknowledging that some users with specific characteristics (for example, social network and the level of knowledge about/emotional attachment to environmental matters which in turn might depend on certain socio-demographic traits) might be motivated differently to use ICTs sustainably (for example, protection of the environment or material benefit). However, the environmental component is present at all levels of the digital divide/stratification. At the first level, it concerns the sustainability of the infrastructures/devices available to access the Internet (and their related costs). The second level includes the capabilities and skills to use digital technologies for specific (environmentally friendly) purposes. The third level concerns the benefits that users can get from the digital experience, and these also include environmental benefits. Moreover, the third level of the digital divide also encompasses the capacity to handle the negative outcomes arising from the inappropriate use of digital technologies. This aspect must be viewed from an individual perspective, involving, for instance, coping with cyberbullying, reducing social anxiety, safeguarding personal privacy, and preventing fraud. At the social level, it encompasses addressing issues like misinformation, disinformation, hate speech, and the decline in physical activities due to digital reliance that might increase the cost for the national health system. Additionally, on an environmental scale, dealing with negative outcomes involves efforts to reduce the digital carbon footprint resulting from digital activities that contribute to environmental degradation. Furthermore, it involves addressing the increasing electronic waste deriving from the rapid replacement of digital devices, which poses significant environmental hazards. Therefore, a comprehensive strategy involves not only bridging access disparities but also, and equally importantly, reducing inequalities in digital competencies and environmental understanding by promoting digital and environmental literacy. This encompasses equipping individuals with digital skills and cultivating the necessary attitudes to exploit the advantages of digital technologies while concurrently mitigating potential negative consequences that may affect individuals, society, and the environment due to their unsustainable usage.

## 9.5 Conclusions

This chapter used two studies conducted by Ruiu et al. (2023a) exploring digital poverty and the digital-environmental habitus of parents in England. In doing so, it aimed to shed light on the intricate interplay between digital technology use, environmental consciousness, and socio-economic backgrounds. The COVID-19 pandemic accelerated digitalization, making even more urgent the need for creating favorable circumstances for tackling digital-environmental poverty and equipping citizens with eco-friendly technology skills. At the same time, we observed how environmental poverty can trigger a vicious cycle that also increases digital poverty. This is because, on the one hand, digital technologies and skills might become secondary to other essential needs (such as heating); on the other hand, they might increase the energy demand, which also exacerbates the economic problem. Moreover, digital skills can advantage users in getting knowledge about the environment and limit their ecological footprint (not only in digital terms). This is especially true when considering the changing landscape of digital technologies that also include the invisible integration of tools like AI and IoT in users' everyday lives. These technological innovations simplify the use of technologies by eliminating the need for users to learn specific hardware and software skills. They also support the efficient and eco-friendly management of resources in households by connecting people, processes, data, and things in an "Internet of everything" (Banafa, 2016). However, this convenience and simplification require reducing users' autonomy. Consequently, users need to be equipped with critical skills to interpret the data and information provided by and to these systems. Furthermore, users need strategic skills to determine what data is collected, and how and why the AI or IoT system collects and shares this data across a complex network of information (Van Deursen & Mossberger, 2018). Finally, they also need to cultivate their environmental awareness skills, which enable them to understand the environmental implications of these technologies, in terms of both their impact and the broader ecological consequences. Users must be able to weigh the benefits and disadvantages for both themselves and the environment, making informed and sustainable decisions about their digital technology use. In light of these emerging challenges and opportunities, this chapter suggested including the digital-environmental habitus concept in both the theoretical and empirical toolkits. This concept allows us to capture the interconnections between digital and environmental dimensions while showing the importance of fostering environmental awareness and understanding alongside digital literacy skills. Recognizing the nuances in digital behaviors and their underlying motivations, whether driven by environmental consciousness or practical benefits, is a first step for formulating multilevel policies to address intricate challenges like digital and environmental poverty. The studies reviewed in this chapter showed some indicators of digital poverty, including education, gender, age, and income, also influence environmental awareness and engagement among digital users (in this case parents). Effective policymaking should not merely bridge disparities in digital access but also address inequalities in digital competencies, nurturing eco-friendly attitudes and skills to maximize the benefits of digital technologies while mitigating their negative impacts. This interpretation implies that the skill to manage the adverse effects of digital uses, as suggested by the third level of the digital divide, should also include the ability to mitigate the degradation of the environment resulting from digital technology behavior.

Without the implementation of measures that consider the intersections of digital, environmental, and social inequalities, the detrimental cycles triggered by the intersecting dimensions of poverty may persist. The COVID-19 pandemic represents a dramatic shift that necessitates the immediate implementation of interventions that address environmental, socioeconomic, and digital inequalities simultaneously to narrow the gap.

The next chapter presents both the positives and negatives of existing practices at each level of the DPF presented throughout the book. It will draw some recommendations that might be useful to develop interventions aimed at tackling digital-environmental poverty as two dimensions of the same social challenge.

## References

Abrahams, J., & Ingram, N. (2013). The chameleon habitus: Exploring local students' negotiations of multiple fields. *Sociological Research Online, 18*(4), 21–34.

Akerlof, K., Maibach, E. W., Fitzgerald, D., Cedeno, A. Y., & Neuman, A. (2013). Do people "personally experience" global warming, and if so how, and does it matter? *Global Environmental Change, 23*, 81–91.

Al-Kumaim, N. H., Shabbir, M. S., Alfarisi, S., Hassan, S. H., Alhazmi, A. K., Hishan, S. S., & Al-Good Things Foundation. (2022). *Digital national, UK.* https://www.goodthingsfoundation.org/insights/building-a-digital-nation/

Arlt, D., Hoppe, I., & Wolling, J. (2011). Climate change and media usage: Effects on problem awareness and behavioural intentions. *International Communication Gazzette, 73*(1–2), 45–63.

Banafa, A. (2016). The internet of everything (IOE). *Open Mind.* https://www.bbvaopenmind.com/en/technology/digital-world/the-internet-of-everything-ioe/

Barbu, A., Catană, Ș.-A., Deselnicu, D. C., Cioca, L.-I., & Ioanid, A. (2022). Factors influencing consumer behaviour toward green products: A systematic literature review. *International Journal of Environmental Research and Public Health, 19*, 16568. https://doi.org/10.3390/ijerph192416568

Barrantes, R. (2007). Analysis of ICT demand: What is digital poverty and how to measure it? In H. Glaperin & J. Mariscal (Eds.), *Digital poverty: Latin American and Caribbean perspectives* (pp. 29–54). Practical Action Publishing.

Bourdieu, P. (1977). *Outline of a theory of practice*. Cambridge University Press.

Bourdieu, P. (1990). *The logic of practice. Stanford*. Stanford University Press.

Bourdieu, P. (2002). Habitus. In J. Hillier & E. Rooksby (Eds.), *Habitus: A sense of place* (pp. 27–34). Ashgate.

Bourdieu, P., & Wacquant, L. (1992). *An invitation to reflexive sociology*. University of Chicago Press.

Bradley, G. L., Babutsidze, Z., Chai, A., & Reser, J. P. (2020). The role of climate change risk perception, response efficacy, and psychological adaptation in pro-environmental behaviour: A two-nation study. *Journal of Environmental Psychology, 68*, 101410. https://doi.org/10.1016/j.jenvp.2020.101410

Brochado, A., Teiga, N., & Oliveira-Brochado, F. (2017). The ecological conscious consumer behaviour: Are the activists different? *International Journal of Consumption Studies, 41*, 138–146.

Brulle, R. J., & Norgaard, K. M. (2019). Avoiding cultural trauma: Climate change and social inertia. *Environmental Politics, 28*(5), 886–908.

Costa, C., Burke, B., & Murphy, M. (2019). Capturing habitus: Theory, method and reflexivity. *International Journal of Research & Method in Education, 42*(1), 19–32.

Crossley, N. (2002). *Making sense of social movements*. Open University Press.

De Canio, F., Martinelli, E., & Endrighi, E. (2021). Enhancing consumers' pro-environmental purchase intentions: The moderating role of environmental concern. *International Journal of Retail & Distribution Management, 49*(9), 1312–1329.

Demski, C., Capstick, S., Pidgeon, N., Sposato, R. G., & Spence, A. (2017). Experience of extreme weather affects climate change mitigation and adaptation responses. *Climatic Change, 140*, 149–164.

Di Maggio, P. (1979). Review essay on Pierre Bourdieu. *American Journal of Sociology, 84*, 1460–1474.

Digital Poverty Alliance. (2022). *How we define digital poverty & inequality*. https://digitalpovertyalliance.org/ukdigital-poverty-evidence-review-2022/introduction-myths-and-shifts/

Elavarasan, R. M., & Pugazhendhi, R. (2020). Restructured society and environment: A review on potential technological strategies to control the COVID-19 pandemic. *Science of the Total Environment, 725*, 138858.

Fornwagner, H., & Hauser, O. P. (2021). Climate action for (my) children. *Environmental and Resource Economics, 81*, 95–130.

Frondel, F., Simora, M., & Sommer, S. (2017). Risk perception of climate change: Empirical evidence from Germany. *Ecological Economics, 137*, 173–183.

Galvani, A., Lew, A. A., & Perez, M. S. (2020). COVID-19 is expanding global consciousness and the sustainability of travel and tourism. *Tourism Geographies, 22*(3), 567–576.

Gazzola, P., Pavione, E., & Pezzetti, R. (2017). Sustainable consumption in the luxury industry: Towards a new paradigm in China's high-end demand. *Proceedings of the 2nd Czech-China scientific conference 2016*. https://www.intechopen.com/chapters/53515

Good Things Foundation (2022). Digital National, UK. https://www.goodthingsfoundation.org/insights/building-adigital-nation/

Gov.UK. (2022). *A plan for digital health and social care*. https://www.gov.uk/government/publications/a-plan-for-digital-health-and-social-care/a-plan-for-digital-health-and-social-care

Greenhalgh, T., & Stones, R. (2010). Theorising big IT programmes in healthcare: Strong structuration theory meets actor-network theory. *Social Science & Medicine, 70*(9), 1285–1294.

Hutton, G. (2021). *Tackling the digital divide*. UK Parliament. https://commonslibrary.parliament.uk/research-briefings/cdp-2021-0175/

Ingram, N. (2011). Within school and beyond the gate: The complexities of being educationally successful and working class. *Sociology, 45*(2), 287–302.

Kumar, A., Prakash, G., & Kumar, G. (2021). Does environmentally responsible purchase intention matter for consumers? A predictive sustainable model developed through an empirical study. *Journal of Retailing and Consumer Services, 58*. https://doi.org/10.1016/j.jretconser.2020.102270

Kumar, R., Saha, R., Sekar, P. C., & Dahiya, R. (2019). Examining the role of external factors in influencing green behaviour among young Indian consumers. *Young Consumers, 20*(4), 380–398.

Liddell, C., & Morris, C. (2010). Fuel poverty and human health: A review of recent evidence. *Energy Policy, 38*(6), 2987–2997.

Lujala, P., Lein, H., & Rød, J. K. (2015). Climate change, natural hazards, and risk perception: The role of proximity and personal experience. *Local Environment, 20*, 489–509.

Marquart-Pyatt, S. T., McCright, A. M., Dietz, T., & Dunlap, R. E. (2014). Politics eclipses climate extremes for climate change perceptions. *Global Environmental Change, 29*, 246–257.

Mubarak, F., Sumi, R., & Kantola, S. P. (2020). Confirming the links between socio-economic variables and digitalization worldwide: The unsettled debate on digital divide. *Journal of Information, Communication and Ethics in Society, 18*(3), 415–430.

Muranko, Z., Andrews, D., Newton, E. J., Chaer, I., & Proudman, P. (2018). The pro-circular change model (P-CCM): Proposing a framework facilitating

behavioural change towards a circular economy. *Resources, Conservation and Recycling, 135*, 132–140.
National Institute of Economic and Social Research. (2020). *Failure to tackle digital skills divide will worsen regional inequality*. https://www.niesr.ac.uk/blog/failure-tackle-digitalskills-divide-will-worsen-regional-inequality
Neves, B. B., Waycott, J., & Malta, S. (2018). Old and afraid of new communication technologies? Reconceptualising and contesting the 'age-based digital divide'. *Journal of Sociology, 54*(2), 236–248.
Ofcom. (2020). *Technology tracker 2020*. https://www.ofcom.org.uk/__data/assets/pdf_file/0037/194878/technology-tracker-2020-uk-dataTables.pdf
Ofcom. (2022). *Online nation 2022*. https://www.ofcom.org.uk/__data/assets/pdf_file/0023/238361/online-nation-2022-report.pdf
Östman, J. (2014). The influence of media use on environmental engagement: A political socialization approach. *Environmental Communication A Journal of Nature and Culture, 8*(1), 92–109.
Owen, A., & Barrett, J. (2020). Reducing inequality resulting from UK low-carbon policy. *Climate Policy, 20*(10), 1193–1208.
Piroddi, C. (2021). Hope, habitus and social recognition: A Bourdieusian proposal. *The Theory of Social Behaviour, 51*(4), 619–635.
Reay, D. (2004). 'It's all becoming a habitus'. Beyond the habitual use of habitus in educational research. *British Journal of Sociology of Education, 25*(4), 431–444.
Ricci, E. C., Banterle, A., & Stranieri, S. (2018). Trust to go green: An exploration of consumer intentions for eco-friendly convenience. *Food. Ecol. Econ., 148*, 54–65.
Roberts, J. A. (1996). Green consumers in the 1990s: Profile and implications for advertising. *Journal of Business Research, 36*, 217–231.
Rosa, C. D., & Collado, S. (2019). Experiences in nature and environmental attitudes and Behaviours: Setting the ground for future research. *Frontiers in Psychology, 10*, 763. https://doi.org/10.3389/fpsyg.2019.00763
Ruiu, M. L., Ragnedda, M., Addeo, F., & Ruiu, G. (2023b). Investigating how the interaction between individual and circumstantial determinants influence the emergence of digital poverty: A post-pandemic survey among families with children in England. *Information, Communication & Society*. https://doi.org/10.1080/1369118X.2023.2166359
Ruiu, M. L., Ruiu, G., & Ragnedda, M. (2021). Conceptualizing techno-environmental habitus. *First Monday, 26*(11). https://doi.org/10.5210/fm.v26i11.12353
Ruiu, M. L., Ruiu, G., & Ragnedda, M. (2023a). Digital–environmental habitus of families in England in times of pandemic. *New Media & Society, 0*(0). https://doi.org/10.1177/14614448221146716
Schmidt, M. (1997). Habitus revisited. *The American Behavioural Scientist, 40*(4), 444–453.

Shah, Z., Wei, L., & Ghani, U. (2021). The use of social networking sites and pro-environmental behaviours: A mediation and moderation model. *International Journal of Environmental Research and Public Health, 18*(4), 1085.

Shamsi, M. A., Chaudhary, A., Anwar, I., Dasgupta, R., & Sharma, S. (2022). Nexus between environmental consciousness and consumers' purchase intention toward circular textile products in India: A moderated-mediation approach. *Sustainability, 14*, 12953. https://doi.org/10.3390/su142012953

Singh, S. (2022). Can habitus explain individual particularities? Critically appreciating the operationalization of relational logic in field theory. *Sociological Theory, 40*(1), 28–50.

Snell, C. J., Bevan, M. A., & Thomson, H. R. (2014). *Fuel poverty and disabled people: The impact of policy change*. Research Report. Centre for Housing Policy, University of York.

Sparviero, S. (2021). The contribution of global media to ethical capitalism. In J. Dal Yong (Ed.), *The Routledge handbook of digital media and globalization* (pp. 55–65). Routledge.

Sparviero, S., & Ragnedda, M. (2021). Towards digital sustainability: The long journey to the sustainable development goals 2030. *Digital Policy, Regulation and Governance, 23*(3), 216–228.

Stones, R. (2005). *Old and afraid of new communication technologies? Reconceptualizing and contesting the 'age-based digital divide' structuration theory*. Palgrave.

Streimikiene, D., Lekavičius, V., Baležentis, T., Kyriakopoulos, G. L., & Abrhám, J. (2020). Climate change mitigation policies targeting households and addressing energy poverty in European Union. *Energies, 13*(13), 3389. https://doi.org/10.3390/en13133389

van der Linden, S. (2015). The social-psychological determinants of climate change risk perceptions: Towards a comprehensive model. *Journal of Environmental Psychology, 41*, 112–124.

Van Deursen, A. J. A. M., & Mossberger, K. (2018). Any thing for anyone? A new digital divide in internet-of-things skills. *Policy and Internet, 10*(2), 122–140.

Zhang, N., & Skorics, M. M. (2018). Media use and environmental engagement: Examining differential gains from news media and social media. *International Journal of Communication, 12*. https://ijoc.org/index.php/ijoc/article/view/7650

CHAPTER 10

# Developing Digital-Environmental Sustainability

## 10.1 Introduction

This chapter reflects on the salient aspects that emerged throughout the analysis of both digital and environmental policy frameworks, as well as existing practices, to provide some recommendations for interventions aimed at addressing digital-environmental poverty as dimensions of the same social challenge. In so doing, it contextualizes policies and examples proposed throughout the book, encompassing models from Western and non-Western countries. The review aligns with the Action Plan developed by the Coalition for Digital Environmental Sustainability—CODES ("Sustainable Planet in the Digital Age," CODES, 2022). This plan offers a framework for advancing digital sustainability through collaborative efforts between private and public sectors. Moreover, in light of the empirical study and the practices presented in the previous chapters, it provides some recommendations toward mixed approaches based on interpreting poverty as multidimensional (including its monetary, social, digital, and environmental dimensions).

Access to tools and the ability to use them beneficially for both users and society (including the natural environment) are the bases of sustainable principles. This implies that policies should address the social inequality and fragmentation brought on by the use of technology to empower



M. L. Ruiu, M. Ragnedda, *Digital-Environmental Poverty*, Palgrave Studies in Digital Inequalities,
https://doi.org/10.1007/978-3-031-56184-9_10

people to serve themselves. This chapter investigates the UK policy landscape described in the previous section in light of the world's digital competitiveness trying to understand what can be learned from the UK approach to digital poverty in both positive and negative terms. This helps us understand why the UK lost positions in the G20 digital ranking (European Center for Digital Competitiveness, 2021). This chapter also considers the private/public collaboration best practices, as described in Chap. 8, to explore the value of implementing mixed approaches that simultaneously address environmental and digital poverty. It suggests that the UK government—although this applies to almost all governments and states worldwide—might seek collaboration with such private actors, with the support of scientific committees to simultaneously tackle digital and environmental risks. These considerations are then compared and contrasted with the eco-civilization example introduced in Chap. 7. Analyzing the policy landscape in the UK in both environmental and digital terms, the public-private partnership emerged to be a distinctive element for tackling digital poverty at all levels but also environmental-related concerns. At the same time, it examines the eco-civilization project in China, which draws upon the principle of "Unity of Man and Nature" and the collaboration between the research community, the private sector, nonprofit organizations, and the wider public (Huang & Westman, 2021). The private-public cooperation, in this case, results from a combination of government-driven policies, supported by a disciplinary and control apparatus, and neoliberal principles (Wang et al., 2022). Despite criticalities in terms of adopting authoritarian environmentalism, the Chinese example has shown the centrality of the government in structuring the environmental orientation of society. However, it will emphasize that while a public-private partnership may be necessary under certain conditions to address digital-environmental poverty on all fronts, governments and policymakers must support and guide the process to ensure that digitalization is accompanied by both socioeconomic benefits for the entire population and environmental benefits on a global scale.

## 10.2 Toward Digital-Environmental Sustainability

To explore the efficacy of the private-public approach and the case studies presented in the previous chapters, we use the Action Plan developed by the CODES (2022) that identifies three shifts and 18 Strategic Priorities to Achieve a Sustainable Planet in the Digital Age between 2022 and

2025. CODES is a global alliance of governments, companies, and civil society launched in March 2021 by UNEP, UNDP, the International Science Council, the German Environment Agency, the Kenyan Ministry of Environment and Forestry, Future Earth, and Sustainability in the Digital Age. It aims to enhance digital transformation for sustainability and climate action (UNEP, 2021), and advance digital, environmental, and social sustainability while mitigating potential negatives and unintended consequences.

We use this plan, developed with multistakeholder participation, to show how mixed policies at the structural-regulative level might be potentially effective in combating digital-socio-environmental poverty by fostering the emergence of circumstances that promote individual conversion to sustainable ICT use. The three shifts proposed by the action plan aim to change the structural interrelationship between digital and environmental sustainability. At the same time, they can function at the individual, meso, and macro levels, thanks to policy interventions that create favorable conditions for both individuals and businesses to adopt and sustain eco-friendly digital practices, all while preventing exclusion from the digital realm and mitigating negative environmental impacts.

The three shifts are strongly interconnected: the first aims to create the conditions for digital, social, and environmental alignment through dialogue, understanding, and action; the second is associated with preventing negative impacts and socio-digital-environmental inequalities; the third is concerned with enhancing innovation (see Table 10.1).

Shift 1 relates to "Enable Alignment" and includes six enablers (Connecting Communities and Transformations, Developing Digital Competencies, Harnessing Science and Systems Thinking, Advancing Multilateral Action, Building Pioneering Coalitions, and Adopting Norms and Standards). This shift represents the first step necessary to merge digital and sustainable goals at the structural level. This, in turn, facilitates the creation of conditions favorable for the participation of multiple actors from academia, organizations, and civil society to participate in the transformation process.

Connecting Communities and Transformation refers to the need to start an integrated dialogue between the digital and sustainability communities, which need to be incentivized by national and international policy agendas and organizations, research and education programs, technology development, and civil society. Therefore, this first pillar aims to create the foundations for participative governance by creating the

**Table 10.1** Adapted from the Action Plan developed by the CODES (2022)

| *Transversal principles* | *Shifts* | *Guiding principle* | *Levels of interaction* | *Enablers* |
|---|---|---|---|---|
| 1) Activating multistakeholder partnerships at multiple levels (see Sect. 10.5.1) | **Shift 1**: Enable Alignment<br>**General aim**: Aligning vision, values, and objectives of the digital age with sustainable development | Collaborative alignment across private/public actors | Digital and sustainable goals alignment at the structural level to create the conditions for digital, social, and environmental alignment through dialogue, understanding, and action | 1) Connecting Communities and Transformations<br>2) Developing Digital Competencies<br>3) Harnessing Science and Systems Thinking<br>4) Advancing Multilateral Action<br>5) Building Pioneering Coalitions<br>6) Adopting Norms and Standards |
| 2) Intersecting policies, standards, regulations, infrastructure, and governance frameworks to catalyze digital sustainability (see Sect. 10.5.2) | **Shift 2**: Mitigate Negative Impacts<br>**General aim**: Ensuring sustainable digitalization to mitigate negative environmental and social impact | Social, digital, and environmental interplay | Enhancement of digitalization as responsible, ethical, equal, and sustainable at the circumstantial level to prevent negative impacts and socio-digital-environmental inequalities at both the individual and societal levels | 1) Reducing Energy and Emissions<br>2) Minimizing Material Base<br>3) Addressing Consumption Drivers<br>4) Mitigating Misinformation<br>5) Closing the Digital Divide<br>6) Preventing Rights Violations |
| 3) Triggering change at the system level or sector level and different scales (from local to global) (see Sect. 10.5.3) | **Shift 3**: Accelerate Innovation<br>**General aim**: Directing innovation efforts toward digitalization for sustainability | Cooperative and collaborative approach to drive technological innovation in line with sustainability goals | Collaborative approach to redirect the innovative potential of digital technologies toward achieving sustainability goals at all levels | 1) Planetary Digital Twin<br>2) Sustainable Circular Economy<br>3) Sustainable Consumption<br>4) Knowledge Commons<br>5) Governance Breakthroughs<br>6) Green, Digital, and Just Transition |

conditions for a plurality of actors to contribute to the decision-making process as both individuals and collectivity.

The second enabler, Developing Digital Competencies, refers to the public sector and policymakers that need to understand both the environmental opportunities and risks of digital transformation. At the same time, businesses and ICT-related scientists need to know how their products and services impact the real world due to the activation of certain social responses (for example, in terms of consumption practices). Digital and sustainability literacy has been suggested to be essential to achieving this goal. This step is needed to promote literacy and create the circumstances for knowledge to circulate and be available for private and public agents.

This is also connected to the third enabler, Harnessing Science and Systems Thinking, which calls for a science-based and holistic approach to understanding how digital technologies impact key economic, social, and environmental systems and how they can be aligned toward sustainability outcomes.

In addition to dialogue, practical, policy, and scientific knowledge, this shift also includes collaborative action. In this direction, the fourth enabler refers to Advancing Multilateral Action by specifically emphasizing the value of cooperation and co-creation between governments, the private sector, and civil society. Furthermore, Building Pioneering Coalitions reinforces more strongly the need for formalizing coalitions between governments, academia, private sector actors, and civil society organizations.

Finally, Norms and Global Standards are needed to standardize how digital impacts are measured and norms can be implemented to achieve certain global goals.

While shift 1 is more concerned with aligning the structural, circumstantial, and individual determinants toward digital and environmental sustainability, shift 2 focuses on how such alignment can help generate circumstances that mitigate the negative impacts and identifies six priorities (Reducing Energy and Emissions, Minimizing Material Base, Addressing Consumption Drivers, Mitigating Misinformation, Closing the Digital Divide, and Preventing Rights Violations) to ensure that the circumstances created favor digitalization as responsible, ethical, equal, and sustainable.

The first negative impact is connected to Reducing Energy and Emissions, which refers to setting certain standards to measure and reduce the energy consumption of ICTs, particularly in light of the rise of new instruments (for example, the high energy demand required by cryptocurrency mining).

A second negative impact can be prevented by Minimizing the Material Base, which refers to the need to reduce material use (for example, extraction of minerals) and waste linked to digitalization.

Moreover, negative impacts can be associated with pervasive techniques of digital marketing that can cause overconsumption. In this direction, the third pillar refers to Addressing (and regulating) Consumption Drivers that accelerate the production and consumption of products and services through, for example, product customization, influencer endorsements, personalized advertising, digital nudging, and 24/7 opportunities for purchasing.

Further emphasizing a need for information and knowledge circulation already included in shift 1, the fourth pillar of shift 2 refers to Mitigating Misinformation as a priority to prevent the damage caused by misinformation and disinformation about sustainability. It stresses the importance of making trusted sources more visible and flagging/removing misinfor mation-containing articles.

The two final priorities of shift 2 more strongly refer to the need for creating structural conditions that prevent social and digital exclusion due to discriminatory circumstances that can create unbalances. The fifth enabler refers to Closing the Digital Divide in an environmentally and socially sustainable manner, which must be reached through both digital infrastructures and digital literacy building.

Finally, the sixth pillar refers to Preventing Rights Violations due to potential abuses connected to land use conflicts in mining minerals needed to power a green digital future; digital surveillance of and against environmental and human rights defenders, whistleblowers, journalists, and political dissidents; violations of online data privacy by private and public actors.

Shift 3 concerns Accelerating Innovation through six enablers (Planetary Digital Twin, Sustainable Circular Economy, Sustainable Consumption, Knowledge Commons, Governance Breakthroughs, and Green, Digital, and Just Transition) that aim to redirect the innovative potential of digital technologies toward achieving sustainability goals. It aligns structural, circumstantial, and individual components of accelerating innovation with the guiding principle of digital-environmental sustainability.

The first enabler is based on the understanding of the digital and environmental realms as twins. Building Planetary Digital Twin prioritizes investments in innovations for planetary health and interactions with economic and social systems. For instance, digital innovations can facilitate automated monitoring of risks, and ecosystem services, as well as support decision-making for achieving sustainable goals. This priority is strongly connected to the previous shifts by also emphasizing the need to support and integrate citizen participation in the process (and create the conditions for equal participation) by validating their contributions and observations into the digital twin ecosystems.

Catalyzing Sustainable Circular Economy prioritizes innovations toward advancing decarbonization, dematerialization, detoxification, and circularity throughout production processes. It is suggested that digital product passports and eco-labels to hold sustainability information on their lifecycle can inform about the product's origin, composition, environmental and carbon performance, and repair and dismantling possibilities. This can be connected to the previous shift needed to avoid the negative impact on the environment (for example, due to high energy demand) and make information available and transparent for citizens.

In a similar direction, Empowering Sustainable Consumption refers to innovations that create circumstances that empower sustainable lifestyles, behaviors, and collaboration. In this category, both gaming and ethical nudging are included as potential tools for creating favorable conditions for sustainable consumption.

Innovations also require the promotion of active citizen participation through two additional pillars related to knowledge and participatory governance. Creating Knowledge Commons prioritizes digital tools that facilitate inclusive and cooperative forms of knowledge production (for example, citizen and open science). This enabler sets the conditions to facilitate knowledge sharing for educational, scientific, or practical purposes. In this direction, Heidel et al. (2022) suggest that knowledge commons can help connect the climate justice and digital rights movements by addressing misinformation around climate change on social media, understanding how intellectual property can limit knowledge about the climate crisis, building new narratives for a more just, inclusive, and equitable Internet, using a climate lens to analyze digital rights issues (such as privacy, surveillance, or artificial intelligence), and understanding how climate change might affect digital rights. However, this also requires setting standards for managing data, public funding and data for open science, research and knowledge, open science standards, investments in digital literacy (aimed at making vulnerable groups heard), education, and digital knowledge.

Supporting Governance Breakthroughs is built-in networked, agile, and collaborative governance that uses digital tools to achieve sustainability outcomes and regulatory compliance. It is suggested that AI can help improve the availability of real-time information, evaluate scenarios, and consider multiple impacts related to different realms. This in turn can facilitate public participation in decision-making as well as crowdsourcing governance priorities and solutions from citizens and citizen science.

Finally, Realizing Green, Digital, Just Transition prioritizes the transition to a green, digital, and just economy for sustainable development in multiple sectors of society and is facilitated by the collaboration between local businesses, entrepreneurs, and academia.

The plan conceptualizes the process of digitalization as intertwined with social and environmental determinants and suggests that structural changes are needed to create favorable circumstances for individuals and businesses to be engaged and play an active role in tackling digital-environmental challenges. Collective and collaborative action, inclusiveness, and globally representative leadership are identified as essential to shaping the digitalization process sustainably and equitably (CODES, 2022).

Analyzing the foundation principles of the three macro shifts included in the CODES Action Plan to enhance digital-environmental sustainability at multiple levels could be useful to identify some valuable contributions of the approaches presented in this book, as well as some weaknesses in creating structural conditions that encourage the rise of circumstances that are favorable for digital-environmental sustainability and digital poverty reduction. The next paragraphs will use the principles guiding the shifts of the Action Plan developed by CODES (2022) to better frame the strengths and weaknesses of diverse types of private-public relationships analyzed throughout the book.

## 10.3 Using the CODES Guiding Principles to Interpret the Public-Private Partnerships in the UK

This paragraph uses the principles guiding the three shifts of the CODES Action Plan to interpret the strengths and weaknesses of the UK private-public relationships. Such a plan emphasizes the value of multistakeholder participation for developing policies aimed at fighting digital and environmental challenges simultaneously by creating certain conditions that align structural and individual levels toward the development and use of digital technologies in a sustainable manner. The previous paragraph also highlighted the importance of developing both private and public consciousness toward a digital sustainable orientation, which simultaneously takes into account the need for digital inclusion against all levels of the digital divide/stratification.

The first shift toward digital-environmental sustainability and mitigation of digital-environmental poverty is connected to creating the conditions for digital, social, and environmental alignment through several enablers that aim to encode environmental and social sustainability in the digital revolution. Such an alignment comes through participatory governance, interdisciplinary literacy, recognition of overlapping between economic, social, and environmental systems, multilevel collaboration and multilateral action, and definition of global standards.

Following its guiding principle, this shift conceptualizes digital-environmental sustainability as based on a multilevel platform of dialogue and collaboration between local and international bodies and institutions, as well as private and public agents, to enhance collaborative governance. This is observable, to some degree, in the UK approach in the context of overlapping between digital and environmental policies. One of the criticalities in the UK policy landscape pertains to the lack of anticipation of the issues arising from the digitalization of society. For instance, the focus has been on addressing the first level of the digital divide since the 1990s when the digital divide began to emerge in the scientific debate as a binary division between people who had access to ICTs and those who did not (Dewan & Riggins, 2005). The foundation of this approach lies in increasing access and connectivity for citizens, to reduce the digital gap in accessing ICTs. While such an approach to universal access has contributed toward reducing the first level of the digital divide, the digital acceleration due to the pandemic has shown that during lockdowns 1 in 20 citizens was still "hardly digitally excluded." Therefore, they have no independent access to the Internet and are still vulnerable to this first level of the digital divide (Abey, 2022; Watts, 2020). However, as the understanding of the digital divide evolved beyond the simple division between the "have and have-not" (Leavitt, 2002) and emphasized the importance of skills and literacy, autonomy in online navigating, and the quality of connectivity (DiMaggio et al., 2004; Hargittai, 2002), the UK policy approach to addressing inequalities has transitioned toward a more decentralized approach with emphasis on fostering private-public partnerships (DCMS, 2022). The previous chapter identified some macro areas in which such overlapping happened in moving online physical functions and services where possible, enhancing the efficiency of ICTs and managing their impact on pollution and waste, and favoring the private-public dialogue. Developing overlapping by adopting a collaborative approach is the first step, identified by the CODES Action Plan, in connecting communities and transformations to combat poverty. In this direction, the CODES Action Plan encourages developing interdisciplinary digital sustainability skill sets in both public and private sectors to understand both the environmental opportunities and risks of digital in order to produce a more comprehensive vision that interprets social, digital, and environmental poverty as interconnected dimensions.

The UK Digital Strategy has increasingly concentrated on developing skill sets among the government and businesses and, to a lesser extent, considered the role of citizens. Moreover, such an approach has not addressed how the interplay between environmental and digital factors can widen social inequalities. Therefore, even though there is increasing recognition of the overlapping between the digital and environmental fields, interventions in tackling both issues as two faces of poverty at the macro-structural level are still fragmented, and both concepts of environmental and digital poverty are rarely mentioned in the regulatory framework. The participatory approaches described by the CODES framework also include citizens' participation and education, which is an area that could be further developed in the UK private-public digital-environmental approach, because it's still screwed toward market-led solutions. However, considering the e-participation Index developed by the UN (2022), which includes an informative level (e-information availability), citizens' inputs to governments (e-consultation), and opportunities to contribute to the policy-making process (e-decision-making), the UK ranks sixth among the 193 UN member states. However, as highlighted by Rawat and Morris (2022), the mere provision of e-infrastructure and channels to access and participate in public matters does not necessarily translate into e-participation. By contrast, in addition to providing digital and environmental literacy, governments also need to encourage the public to provide inputs into policymaking by creating a culture of participation and showing how their voices are heard. Moreover, as a member of the Open Government Partnership (an international initiative aimed at promoting transparency, empowering citizens, fighting corruption, and harnessing new technologies to strengthen governance) (OGP, 2023) since 2011, every two years the UK government must develop an open national action plan (Gov.UK, 2022), in collaboration with civil society. However, the fifth plan (2021–2023) saw the rise of controversies in how civil society was limitedly involved in its development and, especially, in further amendments. Moreover, even though the government and civil society participants agreed about the inclusion of themes related to the environment (including natural resources and climate change) at a stakeholder meeting in December 2020, these themes were later excluded because "the working groups could not agree on a set of draft activities that the Cabinet Office considered workable" (OGP, 2022).

The guiding principles of Shift 2 and Shift 3 of the CODES Action Plan are strongly interconnected in terms of enhancing innovation (shift 3) while limiting the negative consequences of such acceleration (shift 2). Shift 2 focuses on creating circumstances that mitigate the negative impacts of digital transformation and enhance digitalization as responsible, ethical, equal, and sustainable. Reducing Energy and Emissions of ICTs as well as material use and waste linked to digitalization, reducing overconsumption, mitigating misinformation and disinformation about sustainability while closing the digital divide in an environmentally and socially sustainable manner, and preventing rights violations due to potential abuses connected to land use conflicts are all fundamental enablers of such conditions.

Shift 3 includes accelerating innovation through the cooperation of governments, development partners, the private sector, informal economy actors, local communities, and academia to drive the innovative character of digital technologies toward achieving sustainability goals.

Using the neoliberal approach described when referring to the UK example, it is possible to identify several steps in improving digital infrastructures, accelerating innovation (for example, developing a circular economy and digital twins), as well as providing online media and digital literacy strategies. In the direction of generating innovation for improving efficiency, not only in the management of digital and electronic waste, as highlighted in Chap. 8, the UK government committed to the UK's National Digital Twin Programme aimed at developing a digital replica of the built environment (such as buildings, roads, railways, energy systems, and water networks) and interconnected projects to create collaboration between entrepreneurs, academics, and policymakers, at multiple levels. The program is still under development and definition, but developing digital twins requires a massive amount of data that in turn necessitates time (for example, for machine learning not necessarily aligned to socio-environmental evolution) and technological advances (for example, for developing nanotechnologies capable of recording the information needed). This is directly connected to the potential negative impact that a biased replica of already existing unbalances in the socio-environmental system could reproduce and its discriminatory effects. The concept of optimization, which is the final aim of developing digital twins, is driven by underlying principles, which reflect the driving societal paradigms that set certain priorities (for example, economic growth or, by contrast, sustainable development) (Helbing & Argota Sánchez-Vaquerizo, 2022). In this sense, the technological-driven approach of twinning might be proven to be insufficient to avoid some negative consequences of technologies on socio-environmental and digital inequalities. It also requires a level of competencies and skills that might exclude citizens from participating in shaping, accessing, understanding (both benefits and risks), and benefiting from these technologies further enlarging the digital divide, and social and environmental inequalities along with diminishing public awareness and engagement if not carefully directed. The twinning process also poses questions related to privacy-related concerns on how the data needed to create the digital replica are collected and used. In this sense, the participation of the government in a collaborative partnership is pivotal to avoid the twinning approach being exclusively guided by technical and market drivers, and it should recognize twinning as an act of governance, which has socio-environmental impacts (Purcell et al. (2023)) and requires negotiation between multiple actors (Solman et al., 2022), including citizens.

Additional overlapping between digital and environmental interventions has been presented in the previous chapter in relation to some initiatives that the UK is carrying out to activate a circular economy while reducing the negative impacts connected to the generation of e-waste. The enhancement of a circular economy is also emphasized by the CODES plan as innovative in combining digital and environmental sustainability. Chapter 8 mentioned a series of strategies (for example, the Resources and Waste Strategy for England, Beyond Recycling for Wales, Making Things Last for Scotland, and the Northern Ireland Environmental Strategy) as integral to the UK 25-Year Environment Plan for England to recycle and reuse materials (Gov.UK, 2018a). Specifically, the legislation around Waste Electrical and Electronic Equipment recycling (WEEE) recycling has evolved, but it still struggles to challenge the increasing production of e-waste and inappropriate disposal of electronic and electric equipment (Ali & Shirazi, 2023). This is due to scarce financial support (Sundar et al., 2023), but also limited guidance and awareness of e-waste management (at the household level).

Some steps have moved to ensure greener digital technologies and sustainable working practices, as well as to identify driving principles for minimizing waste and embracing a circular economy; using resources more sustainably and efficiently; ensuring ICT sustainability in social, economic, and ethical terms; mitigating and adapting to climate change; analyzing the whole Life Costing; and seeking Innovation opportunities (Gov.UK, 2018b). However, despite the introduction of some regulations, the lack of guidelines and financial support for e-waste still represents a criticality to the realization of a circular economy due to the lack of processing technologies, lack of returns and profits, lack of expert knowledge, lack of effective guidance and standards for the proper collection methods, and lack of proper knowledge (Sundar et al., 2023).

The digital-environmental overlapping is also connected to the promotion of skills and competencies, which according to the second shift of the CODES plan is pivotal in achieving digital-environmental sustainability. In the UK context, several initiatives have been promoted since the introduction of the Digital Strategy 2017. Some of these initiatives have been more oriented toward increasing the acquisition of formal qualifications, while some others, such as the Digital Inclusion Fund, have focused on specific groups by providing skills, especially to older and disabled individuals. Moreover, the private-public Digital Skills Partnership has mainly focused on providing high-level digital skills and has only marginally considered essential competencies to boost confidence in navigating online (Abey, 2022). The UK government also launched an online Media Literacy Framework in July 2021 (DCMS, 2021), alongside the Online Safety Bill, particularly focused on providing skills that enable users to avoid harm online and filter misinformation/disinformation. However, while the strategy sets some fundamental steps in improving the online experience of citizens and consumers, it is heavily based on online safety and scarcely considers digital literacy as a whole. As highlighted by Livingstone (2021), it also puts great responsibility on users to manage and control who accesses their data online but scarcely considers the role of businesses in establishing where and how their data are used. Businesses are involved by encouraging them to support the literacy process through design and providing users with the necessary tools to recognize misleading content.

On the other hand, some concerns have also been raised about the strategy's reliance on the voluntary sector, and commercial media companies, while scarcely considering the need for comprehensive programs of media education in school. It also neglects to consider how media education in schools has been affected by the lack of time and space in the curriculum (MEA, 2021). Voluntary organizations have, indeed, played a valuable role in implementing community-based initiatives to increase essential skills in community centers to enhance participation. They also have played a role in delivering business-financed online training (for example, BT's Skills for Tomorrow delivered by the Good Thing Foundation) through in-person learning, but also by partnering with companies to provide data access and distributing devices to those in need (see Abey, 2022 for a review). However, it has been shown that such initiatives do not receive sufficient financial support for the type and scale of intervention they need. In 2021, for example, 21% of UK adult users stated that they did not feel confident online, the same percentage only used smartphones to navigate the Internet, and 19% did not possess basic skills to navigate the Internet (Abey, 2022). The public-private partnership model adopted by conservative approaches has been oriented toward market-based solutions with a lack of sufficient financial resources by the public sector and confidence in the private commitment to social support. This is supported by, for instance, the encouragement by Ofcom (2023) to Internet providers to offer social tariffs to help customers on low incomes. The nature of such provisions also affects the quality of the service, prices, and eligibility conditions. Similarly, Flynn et al. (2019) emphasize that such a model of governance, driven by a neoliberal orientation, risks undermining concerted approaches to environmental protection due to profit-oriented management of the environment, driven by its monetization and the dependence on voluntary participation in the process.

Another condition included in Shift 2 is represented by respect for human rights such as freedom of expression, privacy, indigenous land rights, and child rights. Neoliberal approaches to environmental governance show how the deregulation of neoliberal settings has produced what has been referred to as "surveillance capitalism" (Lyon, 2019; Zuboff, 2015, 2019), which differs from traditional market mechanisms due to its orientation to anticipate behaviors to generate profit. The Data Protection and Digital Information (No. 2) Bill, under consideration by the House of Commons at the time of writing, proposes some changes to the Data Protection Act 2018 and the UK General Data Protection Regulation. However, the Bill has been criticized in an open letter to the secretary of the state for the Department of Science, Innovation and Technology, signed by 26 civil rights groups because it reduces data subjects' rights while giving more power to private companies (also expanding the areas in which automated decisions can be taken), weakens accountability requirements (by, for example, removing the requirement of consulting with people affected by high-risk data processing and reducing paperwork that will remove obligations for companies to keep records of many operations, for example, data processing operations), and reduces the independence of the Information Commissioner's Office while empowering the Secretary of State over data protection (Burke, 2023; ORG, 2023). The draft of the UK Online Safety Bill assigns Ofcom the task of defining Codes of Practice that can regulate content. This has been highlighted as a concern of a potential "democratic deficit" in the Bill. This is also due to some interpretative spaces left in the Bill when referring to, for example, content that can arm "child of ordinary sensibilities" and "reasonable ground" to identify risks online (Gov.UK, 2021). It is also not clear how legitimate techniques of persuasion through marketing are distinguished from harmful manipulation (Trengove et al., 2022). Consider the example of nudging described in Chap. 7. On the one hand, some studies showed that it could be valuable for empowering sustainable consumption. On the other hand, we have also highlighted that for those who are induced to choose eco-friendly options through persuasive strategies, their level of environmental poverty (in terms of awareness, engagement, and motivation) might not be affected. The CODES plan, for example, includes ethical digital nudging as a strategy to empower sustainable consumption, sustainable lifestyles, behaviors, and collaboration.

## 10.4 Using the CODES Guiding Principles to Interpret the Public-Private Collaboration in the Eco-civilization Project

While a traditional neoliberal approach to the management of the environment might put a too strong emphasis on economic profits, the Chinese eco-civilization project has conceptualized the environment as encoded in the structure of society and as a shaping force of the regulatory framework. This is theoretically in line with the alignment of values, vision, and objectives toward sustainable development as envisaged by the CODES Plan. The ecological civilization project is embedded into Chinese traditional culture and grounded in the principle of "Unity of Man and Nature." Theoretically, it also inspires mobilization across multiple levels of society, including the research community, the private sector, non-profit organizations, and the wider public (Huang & Westman, 2021). Wang et al. (2022) interpret Chinese environmental management as a combination of sovereign governmentality (top-down imposition backed by the threat of punishment), neoliberal governmentality (market based through monetary exchange and incentives), disciplinary environmentality (aimed at producing self-regulation thanks to the internalization of norms and values), and truth governmentality (based on the principle of regulation rather than the exercise of power, see Foucault, 2008). However, Huang and Westman (2021) acknowledge that the interpretation of the relationship between society and nature can vary across cultures within the nation, and this understanding is heavily influenced by local knowledge and material conditions. Consequently, the practical application of the theoretical relationship between nature and society might differ based on local perspectives. This approach has prompted major Global Digital Businesses, such as the Ant Group (part of the Alibaba Group), to create favorable conditions for addressing certain environmental issues and encouraging citizens to actively participate in the transition. However, it has also shown weaknesses, particularly in terms of its authoritarian and hierarchical tendencies. Moreover, the eco-civilization process must be contextualized in the world's largest coal-consuming country, which, despite record investments in low-carbon electricity generation, still approves new coal plant permits for economic growth. However, analysis for Carbon Brief (Myllyvirta, 2023) estimates that if the pace of expansion of solar and wind capacity in China was maintained, the use of fossil fuels would enter a period of structural decline. Therefore, on the one hand, these premises set the ground for the activation of the ecological civilization process, but economic growth remains a guiding principle. The investment in new coal plants shows that economic growth is still a priority over environmental concerns. At the same time, the mixed approach between neoliberal governmentality and disciplinary environmentality could encourage a gradual reduction of fossil fuel use, especially considering that the low-carbon capacity of the country already exceeds some targets established by the government for solar and wind installation (Myllyvirta, 2023). The environmental outcome of this process largely depends on the country's ability to prioritize the reduction of $CO_2$ over capitalist interests. Following a Treadmill of Production theory (ToP) perspective, the alternative scenario, in line with economic growth drivers, might involve the use of technological development and increasing energy capacity as a mere accelerator of production, alongside traditional energy production systems.

Similar to the UK, China has also invested in the development of a circular economy. However, China takes a multi-governmentality approach led by the state. As part of this strategy, the Chinese government uses standards to guide socioeconomic changes. For example, they have established a national standard for waste quality on imported waste from the West to limit polluting recycling activities. In this direction, the Chinese government issued a series of interventions over time combining top-down and market-based approaches to the management of e-waste. To enhance economic development from an ecological modernization perspective, while preserving ecological health, the Chinese government has issued a policy apparatus industrially oriented through eco-industrial parks to enhance the circular economy (Zhu & Cote, 2004). In 2002, China ratified the Basel Convention, an international agreement restricting international trade of hazardous waste, which joined in 1995, against the introduction of hazardous e-waste components (Duan et al., 2016). In 2009, regulations on the management and safe disposal of e-waste were announced (Sthiannopkao & Wong, 2013), and the "old for new" Replacement Home Appliance Policy encouraged recycling by applying a deduction to the purchase of new appliances if old products were returned by consumers (Han et al., 2022). In 2011, the government issued the Chinese Management Regulation for WEEE Recycling and Disposal, which set both goals for the collection and recycling of e-waste (Xiao, 2023). The year after, the Ministry of Finance announced the measures for WEEE Recovery Fund. Accordingly, manufacturers of electrical and electronic products contribute to the waste electrical appliance disposal fund to cover the costs of processing such waste (Liu et al., 2023). Such an evolution enhanced the formation of formal WEEE recycling companies, followed by the active engagement of manufacturers and recycling enterprises in reusing material. The literature highlights that the most effective policies in China are based on the extended producer responsibility, which attributes the responsibility of recycling and disposing of e-waste to the producers (Zeng et al., 2017). In this direction, in 2022, the National Development and Reform Commission of China released a list of six Chinese enterprises involved in meeting recycling targets (Li et al., 2023). China was responsible for 10.1 million tons of e-waste in 2019, and households, institutions, and manufacturers represent the major contributors to e-waste (Ongondo et al., 2011). However, in addition to domestic production, a challenge arises from illegal exports from other countries, with 90% of the total exported e-waste by the US to Asia ending up in China (Thakur & Kumar, 2022). To tackle such a problem of imported waste, the government issued "A Plan for Reforming the Solid Waste Import Administration System." The plan, also known as "Operation National Sword" (enacted in 2018), enforces stringent regulations on imported waste and adds more than 20 types of solid waste to the list of forbidden waste imports. The plan also increased quality standards, reduced the contamination levels acceptable, reduced the number of ports receiving waste, and intensified controls. Examining the effects of the implementation of the ban in five e-waste disposal hubs in China, Guo et al. (2023) found that since its implementation local air pollution decreased.

Moreover, in 2020, the National Development and Reform Commission enacted the "Implementation Plan on Improving the Recycling and Processing System of Waste Home Appliances and Promoting the Renewal and Consumption of Household Appliances," involving local governments in improving the recycling and disposal practice (Xiao, 2023).

The state-led environmentalism has made China subject to study, especially for the incorporation of environmental concerns into business activities to increase environmental profitability and transform it into an "opportunity" (Park et al., 2010). Using a case-study approach to explore the effects of e-waste regulation in Guiyu, China, Wang et al. (2022) theorize that Chinese "Truth governmentality" is supported by the discourse of ecological modernization to replace informal e-waste channels with formal companies; "Disciplinary governmentality" is based on spatial surveillance, registration, statistics, and scientific knowledge; and "Neoliberal governmentality" is also part of the approach because of the economic incentives at play. The study showed that the implementation of such a combined approach achieved the goal of imposing state authority at the local level producing improvement of the environmental conditions, but it also caused drawbacks due to the monopolization of the e-waste business by larger companies and the increasing unemployment of pre-existent informal workers. In this direction, despite the alignment of values and objectives between digital and environmental challenges, the collaborative approach envisaged by the CODES plan is affected by an authoritarian stance.

The Chinese approach to e-waste is strongly oriented to technological innovation, also reflecting the emphasis put on the need to develop and improve environmentally friendly technologies for social change since the publication of the "Central Document No.12: Opinions of the Central

Committee of the Communist Party of China and the State Council on Further Promoting the Development of Ecological Civilization" (Geal & Ely, 2018). This makes the ecological civilization project closer to ecological modernization principles at multiple levels. In this direction, the "Action Plan on Fostering Civic Awareness of Ecological Civilization" integrates ecological civilization into school education. Moreover, environmental NGOs have implemented initiatives, such as in the case of Greenpeace's cleantech incubator Powerlab and the "Wildlife-Free E-Commerce Initiative" launched and coordinated by China Biodiversity Conservation and Green Development Foundation (Huang & Westman, 2021). However, the success of ecological civilization realization in China depends largely on citizen engagement in ecological civilization behavior (Wang et al., 2020). Its foundations also lay on the development of consciousness about the green development concept and lifestyle (Liu & Liu, 2021) and on the involvement of citizens and consumers in the process of implementing policies, which in turn needs to combine digital and environmental sustainability with social benefits and needs. Some studies have explained users' intention to recycle e-waste by exploring its interaction with several variables, including norms (both subjective norms, which derive from social pressure to perform certain behaviors, and self-expected norms, which reflect their moral obligations), personality (more or less oriented to new action), utility/benefits (in relation to its convenience), environmental attitudes and knowledge, demographics, and knowledge of recycling channels (see Lyu et al., 2023 for a review).

As highlighted in Chap. 4, the debate around the theoretical foundation of ecological rationality is still in development due to its contradictory relationship with economic rationality. Despite the multi-governmentality approach adopted by the Chinese state, a great portion of domestic e-waste is still handled by informal recyclers, and only about 15% of e-waste is formally recycled every year (Forti et al., 2020). Along with the increasing formalization of the e-waste recycling system, there is still an informal channel of unsupervised collection activities of paddlers, which is based on the manual dismantling and release of hazardous substances in the natural environment. This also depends on the benefits deriving from door-to-door collection service via paddlers who offer advantageous prices (Ramzan et al., 2019) and avoid fees for disposing of e-waste through formal channels. Financial factors are, indeed, identified in the scientific debate as a major external determinant of the recycling behaviors of consumers (Shevchenko et al., 2019) in addition to internal motivation

(Zhong & Huang, 2016; Zhong et al., 2022) and awareness (Chi et al., 2014). For example, in exploring households' intentions to pay a fee for recycling e-waste in Zhuhai City, Cai et al. (2020) found that the majority of respondents recognize the negative impact of e-waste on both environment and human health, but they attribute the responsibility for paying to both the government and manufacturers. To make the management more efficient a smart system of e-waste collection has been developed by integrating IoT and AI to create an Internet-based e-waste collection. However, such an approach has been found to still be in its early stages to appeal to consumers who might have limited knowledge about smart e-waste collection mechanisms and are, instead, more familiar with informal practices of e-waste management (Han et al., 2022). They might also have privacy concerns about how online platforms use their data, the fairness of costs, and a lack of transparency in the process of disposal/recycling (Lyu et al., 2023). Therefore, a more comprehensive approach to the informal recycling system should consider the traditional practices and perspectives of both paddlers and consumers, recognizing them as integral to everyday practice. This approach lays the foundation for the integration of informal practices into the formal system while preserving the socio-environmental benefits and local employment, and therefore avoiding the negative consequences of a shift toward digital-environmental sustainability (Shift 2 of the Action Plan). For instance, Steuer et al. (2018) proposed the incorporation of informal collectors into the formal system rather than banning informal channels. By contrast, other studies suggest that increasing punitive measures may be more effective than subsidies in addressing illegal activities and improving the collection and recycling system (Wang & Huo, 2023).

The connections between environmental and digital poverty in China are also shown in other fields, suggesting that the development of the digital economy may contribute toward reducing household energy poverty, whereas the digital divide may, by contrast, increase the energy poverty of households. Luan et al. (2023) found that the digital divide negatively affects the alleviation of energy poverty, especially in low-income households, older households, and rural households. It hinders the reduction of energy poverty by increasing income poverty and credit constraints, reducing employment, and weakening social capital.

This is also connected to the promotion of digital skills and competencies, which according to the second shift of the CODES plan is pivotal in achieving digital-environmental sustainability.

China's environmental education is restricted to certain sectors (for example, professional schools, and primary and secondary schools), and this might affect the participation of citizens in the ecological civilization. At the same time, the unbalances between richer urban areas and poorer rural areas might require a different approach to digital, environmental, and financial poverty to address techno-environmental challenges (Zhou, 2021). The acquisition of digital skills is also connected to understanding the impacts of technology use and surveillance, which is integral to the disciplinary governmentality of the Chinese government. In 2017, a policy plan revealed the government's intention to make the country a global leader in AI by 2030 and employ AI to support and maintain social stability (Qiang, 2019). The Chinese approach has increasingly used digital technologies to monitor and control society by increasing, for example, Internet providers' responsibilities of removing and reporting offending content. It also limits the freedom of "spreading rumors" online as well as the organization of protests, restricting access to certain websites and social media, hiring "monitors" of online postings, using voice-recognition, facial-recognition technology, and AI-equipped cameras. This approach also includes creating DNA databases that include not only individuals who have been convicted but also those considered "high-risk" subjects (see Qiang, 2019 for a review). Some scholars have referred to this authoritarian approach as "digital Leninism" (Heilmann, 2016), which aims to implement a capillary control of society. This has led to the affirmation of a surveillance system that is spread and diffused in society and involves multiple actors, including private companies such as Alipay social credit system (Sesame Credit), based on credit history; behavior and preference; fulfillment capacity; personal and demographic characteristics; and social relationships, which are used to calculate risks in economic exchanges. In this sense, surveillance no longer needs to be enforced but uses seduction to make users comply with the rules (Chong, 2019).

However, the implementation of such systems does not necessarily eradicate pre-existing social inequalities. On the contrary, these technologies have played a significant role in exacerbating an asymmetrical accumulation of data, with particularly detrimental consequences for marginalized communities. This phenomenon is evident in regions like western Xinjiang, where the consequences of data-driven processes are evident. An illustrative case is a practice initiated in September 2016, where individuals applying for passports in Xinjiang were compelled to surrender their biometric data and even provide blood samples for DNA information collection (Qiang, 2019). This exemplifies how emerging technologies can be wielded in ways that accentuate disparities and subject certain populations to sorting and discrimination (Lyon, 2007). Such cases show the need for a comprehensive examination of the intricate relationship between technology, data accumulation, and its impact on social inequalities, emphasizing the need to analyze the potential consequences of these systems.

Moreover, digital behavior becomes integral to the social credit system that provides a score by crossmatching offline and online activities, which influences not only access to loans but also other aspects such as applications for jobs and visas. Different from traditional forms of surveillance aimed at tracking and collecting specific information, big data surveillance is based on automated methods that collect, monitor, and conserve information about everyone and everything constantly and invisibly (Andrejevic & Gates, 2014) by enlarging the power gap between state power and citizens (Tufekci, 2014). Such a self-regulative disciplinary approach has been compared to a digital version of Bentham's panopticon, by increasing the effectiveness of the surveillance system while limiting the physical presence of guardians. Surveillance through the social credit system aims to create a "corporate–state nexus," forcing private companies to share data collected to improve state surveillance (Liang et al., 2018). At the same time, this has pushed companies to address environmental obligations (for example, reducing resource consumption and environmental damage) to gain social credit (Aho & Duffield, 2020). In turn, private companies, such as the Ant Group, are encouraged to create additional conditions for users to contribute to their environmental orientation by, for instance, creating apps, such as Ant Forest. This potentially generates win-win situations in which citizens can actively contribute to reforestation while learning about the value of taking care of the natural environment as a civic duty. At the same time, the Ant Group (and Alibaba) collects credits for its environmental engagement. However, even though the social credit system has been created to enhance moral behavior, financial reliability, and social control, it raises numerous concerns about privacy violations by creating a continuous flow of data exchange between private businesses and the government. Such a system is the result of a hierarchical configuration of the government-corporation-public collaboration that is also reflected in the country's digital-environmental approach. This might be partially in line with the digital and green transition for sustainable development facilitated by the collaboration between local businesses, entrepreneurs, and academia, auspicated by the CODES Action Plan. However, this enabler also includes the transition to a just economy that in such a government-corporation-public approach seems to be screwed toward the government (but also the profit side) of the relationship.

This is because such an approach to both digital and environmental management is government led and only participated by companies and the public (Duan et al., 2020). At the same time, some studies have found that government supervision produces positive outcomes in environmental governance and pushes enterprises to limit their environmental impacts. The positive governance outcomes are also increased by citizen active participation (Chen et al., 2019). An illustrative example is the "smelly waters" app in Guangzhou, which encourages citizens to report data and monitor businesses' environmental impact (Hsu et al., 2020). This seems to respond to the promotion of active citizen participation to support Governance Breakthroughs that use digital tools to achieve sustainability outcomes through knowledge and participatory governance, as highlighted by the CODES Action Plan. Creating Knowledge Commons via digital tools is encouraged to facilitate inclusive and cooperative forms of knowledge production (for example, citizen science).

At the same time, this also requires not violating citizens' privacy and transparency in how the data collected will be used and what responses will be implemented. It also requires digital literacy (aimed at making vulnerable groups heard), education, and digital knowledge. However, citizens' participation in the smelly water case and other forms of hierarchical management of both the digital and environmental fields must be intended as their capacity to monitor and report to the central government, rather than actively participate in the decision-making.

## 10.5 Private-Public Partnerships as a "Win-Win" Approach to Environment and Digital Policy Integration

Using the guiding principles of the action plan developed by the CODES (2022), we now identify some strengths and weaknesses of the neoliberal and multi-governmentality approaches described so far using the case studies of the UK and China. We also explore how these principles are reflected in the revisited DPF. The plan can help address the need to conceptualize poverty in the digital era as a combination of the digitalization process and social and environmental determinants. It also suggests that structural changes need to align with individual determinants to create favorable circumstances for individuals and businesses to play an active role in tackling digital-environmental challenges. We have identified some fundamental principles that are transversal to the plan (see Table 10.1) and which can also be applied as indicators to evaluate initiatives aimed at digital and environmental sustainability. These are represented by the multistakeholder nature of the initiatives that need public-private (including citizens) partnerships at multiple levels, as well as leadership based on a multistakeholder approach (Sect. 10.5.1); directly connected to this is the intersectionality of policies, standards, regulations, infrastructure, and governance frameworks needed to catalyze digital sustainability, sustained political attention, and financial support (at least three to six years); accountability, thanks to performance indicators and milestones in consultations with related stakeholders (Sect. 10.5.2); and trigger for change at the system level or sector level and different scales (from local to global) (Sect. 10.5.3).

### *10.5.1 Multistakeholder Initiatives*

Examining the UK as an example of a market-based approach to digital-environmental governance, this chapter emphasized the potential for activating multistakeholder approaches which include public and private actors in the decision-making. However, despite the urgency of environmental threats to society's well-being (including climate change), the intersections between digital and environmental matters are still limited, and intervention appears to be fragmented in initiatives with specific focus either on the socio-environmental inequalities or on digital inequalities. While the neoliberal orientation of the UK approach has promoted public-private partnerships in dealing with digital and environmental challenges, citizens' participation and education on such overlapping are still underdeveloped. This can be understood, using Hatzisavvidou's work (2020) on the construction of the environmental state in Britain, as integral to neoliberal discourses, which in turn has forged common sense in approaching and understanding the environmental crisis. The author suggests a need for changing the language and rhetoric and disentangling it from an economic paradigm conventionally based on evaluation, efficiency, and competitiveness. Chapter 8 referred to some carbon credit projects, such as UK Woodland Carbon and the UK Peatland Code, based on trading units or credits on the market. We have also highlighted the criticalities related to monitoring and evaluating the real contribution of such initiatives to mitigate environmental degradation. Chapter 7 considered initiatives driven by private businesses outside the UK, such as the aforementioned example of blockchain-based Single.Earth. The project aims to create a digital twin of nature using AI and big data to monitor its health. However, the outcomes are still uncertain and controversial. Single.Earth's approach is still based on a conceptualization of nature as per its economic value, but it also shows the potential of combining digital and environmental dimensions to create favorable circumstances for nature-based solutions. When discussing the digital-environmental habitus of families in England, we referred to a benefit-oriented approach shown by respondents when engaging with the environment. Therefore, experiences like Single.Earth have the potential to become powerful motivators for not only businesses but also private citizens to engage in environmental protection while simultaneously benefiting from it. These experiences necessitate, however, to be integrated into a wider global/national vision, which balances economic profits with socio-environmental and digital sustainability. In this context, the role of governments becomes pivotal to harness the full potential of these initiatives and monitor that they do not veer excessively toward profit-driven motives at the expense of the broader sustainability goal.

On the other hand, the authoritarian and hierarchical multi-governmentality approach adopted by China has produced controversial effects in terms of multistakeholder participation. We referred to a multi-governmentality approach of China (Wang et al., 2022) that combines sovereign governmentality (predominant) with neoliberal governmentality, disciplinary environmentality, and truth governmentality. This strategy has encouraged dialogue between the state and private companies, which in turn creates conditions (for example, in the case of Alipay Ant Forest) to actively participate in environmental protection. On the other hand, the limited space of negotiation available to businesses, and even less to citizens, has shifted this relationship toward the state authority. We emphasized in Chap. 7 that some studies found that a benefit-oriented approach motivates Alipay users to join the Ant Forest project, which includes both intrinsic benefits (enjoyment, social interaction, fulfillment, altruism) and extrinsic benefits (external rewards, competition) (Wang et al., 2022). The example of Alipay has shown that a collaborative approach that combines government commitment, science-informed, private businesses, and non-profit organizations (Zeng et al., 2020) can encourage citizens' engagement in pro-environmental behaviors (Liu, 2022). At the same time, these initiatives might present a "democratic deficit" (Trengove et al., 2022) because they do not provide spaces for negotiation and participation of citizens at the upper levels of the decision-making process. Some examples of citizen involvement can be identified through, for example, citizen science. Citizens participate in environmental governance through technologies by informing the government about environmental health. The aforementioned Smelly Waters app that functions through WeChat, in Guangzhou, enhances citizen-authority digital interaction, with citizens reporting problems, providing data, and supervising businesses' impact on the environment and institutions responding to how these problems have been addressed (Hsu et al., 2020). While state control has forced corporations to engage with environmental problems internally and combines government commitment, science-informed, private businesses, and non-profit organizations (Zeng et al., 2020), it has translated citizens' participation into an informative role. This contributes toward activating processes of empowerment of citizens but is limited to their supervisory and reporting functions, rather than involvement in the decision-making process.

Therefore, after reviewing these examples, it seems that both the neoliberal and multi-governmentality approaches do not completely fulfill the requirement of the CODES plan of multistakeholder empowerment in decision-making. However, the private-public dialogue (including civil society) shows the potential to create favorable conditions for addressing the digital-environmental interplay, if all levels participate equally in both defining and enhancing digital-environmental alignment.

### *10.5.2 Intersectionality of Policies, Standards, Regulations, Infrastructure, Governance Frameworks, and Accountability*

The lack of a comprehensive multistakeholder approach in the strategies described is also reflected in the underdevelopment of areas of intersections between policies, standards, regulations, infrastructure, and governance frameworks in both the environment and the digital realms, and the lack of sustained political attention and financial support. We have referred to the neoliberal approach of the UK example to improve digital infrastructures, accelerate innovation (for example, developing a circular economy, AI-driven innovation, and Digital Twins), as well as provide online media literacy strategies. However, the strategy appears to be primarily focused on technological advancement. This has potential consequences in terms of replicating and exacerbating existing socio-environmental and digital inequalities, as well as excluding citizens who lack the necessary skills to access, understand (both benefits and risks), and benefit from these technologies. Increasing digital and environmental skills is pivotal to citizens' participation in digital-environmental sustainability. However, the neoliberal approach discussed in this context places responsibility on individual users, for example, to protect themselves from online abuses and privacy violations (see Livingstone, 2021). It also tends to provide skills and knowledge that benefit the economic structure (through, for instance, investing in specialized skills and AI-driven innovation) rather than individual well-being. This is further exacerbated by restricting financial support to the pivotal role played by the voluntary sector in supporting media and digital education (Abey, 2022). Digital-environmental sustainability requires that digital skills are provided along with environmental skills and knowledge to provide citizens with the tools necessary to make informed choices about their digital and technological uses and behaviors. This is an important factor considering that consumer expenditure (primarily from heating homes and traveling) is the largest contributor to UK emissions, followed by energy consumption, with 80% coming from fossil fuels (Office for National Statistics, 2023). The public-private partnership has emphasized market-based solutions with scarce financial support by the public sector and confidence in the private commitment to social support.

Moreover, the intersection between digital and environmental realms is represented by the embracement of the circular economy, the adoption of greener digital technologies and sustainable working practices, and the efficient use of technologies. However, the main criticalities identified in such a combined approach are due to a lack of guidelines and financial support for e-waste, unsuitable collection infrastructure (Cole et al., 2019), lack of returns and profits, lack of expert knowledge, lack of effective guidance and standards for the proper collection methods, lack of proper knowledge (Sundar et al., 2023), and lack of deadlines for circularity assessments (Benham, 2023).

Comparing the UK and Chinese use of standards in environmental protection, Flynn et al. (2019) identify the voluntary and private-led efforts as a potential threat to the effectiveness of environmental governance such as in the case of the UK. By contrast, the government-led approach of China has combined top-down and market-based approaches to the management of e-waste (Zhu & Cote, 2004). In this sense, ecological civilization materialization passes through an "ecologizing economy" and an "economizing ecology" by transforming the environment into a profitable opportunity (Park et al., 2010). At the same time, some scholars found that such an approach based on "campaign-style environmental governance" (Liu et al., 2015), which attempts to shape behavior patterns of local governments to facilitate the implementation of wider political projects, was not always successful. Indeed, the occurrence of inspections at the local level in certain contexts caused short-lived responses to show compliance with the rules limited to the time of inspection (Wang et al., 2022). Moreover, despite the authoritarian approach, an informal channel for collecting e-waste persists suggesting that a more participative approach, which is informed by local cultural traits and consolidated social practices, could be more beneficial at multiple levels. Finally, the inequalities between urban and rural areas, as well as different educational opportunities and acquisition of skills, suggest a need for a diversified approach to digital, environmental, and financial poverty (Zhou, 2021).

While in the Chinese example, the establishment of the ecological civilization project helps shape the structural conditions for combining socioeconomic, political, and environmental orientation, in both UK and Chinese examples, the approach to a circular economy is strongly driven by faith in technological innovation. The neoliberal setting is predominantly influenced by private interests, whereas in the case of the multi-governmentality approach is screwed toward the state, which drives the industrial sector to achieve ecological civilization (Wang et al., 2020). In both cases, environmental protection tends to be primarily approached from a profit-oriented perspective, which leaves limited room for citizens to participate in the transformation process. Following Spaargaren and Van Vliet (2000), such controversies cannot be understood in a social vacuum, because they depend on both rules and practices which are interdependent. The ecological rationality of consumption practices and behaviors is simultaneously context dependent and influenced by social values and individual predispositions. This also shows the need to observe how the macro and micro levels interact and how the private-public intersects producing social norms that define citizens' digital-environmental habitus.

When considering strategies to tackle digital-environmental poverty, taking into account existing individual determinants (including both digital aspects such as access, devices and connectivity, support and motivation, and environmental awareness, motivation, and engagement) is pivotal to the success of policies that aim to create circumstantial determinants at the local level which are oriented to digital and socio-environmental sustainability (for example, improving environmental conditions, enhancing participation channels, improving living conditions, financial stability, and health, valorizing the socio-demographic context, considering consolidated lifestyle and behaviors).

### 10.5.3 *Change at the System Level or Sector Level and Different Scales (from Local to Global)*

In terms of triggering system-level or sector-level change at different scales (from local to global), the digital and techno intersections with environmental challenges need to more profoundly involve citizens to take into account existing circumstances at the local level and operate to generate new conditions to enhance their awareness, engagement, participation, and empowerment. This should consider how countries position themselves at the global level and how they can influence inequalities internationally.

The literature shows that oil and gas multinational corporations including UK companies (for example, Shell, British Petroleum, Tullow Oil) have control over the majority of oil and gas resources within oil-rich developing countries (Adams et al., 2019; Rudra & Jensen, 2011). Moreover, in March 2023, the UK released a policy paper on mineral strategy (Gov.UK, 2023), which becomes pivotal for energy security and to meet decarbonizing targets. Despite the emphasis on technological innovation, responsible mining, and maximization of domestic extraction, the paper highlights the dependence of the country on importing these resources. It also refers to the review of "mineral rights-related barriers" to facilitate exploration and extraction internally. At the same time, mineral extraction poses both environmental and social challenges, including pollution, soil erosion, and leaching of chemicals in ground waters. These challenges are evident in the Chinese context where 12 out of the 18 minerals listed in the paper are found. Despite "green" mining techniques and the recycling of resources (Li et al., 2022), these issues persist. Mining activities can alter and worsen existing vulnerabilities in extraction sites (see, for example, Bebbington et al., 2018; Ouoba, 2018; Schueler et al., 2011). This is particularly evident in contexts with scarce attention to human rights, consultation, and consent (see, for example, Owen et al., 2022; Zaremberg & Wong, 2018). This occurs despite the presence of standards and guidelines for meaningful stakeholder engagement in the extractive sector (OECD, 2017).

On the other side, when considering the benefits deriving from reforestation programs promoted by the eco-civilization project, which also includes business-oriented initiatives, it is relevant to consider the externalization of deforestation in other countries. In this direction, Downing et al. (2021) found that the benefits of reforestation in China are counteracted by the socio-environmental consequences of deforestation and cross-sector effects in other countries. This can be attributed to the profit-driven nature of such environmental management, which prioritizes consumption and the associated necessity to source supplies from abroad. This further reinforces a need for a comprehensive approach, which also looks at the international effects of policymaking when considering the positives produced nationally by certain structural conditioning. Moreover, it should be considered how the country positions itself at the global level and how it can influence inequalities internationally.

Therefore, in both orientations, the resource extraction and externalization of environmental damage can produce devastating effects in exacerbating social inequalities (Owen et al., 2022), and the benefit produced internally might cancel the negative externalities produced in other vulnerable contexts.

## 10.6 Conclusion

In this chapter we delved into the multifaceted realm of digital-environmental sustainability, offering some recommendations and insights based on an examination of various approaches and studies. The chapter was framed within the context of the action plan developed by the Coalition for Digital Environmental Sustainability (CODES), which aims to create the conditions for a "Sustainable Planet in the Digital Age." We have identified this approach as the basis for addressing digital-environmental poverty as intertwined dimensions of a common social challenge. The three key shifts identified by the CODES Action Plan need to work in harmony to transform the structural interplay between digital and environmental sustainability and operate across different levels, from the individual to the macro.

We used the framework to support the examination of both Western and non-Western approaches to tackle social-environmental inequalities derived by digital acceleration, by underlining the vital importance of access to digital tools and their beneficial sustainable use for individuals and society at large. One of the primary recommendations articulated in this chapter is the promotion of public-private partnerships as a "win-win" strategy to tackle digital and environmental concerns together. On the one hand, the chapter considered the UK government's collaboration with private entities to address these complex issues. While dynamic collaboration was acknowledged as essential, it showed the need for government oversight to ensure that the digital revolution brings socioeconomic and environmental benefits. On the other hand, it explored the Chinese eco-civilization project, emphasizing the potential counterproductivity of excessive government control of the government in shaping society's digital-environmental orientation.

This underlines the need for collaboration and cooperation among various stakeholders, including governments, businesses, civil society, and academia.

Both approaches show that when there is an unbalanced distribution of power in the public-private relationship (whether screwed toward the market or state direction), the alignment of values and strategies, as well as the mitigation of negatives of innovation processes, becomes challenging. Even though the UK example offers a more decentralized approach as well as opportunities for citizens to actively participate in the decision-making process, the spaces of participation can be still widened to counter-balance the market-led orientation of this approach. On the other hand, the informing role of Chinese citizens might be not sufficient to address the negative consequences of transformation processes that are imposed from the top of the hierarchy. In both cases, in examining Shift 2 and Shift 3 of the CODES Action Plan, which deal with mitigating negative consequences and enhancing innovation, we identified critical areas that need attention. The CODES approach raises concerns about the potential negative ramifications of technology on socio-environmental and digital inequalities, the need for competencies and skills, and the protection of privacy. These areas still need to be addressed by adopting a multistakeholder approach.

While the plan's emphasis on skills and competencies aligns with initiatives undertaken in the UK, there are margins for improvement, particularly in expanding comprehensive media and environmental literacy. Moreover, the reliance on voluntary organizations and commercial media companies has limitations, as these entities often lack the financial support required to effectively address the digital divide. There are also concerns regarding the impact of legislation such as the Data Protection and Digital Information Bill on data subjects' rights and the balance of power between individuals and private companies. Similar considerations apply to the Chinese example, with a nebulous aura surrounding the use of data constantly collected from citizens and organizations.

Finally, we stressed the significance of respecting human rights in digital governance, highlighting how challenging can become to distinguish between legitimate marketing practices or state monitoring functions and harmful manipulation.

To conclude, in this chapter, we reiterated the need for a holistic approach that from one side encompasses the interplay between digital, environmental, and economic poverty and on the other attempts to shape a more equitable and sustainable future for all.

## References


Abey, J. (2022). *Bridging the divide.* Policy Report, Fabian Society. https://fabians.org.uk/wp-content/uploads/2022/04/Bridging-the-Divide-web-file-Fabian-Society.pdf

Adams, D., Adams, K., Ullah, S., & Ullah, F. (2019). Globalisation, governance, accountability and the natural resource 'curse': Implications for socio-economic growth of oil-rich developing countries. *Resources Policy, 61*, 128–140.

Aho, B., & Duffield, R. (2020). Beyond surveillance capitalism: Privacy, regulation and big data in Europe and China. *Economy and Society, 49*(2), 187–212.

Ali, S., & Shirazi, F. (2023). The paradigm of circular economy and an effective electronic waste management. *Sustainability, 15*(3). https://doi.org/10.3390/su15031998

Andrejevic, M., & Gates, K. (2014). Big data surveillance: Introduction. *Surveillance and Society, 12*(2), 185–196.

Bebbington, A. J., et al. (2018). Resource extraction and infrastructure threaten forest cover and community rights. *PNAS, 115*(52), 13164–13173.

Benham, K. (2023). *The UK's critical minerals refresh 2023 – CMA's evaluation.* Critical Mineral Association. https://www.criticalmineral.org/post/the-uk-s-critical-minerals-refresh-2023-cma-s-evaluation

Burke, A. (2023). Data discrimination bill attacks our data protection rights. *Open Rights Group.* https://www.openrightsgroup.org/blog/the-data-discrimination-bill-attacks-our-data-protection-rights/

Cai, K., Song, Q., Peng, S., Yuan, W., Liang, Y., & Li, J. (2020). Uncovering residents' behaviors, attitudes, and WTP for recycling e-waste: A case study of Zhuhai city, China. *Environmental Science and Pollution Research, 27*, 2386–2399.

Chen, Y., Zhang, J., Tadikamalla, P. R., & Gao, X. (2019). The relationship among government, enterprise, and public in environmental governance from the perspective of multi-player evolutionary game. *International Journal of*

*Environment and Public Health, 16*(3351). https://doi.org/10.3390/ijerph16183351

Chi, X. W., Wang, Y. L., & Reuter, M. A. (2014). E-waste collection channels and household recycling behaviours in Taizhou of China. *Journal of Cleaner Production, 80*, 87–95.

Chong, G. P. L. (2019). Cashless China: Securitization of everyday life through Alipay's social credit system—Sesame Credit. *Chinese Journal of Communication, 12*(3). https://doi.org/10.1080/17544750.2019.1583261

CODES. (2022). *Action plan for a sustainable planet in the digital age.* https://www.sparkblue.org/CODES

Cole, C., Gnanapragasam, A., Cooper, T., & Singh, J. (2019). Assessing barriers to reuse of electrical and electronic equipment, a UK perspective. *Resources, Conservation and Recycling, 1.* https://doi.org/10.1016/j.rcrx.2019.100004

DCMS. (2021). *Online media literacy strategy.* https://assets.publishing.service.gov.uk/government/uploads/system/uploads/attachment_data/file/1004233/DCMS_Media_Literacy_Report_Roll_Out_Accessible_PDF.pdf

DCMS. (2022). UK digital strategy. https://www.gov.uk/government/publications/uks-digital-strategy/uk-digital-strategy

Dewan, S., & Riggins, F. J. (2005). The digital divide: Current and future research directions. *Journal of the Association for Information Systems, 6*(12), 298–337.

DiMaggio, P., Hargittai, E., Celeste, C., & Shafer, S. (2004). Digital inequality: From unequal access to differentiated use. In K. Neckerman (Ed.), *Social inequality* (pp. 355–400). Russell Sage Foundation.

Downing, A. S., Wong, G. Y., Dyer, M., Aguiar, A. P., Selomane, O., & Aceituno, A. J. (2021). When the whole is less than the sum of all parts – Tracking global-level impacts of national sustainability initiatives. *Global Environmental Change, 69.* https://doi.org/10.1016/j.gloenvcha.2021.102306

Duan, H., Hu, J., Tan, Q., Liu, L., & Li, W. Y. J. (2016). Systematic characterization of generation and management of e-waste in China. *Environmental Science and Pollution Research, 23*(2), 1929–1943.

Duan, X., Dai, S., Yang, R., Duan, X., & Tang, Y. (2020). Environmental collaborative governance degree of government, corporation, and public. *Sustainability, 12*(1138). https://doi.org/10.3390/su12031138

European Center for Digital Competitiveness. (2021). *Digital raiser report 2021.* https://digital-competitiveness.eu/wp-content/uploads/Digital_Riser_Report-2021.pdf

Flynn, A., Hacking, N., & Xie, L. (2019). Governance of the circular economy: A comparative examination of the use of standards by China and the United Kingdom. *Environmental Innovation and Societal Transitions, 33*, 282–300.

Forti, V., Baldé, C. P., Khuer, R., & Bel, G. (2020). *The Global E-waste Monitor 2020: Quantities, flows and the circular economy potential.* United Nations University (UNU)/United Nations Institute for Training and Research (UNITAR) – Co-hosted SCYCLE Programme, International Telecommuni cation Union (ITU) & International Solid Waste Association (ISWA), Bonn/Geneva/Rotterdam. https://www.itu.int/en/ITU-D/Environment/Documents/Toolbox/GEM_2020_def.pdf

Foucault, M. (2008). *The birth of biopolitics.* Palgrave Macmillan.

Geal, S., & Ely, A. (2018). Narratives and pathways towards an ecological civilization in contemporary China. *The China Quarterly, 236*, 1175–1196.

Gov.UK. (2018a). A Green Future: Our 25 Year Plan to Improve the Environment. https://assets.publishing.service.gov.uk/media/5ab3a67840f0b65bb584297e/25-year-environment-plan.pdf

Gov.UK. (2018b). *The greening government: Sustainable technology strategy 2020 – Sustainable technology for sustainable government.* Policy Paper. https://www.gov.uk/government/publications/greening-government-sustainable-technology-strategy-2020/the-greening-government-sustainable-technology-strategy-2020-sustainable-technology-for-sustainable-government

Gov.UK. (2021). *Draft online safety bill.* https://www.gov.uk/government/publications/draft-online-safety-bill

Gov.UK. (2022). *UK national action plan for open government 2021–2023.* https://www.gov.uk/government/publications/uk-national-action-plan-for-open-government-2021-2023/uk-national-action-plan-for-open-government-2021-2023

Gov.UK. (2023). *Resilience for the future: The UK's critical minerals strategy.* Policy Paper. https://www.gov.uk/government/publications/uk-critical-mineral-strategy/resilience-for-the-future-the-uks-critical-minerals-strategy

Guo, L., Walls, W. D., & Zheng, X. (2023). Waste import bans and environmental quality: Evidence from China's electronic waste disposal towns. *Environmental and Resource Economics, 85*, 65–108.

Han, Y., Shevchenko, T., Dongxu, Q., & Guohou, L. (2022). Smart e-waste management in China: A review. In *Congress on intelligent systems (conference paper)* (pp. 515–553). Springer.

Hargittai, E. (2002). Second-level digital divide: Differences in people's online skills. *First Monday, 7*(4). https://doi.org/10.5210/fm.v7i4.942

Hatzisavvidou, S. (2020). Inventing the environmental state: Neoliberal common sense and the limits to transformation. *Environmental Politics, 29*(1), 96–114.

Heidel, E., Dosemangen, S., & Hoeberling, K. (2022). *Climate justice and knowledge commons: Opportunities for the digital rights space.* Open Environmental Data Project. https://www.fordfoundation.org/wp-content/uploads/2022/07/oedp-and-op-climate_01-07-22.pdf

Heilmann, S. (2016). Leninism upgraded: Xi Jinping's authoritarian innovations. *China Economic Quarterly, 20*(4), 15–22.

Helbing, D., & Argota Sánchez-Vaquerizo, J. (2022). Digital twins: Potentials, ethical issues, and limitations. In *Handbook on the politics and governance of big data and artificial intelligence.* Edward Elgar Publishing. https://doi.org/10.2139/ssrn.4167963

Hsu, A., Weinfurter, A., Tong, J., & Xie, Y. (2020). Black and smelly waters: How citizen-generated transparency is addressing gaps in China's environmental management. *Journal of Environmental Policy & Planning, 22*(1), 138–153.

Huang, P., & Westman, L. (2021). China's imaginary of ecological civilization: A resonance between the state-led discourse and sociocultural dynamics. *Energy Research & Social Science, 81*. https://doi.org/10.1016/j.erss.2021.102253

Leavitt, H. J. (2002). Technology and organizations: Where's the off button? *California Management Review, 44*(2), 126–140.

Li, K., Qin, Y., Zhu, D., & Zhang, S. (2023). Upgrading waste electrical and electronic equipment recycling through extended producer responsibility: A case study. *Circular Economy, 291)*, 2773–1677.

Li, S., Yu, L., Jiang, W., Yu, H., & Wang, X. (2022). The recent progress China has made in green mine construction, part I: Mining groundwater pollution and sustainable mining. *International Journal of Environmental Research and Public Health, 19*(9), 5673.

Liang, F., Das, V., Kostyuk, N., & Hussain, M. M. (2018). Constructing a data-driven society: China's social credit system as a state surveillance infrastructure. *Policy & Internet, 10*, 415–453.

Liu, D., & Liu, L. (2021). Strategy of education of citizens' green development view on the perspective of ecological civilizations. *Journal of Simulation, 9*(6), 111–114.

Liu, K., Tan, Q., Yu, J., & Wang, M. (2023). A global perspective on e-waste recycling. *Circular Economy, 2*(1). https://doi.org/10.1016/j.cec.2023.100028

Liu, N. N., Lo, C. W. H., Zhan, X., & Wang, W. (2015). Campaign-style enforcement and regulatory compliance. *Public Administration Review, 75*(1), 85–95.

Liu, S. (2022). *Ant Forest: Using financial technologies to advance climate solutions in China*. Lincoln Institute of Land Policy.

Livingstone, S. (2021). *A missed opportunity: The new national media literacy strategy of DCMS.* https://blogs.lse.ac.uk/parenting4digitalfuture/2021/11/10/media-literacy-strategy/

Luan, B., Hong, Z., & Junbing, H. (2023). Digital divide and household energy poverty in China. *Energy Economics, 119.* https://doi.org/10.1016/j.eneco.2023.106543

Lyon, D. (2007). Surveillance, security and social sorting: Emerging research priorities. *International Criminal Justice Review, 17*(3), 161–170.

Lyon, D. (2019). Surveillance capitalism, surveillance culture and data politics. In D. Bigo, E. Isin, & E. Ruppert (Eds.), *Data politics. Worlds, subjects, rights* (pp. 64–78). Routledge.

Lyu, T., Chen, H., & Guo, Y. (2023). Investigating innovation diffusion, social influence, and personal inner forces to understand people's participation in online e-waste recycling. *Journal of Retailing and Consumer Services, 73.* https://doi.org/10.1016/j.jretconser.2023.103366

MEA. (2021). *The Media Education Association: A response to the DCMS online media literacy strategy.* https://www.themea.org.uk/post/the-media-education-association-a-response-to-the-dcms-online-media-literacy-strategy

Myllyvirta, L. (2023, November 13). *China's carbon dioxide (CO2) emissions are set to fall in 2024 and could be facing structural decline, due to record growth in the installation of new low-carbon energy sources.* Carbon Brief. https://www.carbonbrief.org/analysis-chinas-emissions-set-to-fall-in-2024-after-record-growth-in-clean-energy/#5

OECD. (2017). *OECD due diligence guidance for meaningful stakeholder engagement in the extractive sector.* OECD. https://doi.org/10.1787/9789264252462-en

Ofcom. (2023). Social tariffs: Cheaper broadband and phone packages. https://www.ofcom.org.uk/phones-telecoms-and-internet/advice-for-consumers/costs-and-billing/social-tariffs

Office for National Statistics. (2023). UK environmental accounts: 2023. https://www.ons.gov.uk/economy/environmentalaccounts/bulletins/ukenvironmentalaccounts/2023

OGP. (2022). United Kingdom action plan review 2021–2023. https://www.opengovpartnership.org/documents/united-kingdom-action-plan-review-2021-2023/#_ftnref4

OGP. (2023). Open government partnership. https://opengovernment.org.uk/about/open-government-partnership/

Ongondo, F. O., Williams, I. D., & Cherrett, T. J. (2011). How are WEEE doing? A global review of the management of electrical and electronic wastes. *Waste Management, 31*(4), 714–730.

ORG. (2023). *Data bill will set back UK economy and rights.* Open Rights Group. https://www.openrightsgroup.org/app/uploads/2023/04/DPDI-briefing-for-second-reading-1.pdf

Ouoba, Y. (2018). Industrial mining land use and poverty in regions of Burkina Faso. *Agricultural Economics, 49*, 511–520.

Owen, J. R., Kemp, D., Harris, J., Lechner, A. M., & Lèbre, É. (2022). Fast track to failure? Energy transition minerals and the future of consultation and consent. *Energy Research and Social Science, 89*, 102665.

Park, J., Sarkis, J., & Wu, Z. (2010). Creating integrated business and environmental value within the context of China's circular economy and ecological modernization. *Journal of Cleaner Production, 18*(15), 1494–1501.

Purcell, W., Neubauer, T., & Mallinger, K. (2023). Digital twins in agriculture: Challenges and opportunities for environmental sustainability. *Current Opinion in Environmental Sustainability, 61.* https://doi.org/10.1016/j.cosust.2022.101252

Qiang, X. (2019). The road to digital unfreedom: President Xi's surveillance state. *Journal of Democracy, 30*(1), 53–67.

Ramzan, S., Liu, C. G., Munir, H. M., & Xu, Y. (2019). Assessing young consumers' awareness and participation in sustainable e-waste management practices: A survey study in Northwest China. *Environmental Science and Pollution Research, 26*, 20003–20013.

Rawat, P., & Morris, C. (2022). *The effects of technology and institutions on e-participation*. Routledge.

Rudra, N. S., & Jensen, N. M. (2011). Globalization and the politics of natural resources. *Comparative Political Studies, 44*, 639–661.

Schueler, V., Kuemmerle, T., & Schröder, H. (2011). Impacts of surface gold mining on land use Systems in Western Ghana. *Ambio, 40*, 528–539.

Shevchenko, T., Laitala, K., & Danko, Y. (2019). Understanding consumer e-waste recycling behaviour: Introducing a new economic incentive to increase the collection rates. *Sustainability, 11*(9), 2656. https://doi.org/10.3390/su11092656

Solman, H., Kirkegaard, J. K., Smits, M., Vliet, B. V., & Bush, S. (2022). Digital twinning as an act of governance in the wind energy sector. *Environmental Science & Policy, 127*, 272–279.

Spaargaren, G., & Van Vliet, B. (2000). Lifestyles, consumption and the environment: The ecological modernization of domestic consumption. *Environmental Politics, 9*(1), 50–76.

Steuer, B., Ramusch, R., & Salhofer, S. (2018). Is there a future for the informal recycling sector in urban China? *Detritus*. https://doi.org/10.31025/2611-4135/2018.13725

Sthiannopkao, S., & Wong, M. H. (2013). Handling e-waste in developed and developing countries: Initiatives, practices, and consequences. *Science of the Total Environment, 463*, 1147–1153.

Sundar, D., Mathiyazhagan, K., Agarwal, V., Janardhanan, M., & Appolloni, A. (2023). From linear to a circular economy in the e-waste management sector: Experience from the transition barriers in the United Kingdom. *Business Strategy and the Environment*. https://doi.org/10.1002/bse.3365

Thakur, P., & Kumar, S. (2022). Evaluation of e-waste status, management strategies, and legislations. *International journal of Environmental Science and Technology, 19*, 6957–6966.

Trengove, M., Kazim, E., Almeida, D., Hilliard, A., Zannone, S., & Lomas, E. (2022). A critical review of the Online Safety Bill. *Patterns, 3*(8). https://doi.org/10.1016/j.patter.2022.100544

Tufekci, Z. (2014). Engineering the public: Big data, surveillance and computational politics. *First Monday, 19*(7), 1–16.

UN. (2022). *UN e-knowledge database*. https://publicadministration.un.org/egovkb/en-us/Data/Country-Information/id/182-United-Kingdom-of-Great-Britain-and-Northern-Ireland

UNEP. (2021). *Launch: Coalition for Digital Environmental Sustainability (CODES)*. https://www.unep.org/events/webinar/launch-coalition-digital-environmental-sustainability-codes

Wang, K., Qian, J., & He, S. (2022). From campaign-style governance to multiple environmentalities: Urban political ecologies of e-waste regulation in Guiyu, China. *Urban Geography*. https://doi.org/10.1080/02723638.2022.2092307

Wang, R., Qi, R., Cheng, J., Zhu, Y., & Lu, P. (2020). The behaviour and cognition of ecological civilization among Chinese university students. *Journal of Cleaner Production, 243*. https://doi.org/10.1016/j.jclepro.2019.118464

Wang, Z., & Huo, J. (2023). Do government intervention measures promote e-waste recycling in China? *Journal of Environmental Management, 342*. https://doi.org/10.1016/j.jenvman.2023.118138

Watts, G. (2020). COVID-19 and the digital divide in the UK. *The Lancet, 2*(8). https://doi.org/10.1016/S2589-7500(20)30169-2

Xiao, H. (2023). Different strategies and management between countries towards Waste Electrical and Electronic Equipment (WEEE) to the realization of sustainability. *SHS Web Conference, 154*. https://doi.org/10.1051/shsconf/202315403010

Zaremberg, G., & Wong, M. T. (2018). Participation on the edge: Prior consultation and extractivism in Latin America. *Journal of Politics in Latin America, 10*, 29–58.

Zeng, X. L., Duan, H. B., Wang, F., & Li, J. H. (2017). Examining environmental management of e-waste: China's experience and lessons. *Renewable and Sustainable Energy Reviews, 72*, 1076–1082.

Zeng, Y., Sarira, T. V., Carrasco, L. R., Chong, K. Y., Friess, D. A., Lee, J. S. H., Koh, L. P., Worthington, T. A., Zhang, Y., & Koh, L. P. (2020). Economic and social constraints on reforestation for climate mitigation in Southeast Asia. *Nature Climate Change, 10*(9), 842–844.

Zhong, H., & Huang, L. (2016). The empirical research on the consumers' willingness to participate in e-waste recycling with a points reward system. *Energy Procedia, 104*, 475–480.

Zhong, H., Zhou, S., Zhao, Z., Zhang, H., Nie, J., & Simayi, P. (2022). An empirical study on the types of consumers and their preferences for e-waste recycling with a points system. *Cleaner and Responsible Consumption, 7*. https://doi.org/10.1016/j.clrc.2022.100087

Zhou, X. (2021). Ecological civilization in China: Challenges and strategies. *Capitalism Nature Socialism, 32*(3), 84–99.

Zhu, Q., & Cote, R. (2004). Integrating green supply chain management into an embryonic eco-industrial development: A case study of the Guitang Group. *Journal of Cleaner Production, 12*(8–10), 1025–1035.

Zuboff, S. (2015). Big other: Surveillance capitalism and the prospects of an information civilization. *Journal of Information Technology, 30*(1), 75–89.

Zuboff, S. (2019). *The age of surveillance capitalism: The fight for a human future at the new frontier of power*. Profile Books.

CHAPTER 11

# Conclusion

This book suggested some theoretical foundations to understand digital-environmental poverty in the context of digital technological acceleration and increasing environmental urgency. In so doing it showed that poverty is an intricate and multifaced phenomenon, which is also context-dependent and, consequently, subject to different perspectives and approaches. The causes and effects of poverty evolve, and our conceptual frameworks and instruments for investigating it also need to adapt. In this direction, the concept of digital poverty has become crucial to understanding marked forms of marginalization. This includes partial or complete exclusion from the digital realm where resources and opportunities have shifted. The acquisition of traditional digital skills might not be sufficient to address digital-environmental poverty. AI-related skills, including AI awareness and competencies, are needed to recognize the risks, for example, associated with algorithmic biases, privacy breaches, and security management. It also involves an understanding of automated judgments made by algorithms, as well as essential skills and competencies required to harness the benefits of digital technologies and address the associated challenges, including potential harm to the natural environment. This is directly connected to the environmental dimension of poverty, which further affects the quality of life. This is not solely due to deprived natural ecosystems, but it is also a consequence of scarce environmental awareness



M. L. Ruiu, M. Ragnedda, *Digital-Environmental Poverty*, Palgrave Studies in Digital Inequalities,
https://doi.org/10.1007/978-3-031-56184-9_11

and limited involvement in pro-environmental behaviors and policy-making aimed at fostering digital-environmental sustainability. This conclusive paragraph aims to provide some takeaways and associated policy recommendations from the book (Table 11.2).

The first takeaway is that despite efforts to incorporate digital and environmental aspects into the conceptualization of poverty (as evidenced by initiatives such as the Millennium Development Goals, Sustainable Development Goals, and CODES plan), there remains a challenge in fully integrating both environmental degradation and digital exclusion into comprehensive policy interventions. Instead, the book emphasized the need to simultaneously consider the various dimensions of poverty, with a specific focus on environmental and digital components, recognizing their interrelated and yet independent nature from economic aspects. Efforts to address poverty should take into account additional factors that contribute to poverty including access to natural and digital resources, society and individual capacity and motivation to utilize them efficiently, a shared understanding of the value of these resources, and the empowerment to participate in decision-making processes. This relates to the need to address the different levels of digital inequalities in conjunction with environmental inequalities (see Table 11.1).

One way to achieve this is, for example, to take into account the resilience of the digital infrastructure in addition to its availability (what we could call the first level of digital-environmental poverty). At this level, access to devices should consider not only the acquisition of tools and broadband but also their environmentally conscious use and recycling when they no longer function. This is directly connected to the acquisition of digital skills (what we might call the second level of digital-environmental poverty) that require educating consumers about proper ICT use and disposal, and raising awareness about e-waste recycling. Moreover, digital skills need to be expanded to encompass the critical capacity to evaluate the environmental impact of digital behavior and leverage ICTs for environmental purposes. Finally, digital skills and tools need to empower users to benefit from their digital experience and improve their capacity to deal with the related negative consequences. At this third level (which we could call the third level of digital-environmental poverty), environmental benefits should also be taken into account (for example, the capacity to combine digital-environmental challenges to benefit the individual and society) and the capacity to respond to potential unintended outcomes (for example, developing best practices to deal with digital pollution). At this level,

**Table 11.1** The three levels of digital-environmental poverty

| |
|---|
| *Takeaway*: Need to integrate both environmental degradation and digital exclusion into comprehensive policy approaches |
| *Policy Recommendation*: Recognize the environmental component at all levels of the digital divide/stratification to formulate integrated interventions by providing access, skills, and motivation for environmentally friendly digital use, thereby reducing their impact on environmental poverty and enhancing well-being. Policies should consider the environmental impact of citizens' use of ICTs, not just government and business efficiency |
| *Takeaway*: Need to employ a multidimensional perspective that simultaneously considers the macro, meso, and micro dimensions of digital-environmental poverty |
| *Policy Recommendation*: Develop green-focused solutions while considering the interplay between structural constraints and individual agency at the meso/circumstantial level. Holistic approaches that consider factors such as access to resources (both digital and natural capital), education (digital and environmental literacy), capacity building, information sharing, citizen empowerment, and efficient, sustainable infrastructure are essential to influence the digital-environmental habitus |
| *Takeaway*: Digital uses and behaviors can be both a cause and a potential alleviation of environmental problems. Theoretically understanding the mechanisms at play at the circumstantial level aids in developing strategies for addressing digital and environmental dimensions at the macro and micro levels |
| *Policy Recommendation*: Develop regulatory frameworks that shape circumstances that empower digital users to be environmentally responsible citizens by involving them in the decisional process. Active participation of digital users is essential for the success of pro-environmental initiatives, enabling structural changes for sustainability and increasing individual awareness, motivation, and engagement in eco-friendly digital behaviors |
| *Takeaway*: Approaches influencing individual digital behaviors (such as nudging) must consider multiple factors across structural, circumstantial, and individual levels |
| *Policy Recommendations* |
| 1. At the individual level, consider implementing "green by default" listing and ranking mechanisms on online platforms. Address privacy concerns, usage barriers, and green scepticism, and consider environmental awareness, motivation, and the role of social networks in shaping digital consumption behaviors |
| 2. Prioritize ethical considerations in AI regulations to encourage sustainable use and responsible data-driven recommendations. This includes monitoring the ethical standards by employing the same AI technology |
| 3. Design comprehensive educational programs to equip users with the skills necessary to critically assess AI-driven suggestions, and understand their influence on behavior and decision-making |
| *Takeaway*: Examples of tokenization, blockchain-based green currencies, and gaming apps can create favorable circumstances for citizen participation in environmental protection. Government oversight and long-term strategy should prioritize citizen education, participation, and engagement in environmental issues |
| *Policy Recommendations:* |

(*continued*)

**Table 11.1** (continued)

1. Establish clear market regulations for carbon markets, monitoring systems, and green currencies, providing guidelines for smaller stakeholders
2. Ensure that investment in carbon markets does not serve as mere compensation for harmful practices
3. Implement digital twins of the environment for real-time monitoring to prevent speculation and protect vulnerable communities
4. Regulate and conduct public investigations into digital currency minting processes before granting permissions
5. Regulations should clarify how digital tools can be used for control, decision-support, and discipline while preventing discrimination (as seen in the social credit model and governmental use of complex algorithms in decision-making)

active participation in the decision-making process could be beneficial to developing collaborative effective practices. These three levels directly impact inequalities in digital-environmental terms and simultaneously depend on the interchange between structural, circumstantial, and individual determinants (see Fig. 5.1). DEP, as discussed throughout this book, signifies the coexistence of a deficiency of basic digital needs and healthy ecosystems. This dual hardship reinforces and is, in turn, reinforced by various other types of inequality.

The policy recommendation tied to this takeaway pertains to the need for a reevaluation of obsolete basic indicators of digital poverty (Table 11.2). This reevaluation should extend beyond the mere provision of digital infrastructure, taking into account not only socioeconomic and cultural factors but also environmental aspects. Focusing on policy intervention aimed solely at increasing access and connectivity (the first level of the digital divide) might not be sufficient to address both digital and environmental levels of individual poverty. While incomes are widely recognized to be a leading driver of digital exclusion and can affect the efficiency of Devices and Connectivity, Access, Capabilities, and Motivations, it is not the only cause of digital inequalities. Factors such as having children with disabilities and additional socio-demographic traits (such as age and education), parental status, lifestyles, and digital behaviors also play a role in predicting certain aspects of digital poverty. Addressing digital poverty needs combined interventions across the three levels of digital divide, ensuring individuals have the means to access, utilize the full potential of the internet, and reap its benefits while managing potential negative consequences. The environmental dimension must be considered at all levels

**Table 11.2** Summary of Takeaways and Policy Recommendations

| *Level* | *Implications* | *Requirement* |
|---|---|---|
| First level of digital-environmental poverty | Scarce availability of environmentally friendly devices and digital infrastructure that might impact and be impacted by natural degradation | Improving the efficiency of devices and digital infrastructure as well as their resilience against natural degradation |
| Second level of digital-environmental poverty | Limited possession of digital skills that affect ICT acquisition, substitution, use, and disposal practices | Providing users with the critical capacity to evaluate the environmental impact of digital behavior and leverage ICTs for environmental purposes |
| Third level of digital-environmental poverty | Limited capability to benefit (in social and environmental terms) from the digital experience and deal with the related negative consequences (including negative impacts of digital uses on the environment) | Empowering individuals to gain benefits through active participation in the decision-making process to develop best practices that benefit both the individual and the environment, as well as models to deal with negative outcomes (e.g., digital pollution) |

of the digital divide/stratification (Table 11.1). At the first level, it pertains to the sustainability of the available digital devices and internet infrastructures (and associated costs). The second level includes the capabilities and skills needed to use digital technologies for specific (environmentally friendly) purposes. The third level involves the benefits users can derive from the digital experience, including environmental advantages. Recognizing the environmental component also means addressing the negative outcomes by reducing the digital carbon footprint resulting from digital activities that contribute to environmental degradation. This entails reducing inequalities in digital competencies, providing individuals with appropriate skills and fostering attitudes to harness the benefits of digital technologies while mitigating their potential negative impacts.

A second takeaway connects efforts to combat digital poverty with a multidimensional approach that simultaneously considers the macro, meso, and micro dimensions of poverty. Environmental poverty is not solely determined by the health of ecosystems; it is also influenced by the perceptions and significance attached to the natural environment. Such a societal understanding, in turn, shapes and is shaped by individual perceptions, values and behaviors. The alignment between industrial/

technological development, economic growth, and global environmental challenges hinges on such socially constructed meanings and values attributed to the environment. When addressing environmental poverty, we applied Giddens's structuration theory and a Bourdesian approach to the cultural component of taste. These approaches helped us understand the dynamic interplay between social practices and individual agency, which represents both a reflection of individuals' backgrounds and a product of their experience within the social context. Together, these approaches facilitate an understanding of how ecological values and associated behaviors must be contextualized within a framework of shared social norms that are both influencing and influenced by these practices.

In our approach, we proposed an enhanced understanding of the DPF from a sociological perspective, by blending Giddens' concept of the duality of structure and Bourdieu's notion of habitus. In our analysis of the determinants within the DPF at the structural, circumstantial, and individual levels, we suggested that the structural determinants (broader socioeconomic, cultural, and political contexts that shape the digital landscape) provide the framework within which agents act according to their individual determinants (in the DPF represented by Device and connectivity, Access, Capabilities, Motivation, and Support). The individual determinants, in turn, influence the individual transformative power to change such a framework. The circumstantial determinants (in the DPF including living conditions, economic stability, family dynamics, health, sociodemographic context, psychosocial factors, lifestyle, and behaviors) serve as an intersectional space between the structural and agentic levels. They contribute to the production and reproduction of regular social practices and display structural properties in time and space through social relations. We have also highlighted parallels with the Bourdesian concept of habitus, which encapsulates the intricate interplay between external factors and individuals' inherent predispositions, shaping their actions within precise fields (including the digital realm).

The policy recommendation arising from this observation is that policymaking should avoid treating environmentally friendly solutions in isolation, disconnected from underlying structural constraints and solely reliant on individual choices and self-identity. Similarly, interpreting digital behavior as solely influenced by structural determinants might lead to an incomplete understanding of the interplay between societal dynamics and technology.

There is a need for holistic approaches that acknowledge the combined influence of various factors. These factors encompass access to resources (both digital and natural), education (digital and environmental literacy), capacity building, information sharing, citizen empowerment, and the development of efficient and sustainable infrastructure. These factors shape the digital-environmental habitus and need to be considered together to create effective policies.

A third takeaway is that digital usage and behaviors can both exacerbate and potentially alleviate societal pressure on the environment. They can harm the environment, but also facilitate economic development and environmental protection. We have observed that advancements in ICTs, AI, IoT, ML, and blockchain can contribute to processes like dematerialization, global networking, information sharing, and increased efficiency and competitiveness, all while reducing $CO_2$ emissions. Digitalization has a broad-reaching effect on consumer behavior, organizations, healthcare, education, and social and environmental dynamics. However, this increased efficiency can also stimulate greater productivity and consumption, potentially leading to a higher carbon footprint due to increasing energy demand for computers and servers, electronic waste, and resource extraction. The dynamic interaction between the environment and digital tools depends on both structural and agentic factors in a circular process. This process affects the distribution of transformative power, which in turn influences our collective understanding of the environmental impacts of digital practices and the formulation of rules and policies. Structural conditions, which encompass natural resources, knowledge, and regulatory frameworks, contribute to shaping both "circumstances" that encourage participation at the meso-level and individual predispositions toward using (digital) technologies in a pro-environmental manner. It is also relevant to note that top-down approaches can hinder stakeholders' commitment to environmental management, as they may lead to a sense of powerlessness among those affected. By contrast, the involvement of various actors from the market, government, civil society, NGOs, local community, and individual citizens has often shown its potential to empower decision-making. At the structural level, neither market-driven responses nor authoritarian environmental approaches can effectively address digital-environmental poverty without considering the responsibilities of citizens, which extend beyond mere reporting. Market-led responses might not be sufficient to address different levels of digital poverty, as a one-size-fits-all approach fails to account for contextual nuances, specific skills shortages, environmental conditions, awareness levels, and engagement dynamics. The Ecological Civilization paradigm offers a holistic vision, guiding regulative frameworks to create opportunities for addressing both environmental and digital challenges. It also encourages eco-innovation by supporting business ideas and involving citizens to contribute to the transition. This paradigm has prompted investments in both industrial digitalization and digital industrialization, furthering the green economy.

On the other hand, the UK private-public approach showed that collaborations between governments, universities, and businesses are emerging to align social, economic, and environmental goals with digital advancements (such as in the case of Digital Twin Hub, in the UK). However, the social impact of such initiatives hinges on the equitable distribution of benefits. Furthermore, public funding is crucial to exploring new solutions that can benefit both citizens and private enterprises. While public-private partnerships may be necessary to address digital poverty comprehensively, governments and policymakers must oversight the process to ensure that digitalization results in socioeconomic benefits for the entire population and has a global environmental impact.

According to this view, the structural determinants of digital-environmental poverty can produce *institutional power* through control over rule-making. This, in turn, has cascading effects on both circumstantial and individual determinants by creating conditions for citizens to participate in digital-environmental decision-making. We also referred to poverty in terms of a different distribution of power, which can be determined at the circumstantial level by *material power* (involving wealth, possessions, and physical means of coercion) and *discursive power* (pertaining to the ability to control the terms of discussion and shape narratives). This level also serves as the foundation for fostering *people-power*, which can lead to increased civic participation, activism, and advocacy.

The policy recommendation tied to this point emphasizes the need for regulatory frameworks to establish conditions that empower digital users to become environmentally responsible citizens through active involvement in the decisional process. Public-private partnerships should involve multiple stakeholders, but governments and policymakers must oversee and guide the process to ensure that digitalization delivers both socioeconomic benefits for the entire population and global environmental advantages. The engagement of digital users is vital for the success of pro-environmental schemes in both directions: advancing structural changes to promote sustainability and enhancing individual awareness, motivation, and engagement in eco-friendly digital behaviors. The range of digital skills to be provided also includes digital participation in civil society.

Directly connected to the previous point, a fourth takeaway pertains to the theoretical understanding of the intersections between digital and environmental dimensions at the circumstantial level, where macro and micro determinants convey. We have defined this meso level as the context in which human agency manifests within the framework of social relationships. In this context, the Bourdesian concepts of field and (digital-environmental) habitus can help understand the variations in attitudes of digital technology users toward the environment. The circumstances that characterize the field result from a combination of both individual traits and structural configuration. The field can be understood as a space where the interplay between *institutional power*, *material power* (which encompasses the possession of various forms of capital including digital and environmental capital) *discursive power*, and *people-power* (as discussed in the third takeaway) materialize and determine the privileges that actors possess and reinforce in the specific context. These privileged positions, in turn, empower agents to accumulate additional capital and power, influencing the field of action. The circumstantial level is where Bourdieu's digital-environmental habitus can be transformed and conditioned by the framework of social relationships established at the structural level. Operational circumstances can contribute to altering the configuration of the digital-environmental habitus. The rapid digital acceleration due to the COVID-19 pandemic has triggered a "dialectical confrontation" between the pre-existing habitus and the new values and behaviors shaped by the evolving digitalized field of action. We used the concept of field to describe how agents position themselves within a social network, while habitus encompasses the absorption of values, perceptions, and behaviors through social practices, depending on these positions. Habitus develops from the unconscious acquisition of cultural, economic, and social capital from the early stages of life, and continually adapts to new contexts. In this sense, it results from a dialectical relationship between structure and agency within a social network of agents operating in specific fields. The ability to transfer competencies and skills from one field to another makes habitus flexible and capable of transformative power. We contend that the digital acceleration of post-COVID-19 societies, coupled with a global environmental crisis, demands increased policy attention to the interplay between digital and environmental habitus. The digital-environmental habitus encompasses both individual perceptions of the environmental impacts of digital technologies (digital carbon footprint), influenced by their internalization of a collective understanding, and the resulting behavioral responses. This concept embodies a dual function, acting as a catalyst for change and as a product of both circumstantial factors (digital field action) and structural configurations (existing systems and norms regulating the social space in digital-environmental terms).

The policy recommendation reiterates the importance of focusing on the circumstantial level to grasp how structural and individual determinants interact.

The fifth takeaway highlights that solely focusing on structural elements may not be sufficient to address digital-environmental poverty, as efforts to influence digital behavior toward sustainability have produced uncertain results. Individual pro-environmental attitudes also depend on factors such as planning, rationality, and the capacity to reflect on the consequences of actions, including their positive outcomes. At the individual level, (digital) nudging has been found to be successful in promoting pro-environmental choices in the digital context under certain circumstances.

The recommended policy approach for enhancing individual engagement in online green consumption involves implementing "green by default" listing and ranking mechanisms on online platforms. By making green products/services more visible than non-eco-friendly alternatives, this approach can nudge users toward making eco-friendly choices. At the same time, these initiatives must be integrated into a wider digital and environmental literacy program for long-term results, as discussed in the previous points.

Additionally, it is essential to consider factors such as privacy concerns, usage barriers, and green scepticism, which can impact the use of gaming apps that engage with pro-environmental behaviors (for example, Ant Forest, see Chap. 7). The development and implementation of these strategies should also consider factors such as environmental awareness, motivation for pro-environmental actions, and the influence of social networks on digital consumption behaviors.

Furthermore, regulations governing AI usage should prioritize ethical considerations, encouraging sustainable uses of digital tools and responsible data-driven recommendations. This could entail deploying AI technology to monitor the ethical standards followed by personal assistants' recommendations.

Finally, to empower citizens, it is crucial to design comprehensive educational programs that provide users with the skills necessary to critically assess AI-driven suggestions, and understand their influence on behavior and decision-making.

The sixth takeaway underscores the importance of further exploring public-private initiatives that can create favorable circumstances for motivating citizens to actively participate in environmental protection. The book referenced examples like tokenization, blockchain-based green currencies, and gaming apps to highlight both their advantages and disadvantages. Initiatives that follow natural capital approaches (such as UK Woodland Carbon and the UK Peatland Code), along with AliPay Ant Forest and Single.Earth, while profit-driven, show potential for involving and engaging citizens in pro-environmental behaviors.

The natural capital approach assigns financial value to natural resources and employs market-based instruments to incentivize stakeholders to engage in environmental conservation. Similarly, blockchain-based green currencies attribute a digital value through the tokenization of natural resources for use in exchange for goods or services. Game-based apps, like Ant Forest, connect the efforts of private businesses, NGOs, and citizens in environmental protection. The benefit-oriented approach of these initiatives has been attractive for households, encouraging them to reduce deforestation and participate in pro-environmental activities. While the scientific debate regarding the benefits of reforestation is ongoing, these collaborative approaches show the potential to effectively address environmental challenges.

Leveraging blockchain technology and automating data acquisition and monitoring processes can improve transparency for both regulators and participants. However, it is crucial to establish regulatory frameworks to mitigate the potential risks of prioritizing economic stakes over the public good. These regulations also help prevent power imbalances that may favor influential actors in the network at the expense of those who rely on those resources for their livelihood.

The associated policy recommendations pertain to the need for government approaches to establish clear market regulations for carbon markets and green currencies. These policies should include guidelines for smaller stakeholders, such as individual farmers and land managers, addressing aspects related to their complementation of public sector programs, business risks, and the standards governing both payments and model effectiveness. Clear standards are also needed to prevent the risk of "phantom credits" that might not truly reflect reductions in carbon emissions, potentially leading to "greenwashing." Some of these criticalities can be addressed by following the Single.Earth example, which involves creating a digital twin of the environment for real-time monitoring of changes. Moreover, it is essential to ensure that the commodification of natural resources does not translate into speculation or become merely a compensation mechanism for harmful practices. This approach must safeguard against the adverse impact on communities living in vulnerable conditions, who might lose access to local resources for the sake of market profit.

Furthermore, it is imperative to conduct thorough investigations when proposing digital currencies, especially in terms of determining the energy consumption of minting processes.

At the same time, monitoring strategies should adopt a context-specific approach (by, for example, leaving flexibility for developing local strategies that can better address concerns raised from specific situations) to avoid the risk of violating citizens' privacy and rights, whether for profit-driven goals or government-imposed nomocracy.

# Index





M. L. Ruiu, M. Ragnedda, *Digital-Environmental Poverty*, Palgrave Studies in Digital Inequalities,
https://doi.org/10.1007/978-3-031-56184-9

The manufacturer's authorised representative in the EU is Springer Nature Customer Service Centre GmbH, Europaplatz 3, 69115 Heidelberg, Germany. If you have any concerns regarding our products, please contact ProductSafety@springernature.com

Printed and bound by CPI Group (UK) Ltd, Croydon, CR0 4YY
30/09/2026
02225507-0003